*Reluctant Cold Warriors*

# Reluctant Cold Warriors

## Economists and National Security

VLADIMIR KONTOROVICH

OXFORD
UNIVERSITY PRESS

# OXFORD
UNIVERSITY PRESS

Oxford University Press is a department of the University of Oxford. It furthers
the University's objective of excellence in research, scholarship, and education
by publishing worldwide. Oxford is a registered trade mark of Oxford University
Press in the UK and certain other countries.

Published in the United States of America by Oxford University Press
198 Madison Avenue, New York, NY 10016, United States of America.

CIP data is on file at the Library of Congress
ISBN 978–0–19–086812–3

1 3 5 7 9 8 6 4 2

Printed by Integrated Books International, United States of America

*To the memory of Isaac Kantorovich, Ada Temkina,*
*and Vladimir Shlapentokh*

# Contents

# *Preface*

IN 1996, I WROTE a chapter on Western misdiagnoses of the Soviet economy for a planned collective volume devoted to the collapse of Communism, which contained sections on economic growth, the military economy, and reform (Kontorovich 1996). The volume did not materialize, and a section on the treatment of the military aspects of the Soviet economy grew into three articles:

"What Did the Soviet Rulers Maximize?" 2009. *Europe-Asia Studies* 61 (9): 1579–1601 (coauthored by Alexander Wein);
"A Cold War Creature Which Sat Out the War." 2014. *Europe-Asia Studies* 66 (5): 811–29;
"The Military Origins of Soviet Industrialization." 2015. *Comparative Economic Studies* 57 (4): 669–92.

These articles have been rewritten to form parts of this book.

I am grateful to the Earhart Foundation and to Haverford College for financial support. Richard Ball, Gregory Brock, Robert Campbell, Janet Ceglowski, Julian Cooper, Robert Davies, Michael Ellman, Richard Ericson, Linda Gerstein, Philip Hanson, Mark Harrison, Gregory Khanin, Frederick Pryor, Peter Rutland, and Vladimir Shlapentokh made valuable suggestions and comments on the drafts of various parts of this book. Lyra Piscitelli edited the manuscript and suggested multiple revisions for consistency and clarity. I thank Amichai Berman, Kenneth Gudel, James Novak, Ioannis Rutledge, Diana Schoder, Alex Wein, and Isaac Wheeler for research assistance and for editing parts of the text.

# Introduction: Why bother with the writings on a defunct economy by authors now at best retired?

## Social science and the prevention of Armageddon

During World War II, social scientists in the United States were mobilized to help with a variety of tasks previously far beyond their professional expertise, from bombing-target selection to military personnel assignment. The newly found use of the social sciences for national security purposes outlasted the war and was one of the reasons for the field's rapid expansion after 1945, fueled by government funding.[1]

One of the new functions of the social scientists working for the Office of Strategic Services (OSS), the wartime precursor of the Central Intelligence Agency (CIA), was advising the government about the nature, capabilities, and prospects of the enemy and allied powers. Previously reserved for generals, journalists, spies, and diplomats, this role was greatly enhanced in subsequent decades, and became a part of the permanent repertory of social science–government relations. But how well did social scientists do the job the government expected of them? I seek to answer this question based on a close look at one academic field, the study of the Soviet economy, called here "Sovietology" for the sake of brevity. The study of all aspects of Soviet society, including politics, society, history, and culture, which is usually denoted as "Sovietology," is called here "Soviet studies."

Two characteristics of Sovietology make it especially useful for studying the connection between national interests and the social sciences. First, it was a made-to-order, single-use field. Most other disciplines mobilized for national security needs, both during and after World War II, had a previous "civilian" history, which shaped their scope and methods. They also had alternative "civilian" contemporary applications, which influenced their development. As will be shown in chapter 1, Sovietology was created from scratch specifically to help the US government fight the Cold War, and expired with the war's end.

Second, the national security demands on Sovietology were especially urgent. It was summoned to life to assist in waging a conflict with the highest imaginable stakes. Armageddon, which the Soviet collapse helped avert, as the title of Kotkin (2001) proclaims, was the worst of several possible bad outcomes. If the Cold War was a war, it could be lost, difficult as this is to imagine now. Or the Soviet system could have endured until today, as Mikhail Gorbachev has gleefully reminded his critics from time to time, and with it the indignities it imposed on its subjects and the stress of conflict borne by the rest of the world. More people could have fallen under its sway, as Ethiopians and Afghans did in its final decades. It took a massive expenditure of resources, the loss of many lives, and great moral and political strain on the free societies to stand their ground during the half century of the Cold War.[2] Given the Sovietologists' knowledge of these stakes, one can assume that the limitations of their work were not for lack of trying.

The assessment of Sovietology's response to national security needs is of far more than historical interest. While the urgency of national security demands has declined in the post–Cold War world, the use of social science has become a permanent feature of the national security system. Across American campuses, people with PhDs and knowledge of difficult languages, are analyzing the unfamiliar societies from which current and future threats to our security may spring, under contract with the federal government or in a federally sponsored center.

An assessment of their predecessors' performance can tell us what may be expected from the national security applications of the social sciences. It is particularly important to identify systematic, predictable biases like those found in other human endeavors. Bureaucrats are known to over-manage and engage in logrolling, universities tend to serve professors rather than students, government regulators become advocates for the industries they are supposed to oversee, and the military often cling to familiar, although obsolete, weapons and strategies.[3] Each of these deviations from an organization's stated purposes can be explained by individual responses to the prevailing incentives. Social sciences, when they inform our security policy about the capabilities, prospects, and intentions of rival countries, may be subject to similar professional deformations. If these are documented, and their origins traced to the incentives provided by the organization of social science, this knowledge can serve as a corrective lens for the users of social science expertise.

## *What we needed to know about the Soviet economy*

The Soviet challenge to the West had many dimensions—diplomacy, propaganda, subversion—but it was military at the core.[4] The imprint it left in American history consists mostly of military or military-related events: the Berlin blockade, the Korean War, the Rosenbergs and the theft of nuclear secrets, the Sputnik panic, the missile gap, the Cuban Missile Crisis, the Vietnam War, President Carter's freedom from "inordinate fear of Communism," President Reagan's Strategic Defense Initiative (SDI), and Governor Michael Dukakis in the tank. The Sputnik, the MiGs of Korea and the SAMs of Vietnam, the missiles of 1962, and those to be parried by the SDI, all had to be designed, tested, and produced before becoming factors in the military and political game. There would have been no Cold War without the Soviet side's unique capacity to produce large quantities of the most advanced weapons systems.

The part of the economy embodying this capacity is called here "the military sector." It comprises a collection of military-related activities carried out both in specialized defense establishments and in civilian ones. It includes research, development, and production for military needs, the creation and maintenance of mobilization stocks and capacity, the acquisition of foreign technology for military production, and industrial dispersion, as well as the planning and financing of these activities. As will be shown in chapter 2, this sector constituted a separate economy within the Soviet economy and was not only unusually large and important, but also uniquely successful.

For Sovietology to serve its intended purpose, it had to fulfill two large tasks.[5] One was the study of the overall economic potential of the USSR, which formed the foundation of its military might, including the size, growth rate, innovativeness, and adaptability of the economy and its main sectors. This task involved, to a greater or lesser degree, most of what economists do in the normal course of their professional lives, and the academic Sovietologists could not have failed to address it. This is admittedly a very crude assessment. Gauging their success would require a topic-by-topic analysis, and no such effort is attempted here.

The second task expected of Sovietology was to inquire into the military sector, the part of the economy directly serving the Cold War. The Sovietologists themselves put this task at the top of their list of promises when lobbying for government funding for their field (see section 1.2). Evaluation of Sovietology's treatment of the military sector is the subject of this book.

## *The widely known, yet previously unmentioned war economy*

The economic decline during the last years of the USSR and the country's eventual collapse gave rise to two new strands of research. One dealt with "transition," or the introduction of market institutions into the formerly centrally planned economy. Writings in this genre often included brief descriptions of the Soviet economy as the departure point in the transition process. Another line of scholarship investigated the Soviet collapse in the context of the country's economic history. In both of these literatures, one can read that "the communist economy was foremost a war economy" (Åslund 2002, 31, 38); "At the heart of the former Soviet economy was a defence industry of quite extraordinary scale. Its priority development over several decades distorted the development of the entire economy" (Cooper 1993, 3); and "The importance of the defence sector is hard to exaggerate" (Hanson 2003, 31). Further, rapid economic growth during and after industrialization had "a strictly military orientation."[6] The economy was designed for military production rather than consumer welfare and was most successful at producing large quantities of military goods.[7]

Serving the needs of the military is said not only to have dominated the life of the Soviet economy, but also to bear much responsibility for its death. The common argument in many explanations of the system's demise is that excessive military spending and attendant economic irrationality depleted the civilian economy and promoted stagnation.[8] Hanson (2003, 247–48) hypothesizes a different, though equally prominent role for arms production in the Soviet demise.

After 1991, disposing of the military industry's inheritance, under the name of conversion, became one of the main issues of transition policy. By my count, over a dozen books on the subject appeared in the West between 1993 and 2006, more than on any other single sector of the post-Soviet economies.

Most of the writers quoted here present the pre-eminence of the military sector as a self-evident fact, without citing any supporting sources, as if conveying common knowledge. Yet such statements would be surprising for a reader of the standard textbooks on the Soviet economy written only a few years earlier.

Consider the encyclopedic 600-page treatise by leading authority and Harvard professor János Kornai (1992). It was published by Princeton University Press and boasts 45 pages of bibliography. Far from speaking of a "militarized" or "war" economy, the book barely mentions military factors, listing the military industry as number seven among 11 priorities in allocation of investment.[9] Another popular textbook, the almost 400-page *Soviet Economic System* by Alec Nove (1986), one of the masters in the field, went through three editions. It has three references to the military in the index, the same number of references as to "planning in ton-kilometers," a technical matter of little systemic importance. None of the references concern "the overexpanded military-industrial complex," which the same author would acknowledge eight years later (Nove 1994, 349).

If the transition writers in the 1990s were correct in their characterization of the Soviet economy, the military sector was a matter of tremendous importance for US national security and, indeed, the survival of the world. One would expect the academic experts on the Soviet economy to explore its every angle and to inform the public back when it mattered. If the Nove and Kornai books are typical of the studies of the Soviet economy during its lifetime, they did not, and it is important to know why.

## *Main findings and methods*

A massive survey of the literature in chapter 3 confirms the suspicion raised by the Kornai and Nove books. Over its lifetime, Sovietology largely ignored the military sector, lavishing its attention instead on civilian sectors of lesser importance to the West and also of lower standing in the Soviet priority ranking. Also, when addressing a subject that, by the Soviets' own account, had important military aspects, Sovietologists tended to ignore credible official military interpretations, and substitute their own contrived civilian ones. I call this phenomenon "civilianization" (chapters 4 and 5).

I establish the neglect of the military sector using a straightforward and transparent method, comparing the number of references to the military and civilian sectors in Sovietological literature. The meaning of civilianization, however, requires some explanation. Sovietologists worked almost exclusively with sources of Soviet origin. Analyzing the economy meant, to a large degree, testing the Soviet-offered data, descriptions, and interpretations for reliability, and using the more reliable ones. Civilianization represents a systematic bias in this process, as the official statements on military significance of economic policies are downplayed irrespective of their reliability. Official statements emphasizing the civilian aspects of the same policies are played up and made to carry more explanatory weight than they are capable of. In asserting this bias, I do not rely on any generalized notions of whether one can or cannot "trust the Soviets," but rather on the detailed economic and historical analysis of specific official pronouncements and the uses to which they were put by Sovietologists (chapters 4 and 5, sections 7.2 and 7.3.3).

The neglect of the military sector in Western literature, though not its civilianization, may be explained by extraordinary Soviet secrecy. However, there is no evidence that Sovietologists were much concerned with secrecy, or were interested in the work of the outsiders who managed to circumvent it. Secrecy made the study of the military sector more difficult, but far from blocked it, as the work of these outsiders demonstrated (section 6.3.2).

Sovietologists neglected the military sector and civilianized its important aspects as a matter of choice, not necessity. Self-interest impelled scholars in the small, low-prestige field to follow the agenda of the larger discipline of economics, which had little concern for military matters.

Investigating socialism's claims of greater efficiency, stability, and equality was seen as the central mission of Sovietology, and such a retrograde part of the economy as the military sector was of no help in that task. Many authors were uneasy about as much as mentioning the military sector and rushed to vouch for the Soviets' purely defensive intent, using unsourced and often inaccurate geopolitical and historical arguments (chapter 7).

The findings of the book suggest a revision of Soviet economic history, though not in the obvious way of introducing new evidence or interpretations. Chapters 4 and 5 draw a picture of the Soviet economy that is more militaristic than that provided by the standard account in Sovietological literature. This is hardly news, as research in Soviet archives after 1991 uncovered a wealth of information on the importance of the military sector in general, and in the First Five-Year Plan, the topic of chapter 5, in particular (Ellman 2008b, 104–5). Yet this avalanche of evidence had little effect on the acceptability of the civilianized account, which outlived both Sovietology and its subject and is well represented in the current literature.

This persistence reflects a characteristic of Sovietological knowledge that I call "fragmentation." Opposing views coexist in the literature, sometimes under the cover of the same textbook, without their adherents confronting each other or even acknowledging each other's existence. Thus, the dominant civilianized accounts of Soviet planners' objectives and of the First Five-Year Plan in Sovietology existed alongside minority positions stressing military factors, but the twain never met. In a fragmented field, evidence produced in favor of one position does not affect the standing of the opposing one, just as the appearance of Kornai's Soft Budget Constraint theory did not lead anyone to question the Adjusted Factor Cost Standard (explained in section 1.3.2).

This book provides the first critical assessment of the standard accounts of two topics, the objectives of central planners and the intent of the First Five-Year Plan. These accounts advance the proposition that the Soviets pursued growth for its own sake, which would make the thrust of their economic policies irrational, and thus put them beyond the pale of economic analysis. The civilianized version of the First Five-Year Plan has additional elements, such as the important role of the 1920s ideological debate—and of a few individual economists involved therein—in originating the plan strategy, as well as the derivation of the plan's stress on investment goods from Marx's writings. I show the weaknesses of these interpretations, and propose a simpler, though less pacific, interpretation of the plan's origins.

## *A disclaimer*

At the center of this book is the failure of an academic field to perform an important task for which, in large measure, it was created. With some chapters documenting the dimensions of this failure, and others exploring its causes, the tone of the book is inevitably critical. This does not mean the author holds his subject in low regard. Americans studying the Soviet economy faced formidable obstacles—the small number of fellow practitioners, the lack of access to the object of study, and the unusual conceptual difficulties of understanding a new type of economy. Despite all this, the field of Sovietology performed many valuable services for society and scholarship in its short life span. My criticism of some aspects of this enterprise is motivated by my belief in its seriousness and worthwhile nature.

The same is true at the level of individual scholars. In this book, I take issue with the writings of the people whose work I value highly and from whom I have learned much. My disagreement with their specific arguments does not necessarily signify a rejection of the articles or books, often excellent, where these arguments appear, or of the broader achievements of their authors.

## Notes

1. Backhouse and Fontaine (2010, 8); Leonard (1991, 262–69) specifically on economics; Crowther-Heyck (2006, 425–26) on post-war years.
2. On resources, see Higgs (1994).
3. Williamson (1985, 148–59); Sykes (1990); Viscusi et al. (1995, 38–39); Keller (2002).
4. National Security Council ([1950] 1975, 64–67); Friedberg (2000, 36–40, 81).
5. There are other valid criteria for judging an academic field. For an evaluation of Sovietology's contributions to the general understanding of society and the common arsenal of research tools, see Ellman (2009).
6. Gaidar (2003, 23); Earle and Komarov (1998, 6); Haynes and Husan (2003, 119); Pomer (2001, 140).
7. Skidelsky (1995, 103, 109, 111); subtitle of Gaddy (1996); Pomfret (2002, 18).
8. Cooper (1993, 1); Layard and Parker (1996, 47–48); Reddaway and Glinski (2001, 259–60). Easterly and Fischer (1995, 347–48, 361) test econometrically the impact of military spending on growth slowdown and find a small negative effect, a common result in such exercises.
9. On page 174, there are also passing references to military expenditures and to political control over armed forces.

# PART I

## Sovietology and The Soviet Military Power

The two protagonists of this book are the academic field of American Sovietology, which was created to help deal with a strategic challenge and received lifetime government support for reasons of national security, and the Soviet economy's unusually large, privileged, and successful military sector, which was the basis of that challenge.

*I*
_____

# The Origin and Structure of Sovietology

THE AMERICAN STUDY of the Soviet economy did not arise from the natural confluence of scholarly interests, as is usual for academic fields, but was created by the efforts of foundations, university administrators, and the government in the space of a few years. The military sector was one of the most important topics that the sponsors of Sovietology expected it to address. To understand how the field dealt with this task, I describe its internal structure, its standing within the discipline of economics, and its relations with other disciplines doing research on the Soviet economy.

## *1.1 The Cold War roots*

The Soviet economy was the greatest economic experiment in history. In 1917, a party that pledged to uproot the entire economic order and replace it with one based on diametrically opposite principles, seized power in a vast country and introduced unprecedented changes—workers' councils to manage factories, the abolition of money, summary executions for the private sale of bread, and the nationalization of most of the non-agricultural economy. In the 1930s, comprehensive central planning of the economy and a policy of rapid industrialization generated record-high reported rates of economic growth with full employment, a stark contrast to the Great Depression the rest of the world was facing (Nove 1992, chs. 3–9). The choice between capitalism and socialism, plan and market, was actively debated in Western countries in the interwar period.

Yet all the novelty and apparent success of the Soviet experiment was not enough to inspire its systematic professional study in the United States (Engerman 1999). Only seven economists with American doctorates devoted themselves full-time to the study of the USSR between 1930 and 1949, a period in which more than 2,400 such degrees were granted.[1] "American economists had shown an almost complete lack of interest in Soviet economic problems" (Gerschenkron 1968, 527). Writings on the Soviet economy through the 1940s would later be characterized as "impressionistic and journalistic," "naïve both politically and economically," and marred by the "absence of measurement."[2] The great debate about the comparative virtues of socialism and capitalism in which von Mises ([1922] 1981), Taylor (1929), Dobb (1933), von Hayek (1935), Lange (1938), and Schumpeter ([1942] 1976) engaged proceeded practically without reference to the Soviet experience. Von Hayek, in his foreword to Brutzkus (1935), noted the lack of information on the Soviet economy, though one of the participants of the debate wrote an early volume on the subject (Dobb 1928).

Serious research on the Soviet economy only started in response to the national security challenge of World War II, as the US government needed to understand the economic potential of its ally. Abram Bergson, "considered to have been the intellectual father of Soviet economic studies in the United States," headed work on the estimates of national income and studies of particular sectors at the Research and Analysis Branch of the OSS (Hardt 2004, 34, 38).

The systematic academic study of the Soviet economy emerged in the United States only in the late 1940s, three decades after the Bolshevik Revolution proclaimed its ideologically motivated revamping of the economy, and two decades after central planning started working its miracles. It was created in response to yet another national security challenge.

After the war, as large parts of Eurasia fell under the sway of the USSR, the European powers and Japan lay devastated, unable to withstand the Soviet pressure. And new weapons put North America itself within the reach of possible strikes.[3] The United States prepared to face this unprecedented challenge not only by increasing defense spending, but also by building new institutions and thoroughly revamping old ones—the armed services, intelligence agencies, the research and development system, and the military industry—for Cold War purposes (Friedberg 2000). A small part of this effort involved creating scholarly fields from scratch, and strengthening existing fields with the purpose of generating knowledge relevant for prosecution of the conflict. The study of the Soviet economy was one such field.[4]

Early practitioners clearly understood the security motivation for the field. "Because the Soviet system is engaged in a deadly race with the market-oriented economies . . . it has prompted systematic study by a number of economic researchers" (Spulber 1961, vii). Reviewing the progress in understanding the Soviet economy in the 1950s, Campbell (1961, 130–31) noted that "the justification for all this research has been the 'need to know' from the national interest point of view."[5] In a bout of post-Sputnik soul searching, the Committee on Economic Development proclaimed, "Nothing is more essential than knowing one's adversary" (Cowles 1958, 9). In a telling metaphor, a British Sovietologist compared the "simple, massive, and original program" for teaching economists the Russian language to the Manhattan Project (Wiles 1961, 87).

Yet unlike the Manhattan Project, the founding of Sovietology was not a purely government effort, but a joint endeavor by public and private entities with a shared understanding of the strategic situation. In the setting up of university research centers, "even though most of the interest and sponsorship have emanated from non-governmental sources [foundations and university administrations], the impulse has still been the realization that the actions of the Russians are going to influence our future in the world" (Campbell 1961, 129, 131).

Later accounts have confirmed this understanding. Millar (1980, 326) writes of earlier generations of Sovietologists relying on the national security significance of their field to obtain tenure in the economics departments, a strategy that had become less effective in the 1970s. Pollack (1996, 40–41) describes early analysts for the RAND Corporation, the birthplace of Soviet studies in his account, as being "spurred by the singular challenges of containment and nuclear deterrence." The website of the Harvard Russian Research Center informs visitors that "the sense of urgency that sparked its creation derived largely from the postwar international situation. The Center's founders believed not only that Russia and Soviet Communism were of great intellectual interest, but also that the training of specialists in this field was vital to deal with the challenge of the Soviet superpower."[6]

## *1.2  Cradle-to-grave national security funding*

Throughout its lifetime, academic Sovietology was supported by federal funding motivated by national security needs. Some of the support was aimed broadly at the institutions or researchers in Soviet studies, or even all area studies, with economics being one of the beneficiaries. Other funding went to specific economics projects.

The longest running source of support was the eloquently named National Defense Education Act, passed in the aftermath of the Sputnik shock in 1958. The act's Title VI provided financing to university area-studies centers. Support for Soviet studies centers under the title fluctuated over time, amounting to over $5 million in 1970, and to $1.6 million in 1983.[7] This funding only covered a fraction of the costs of Soviet studies, since professors' salaries were paid by the universities. While proportions shifted over time, non-governmental sources were said at one point to cover five-sixths of the centers' cost, with the government providing "a critical margin of supplementary support" (US House 1971, 1433). As Kramer (2001, 125) argued for the case of Middle Eastern studies, "Title VI has been the most consistent and predictable source of outside funding."

In 1978, the non-profit, autonomous National Council for Soviet and East European Research (NCSEER) was established at the initiative of the Defense Department, which was also the largest source of its funding, with other government agencies participating.[8] It provided grants to individual scholars for "basic" social science research projects, including those in economics. In the first four years of its existence, the council received more than $4 million of funding. CIA specialists evaluated the council reports on quality and usefulness, and found 21 out of 25 to be good or excellent on both counts.[9]

Under the Soviet–East European Research and Training Act of 1983 (Title VIII of the State Department Authorization Act), about $5 million per year went to support graduate students, subsidize junior faculty positions, and provide other aid to Soviet studies (Harris 1997, 455). While the word "defense" was not in the title, the hearings on the proposed legislation left no doubt about the national security rationale. Prominent former and current officials of the Pentagon, CIA, and State Department testified in favor of increased support in their capacity as the users of Soviet-studies expertise. While most of the testimony was a businesslike discussion of the nuts and bolts of Soviet area-studies organizations, references to "primary adversary," "national security," "the most dangerous . . . foreign entanglement," and the like abounded.[10]

Academic economists also did contract research for the Department of Defense and the CIA directly or through intermediary firms. This type of government support played a crucial role even in the field's founding, when foundations and universities were in the lead. The main steps in creating Sovietology were setting up specialized institutions, sponsoring large-scale projects, training graduate students, and placing them in academic positions (Gerschenkron 1968, 527–28, 530). The first was largely funded by private sources; Columbia University's Russian Institute was established in 1946 with Rockefeller Foundation money, and the Harvard Russian Research Center was founded in 1948 with a grant from the Carnegie Corporation. The crucial second and third steps, large-scale projects that generated the subject matter of the new field and served as training grounds for the graduate students, were accomplished with government funds.

The foundational research undertaking was the reconstruction of the Soviet national income and product accounts, performed at RAND in the 1950s as part of its work for the US Air Force. It included the derivation of current-price national income for the years 1928, 1940, 1944, 1948, and 1949–1955, as well as studies of such topics as price trends in industry, the cost of living and real wages, machinery prices and output, the volume of construction, and farm prices. All this was crowned by the estimation of the real national income in 1928–1955.[11] RAND also co-sponsored a study of the Soviet fixed capital stock in 1928–1962 (Moorsteen and Powell, 1966). A much cited work on the economics of the Soviet firm, Berliner (1957), came out of the Harvard Interview Project financed by the US Air Force (Engerman 2009, 52–62).

These projects provided the new field with a common conceptual and empirical foundation upon which further advances could be built. While professors and graduate students worked at RAND as consultants, RAND employees migrated to academia, in a pattern documented by Mirowski (2002) for economics in general.

In the late 1960s, a new attitude arose among academics, described as "an indiscriminate hostility to the government" and "profound suspicion of all government."[12] It was said to reduce scholars' contribution to public policy and to lead some professors to turn down government contracts. This change in sentiment has been well documented and is undisputed (Engerman 2009, ch. 9), but its effects on the willingness to accept government funding varied over time and across disciplines. In the 1970s, the tension was said to have lessened, and academics resumed paid engagements with the government. After all, Soviet studies, unlike many other fields, attracted no financing from the business sector, the government being its natural funding source (US Senate 1982, 15, 24, 32).

Aversion to government work appears to have had less of an impact on willingness to accept government funding in economics compared to other disciplines. As a graduate student in the late 1970s, I witnessed researchers with quite radical views working on Pentagon- and CIA-funded projects without the slightest compunction through intermediaries such as SRI International, Wharton Econometrics, and Plan Econ, Inc., to name just a few.

National security funding of innovative large projects in Sovietology continued. In the 1970s, the Defense Advanced Research Projects Agency funded the construction of the large-scale econometric model of the Soviet economy at Wharton Econometrics and the Stanford Research Institute by the University of Pennsylvania economists (Green and Higgins 1977). The CIA and the Departments of State and Defense financed the Soviet Interview Project of the late 1970s and 1980s (Engerman 2009, 254).

The fact that Sovietology benefited from an act of Congress with "defense" in its title does not mean that the government expected academics to do research on the military sector. "Although the word 'defense' had a certain magic . . . in loosening the legislative purse strings, it happily has not been construed in narrow terms"[13] All the government-funded projects just described concerned general economics, not the military sector proper. Yet there is also direct evidence that the government gave top priority to academic research on the topic.

In the second half of the 1960s, Soviet studies suffered from a decline in both private foundation and government funding, and by the second half of 1970s, it had become clear that the academic study of the Soviet economy, in particular, was facing the prospect of extinction.[14]

At that time, several projects designed to save and reinvigorate research on Soviet society with the infusion of government funds were being discussed by academics and officials at the CIA and the Pentagon. Thus, a 1978 CIA document titled "The Decay of US Research on the USSR: Need to Explore Remedial Action" listed five initiatives for remediation (Assistant 1978). These proposals emphasized sensitivity to the needs of government "users" of Soviet studies, and promised to prioritize research on the military sector.

A proposal developed at Harvard Russian Research Center had "the size of the Soviet defense effort, the influence of domestic factors on Soviet foreign policy" on its research agenda. When NCSEER was created in 1978, "it was to address . . . three sets of policy concerns: the size and burden of the Soviet defense effort . . . the long-term prospects for the Soviet economy and society . . . and Soviet objectives in long-term political-economic-military relations with the United States" (Engerman 2009, 251).

At about the same time, two senior Sovietologists, Vladimir Treml of Duke and Herbert Levine of the University of Pennsylvania, together with consultant Mark Earle, suggested the creation of a CIA-supported research institute for the study of the USSR. Their proposed research program noted that "among the concerns facing U.S. policymakers today, there is particular emphasis on the interrelationships between economic and military factors." The second of the five proposed research topics was the role of the military in Soviet society, including "the perception and measurement of economic trade-offs in the determination of the share of defense in the national economy," "the nature of the interrelatedness of the civilian and military sectors," and "the nature of interrelatedness of resources committed to domestic political control and those committed to the military." "Pricing in civilian and military industries" was also included (Treml et al. 1977, 4–6). This stress on military-economic issues reflected the Sovietologists' understanding, developed over decades of interaction, of "the most immediate needs of the U.S. Government" (Treml et al. 1977, 9).

Government officials judged the proposals to be too narrow, but there is no indication that they objected to the priorities (Engerman 2009, 252–53). US Army general William Odom, testifying at the Congressional hearings on expanded government support for Soviet studies, pointed to conspicuous lacunae in the academic literature: "Our study of the Soviet economy has ignored the vast non-budgetary allocations to Soviet defense. . . . Many unclassified aspects of Soviet military institutions can be studied in the universities. Yet they have received only spotty attention."[15]

## 1.3 The industrial organization of Sovietology

This section describes the characteristics of a field created by the urgent efforts to learn about the Soviet adversary and maintained by the steady drip of government funding. These characteristics will be used in chapter 7 to help explain why Sovietology performed the way it did. If economics explains human behavior, it should apply to economists as well (Colander 1989, 137). The structure of Sovietology, and its place in the wider academic world, which are detailed here, determined the incentives that its practitioners faced, and thereby their professional choices. "The institutional location of economists is always of paramount importance to understand the intellectual substance of the knowledge they produce" (Fourcade-Gourinchas 2001, 400).

### 1.3.1 Structure and conduct

In an old industrial-organization paradigm, the structure of the market—the number and size distribution of firms—determined the firms' conduct, which in turn determined their performance in terms of profitability (Sutton 2008). This structure-conduct-performance framework helps make sense of the development of Western scholarship on the Soviet economy, though it unfolded in the non-market environment.

The main structural characteristic of Sovietology was its small size relative to other fields of economics. It started out with about ten US- and foreign-trained scholars in the late 1940s. Between 1949 and 1958, 39 PhDs in the Soviet economy were awarded, with the majority of the recipients assuming positions in American universities (Millar 1995, 226). The late 1950s and early 1960s were seen as the time when "the study of the Soviet economy has been effectively transformed into an integral part of the discipline of economics" (Gerschenkron 1968, 531). However, it was, and remained for the rest of its lifetime, a microscopic part of the discipline. Over the whole decade of the 1950s, a total of 42 PhDs in Sovietology were awarded, compared to about 2,500 PhDs in economics. The average annual number of economics PhDs tripled in the 1960s and stayed at that level throughout the 1970s. Newly minted Sovietology degrees numbered 56 and 70 for each decade, less than 1% of the total.[16] Additional specialists who received their degrees in the 1980s brought the total stock of PhDs below 253, all but about 20 of them still active, at least occasionally, at the end of the 1980s (Millar 1995, 226). Alternative estimates, with somewhat different coverage and dates, confirm the minuscule size of the field (see appendix 1.1).

Another characteristic of Sovietology was that the production of new PhDs was highly concentrated. In industrial organization, "concentration ratio" refer to the share of an industry's output produced by a few (usually four or eight) top firms, and is used as a rough indicator of the extent of competition; the higher the ratio, the less competitive the industry. Fully one-half of the 1949–1958 crop of PhDs in Soviet economy were the students of A. Bergson and A. Gerschenkron at Harvard and Columbia universities. Between 1959 and 1968, these two schools produced 40% of PhDs in the field. This was a natural outcome of the minuscule number of scholars at the time of the field's creation. Concentration ratio further fell off in the two succeeding decades (Millar 1995, 226, 228). Still, assuming that ten years is the period necessary for young scholars to find their feet, it may be said that the students of Bergson and Gerschenkron dominated the field for three-quarters of its brief existence.

Along with the small size of the field went its stunted institutional development. The creation of the first American journal devoted to the study of Soviet-type economies (*Journal of Comparative Economics* in 1977) lagged three decades behind the emergence of the field itself.[17] In the pattern observed in general economics at the turn of the twentieth century, important articles by prominent Sovietologists appeared in non-economics journals (Stigler et al. 1995, 332). Thus, Grossman's "Notes for a Theory of the Command Economy," perhaps the most profound article in the field, appeared in *Soviet Studies*, and Bergson's "Toward a New Growth Model" was published in *Problems of Communism*.[18] Underdeveloped professionalization also manifested itself in the unusually large role, by the standards of contemporary economics, played by researchers outside of the formal profession (see section 1.4.1).

Effects of the high degree of concentration are analogous to those of the founder effect in population genetics, resulting in greater uniformity of outlook across researchers. Most specialists in the Soviet economy knew one another personally and were graduate students or grand–graduate students of the few founding personalities. In the words of one of the founders, the "closely knit group . . . produced somewhat excessive loyalties and reticences," leading to "a curious absence or near absence of public disagreement" (Gerschenkron 1968, 534). To a British economist who had been writing about the Soviet economy since the 1930s, the discussions at the first major conference of the new field (published as Bergson 1953a) "resemble the proceedings of the most oleaginous type of Mutual Admiration Society, and critical judgments are few and far between" (Clark 1956, 14). As I will show in the next section, most of the debates that did occur were between American Sovietologists and outsiders of various kinds.

The minuscule size of Sovietology relative to the economics profession also meant that there were not enough specialists to cover the range of problems arising in the analysis of a modern economy. Sovietologists were spread thin, leaving some sub-fields the sole preserve of a single researcher, who naturally had no one with whom to debate his work.

## 1.3.2 Reliability of results

By analogy with the industrial organization paradigm, the structure of Sovietology influenced its practitioners' conduct, which in turn determined the field's performance. One aspect of this influence is obvious: the small number of researchers produced fewer findings than a larger number would have done. Less obviously, the small size of the field, high degree of concentration, and aversion to debate reduced the reliability of Sovietological findings.

Knowledge advances through production of new findings and their subsequent critical examination, which involves checking the internal consistency of theoretical constructs, confronting theory with empirical tests, and replicating empirical results. Consider replication, which assures reliability of research findings by confirming true discoveries and weeding out false ones. Not every kind of replication is effective. Replication by the original discoverers, by teams heavily influenced by the original team or school of thought, or under the conditions when the ruling school of thought is so strong as to control publication venues, may result in spurious confirmation. Thus, independent replication requires a number of researchers in the field, with diverse theoretical allegiances (Ioannidis 2012b, 408).

A large fraction of published results in disciplines such as medicine and psychology turn out not to be reproducible ("Unreliable Research" 2013). False findings are not being weeded out effectively, as incentives in academia favor the production of new findings over their replication. "The claimed discoveries that have no published replication attempts apparently make up the vast majority of psychological science" (Ioannidis 2012a, 650). In the absence of replication, fallacies go unchallenged. And even contradicted findings tend to linger in the literature (Tatsioni et al. 2007).

Until recently, replication has been uncommon in economics. Of the 92 replications appearing in three leading journals over the period of 1965–1989, only 20% fully support the original work, and 65% contradict it (Hubbard and Vetter 1992, 29, 32). Individual incentives in academic economics are stacked against spending one's time on replication (Hamermesh 2007). Many fields of economics have too few researchers, producing monopolies and inbreeding. This, combined with other characteristics of the discipline, leads some authors to rate the credibility of economics literature as moderate to low (Ioannidis and Doucouliagos 2013).

All the factors which reduce reliability of published results in empirical economics apply with even greater force to Sovietology. Replication requires re-running an experiment or re-estimating a statistical model. In Sovietology, there were no experiments. Statistical estimation was less common than in economics at large because of the paucity of data, which also limited the opportunities for "replication with extension" (Hubbard and Vetter 1992, 29). This in itself made the field's findings less reliable. In most cases, critically re-examining the evidence and the validity of consequent conclusions would have to do.

The aversion to debate produced by the small size and high degree of concentration or inbreeding—to use Ioannidis's term (2012b)—in the field made critical examination of earlier findings less likely. Results of unknown reliability too often became part of the knowledge base, something "everybody knows." An important example of this is the universal acceptance of the notion of enterprise managers being bonus maximizers, introduced by Berliner (1957) in a pioneering study. Its logic or supporting evidence had never been critically examined, in contrast to the wide-ranging and profound debate on the profit maximization assumption that occurred in mainstream economics during the 1940s and 1950s.[19] Chapters 4 and 5 of this book will render more examples of the propositions commonly accepted in the field yet lacking empirical support and theoretical consistency.

Findings in Sovietology suffered from a particular form of unreliability that may be called fragmentation. Mutually exclusive theoretical propositions and empirical assertions concerning the very fundamentals of the system were held at the same time, sometimes by the same scholars. Unlike, for example, alternative theories of macroeconomics, they were not held by contending schools in debate. The proponents of one did not acknowledge the existence of the other, much less dispute it.

One example of fragmentation concerns Adjusted Factor Cost Standard (AFCS) and Soft Budget Constraint (SBC). AFCS, the earliest theoretical construct in Sovietology, is considered in the field to be an "enormous achievement" (Ellman 2008a). It provided the theoretical underpinnings for national income accounting in a centrally planned economy, and hence for everything we know about Soviet growth and productivity. SBC is a concept used in the analysis of producer behavior that is central to "the most complete positive theory of the socialist economy . . . to date" (Roland 2008, 147). Developed by János Kornai in Hungary in the late 1970s, it was widely accepted by Sovietologists without regard to its incompatibility with AFCS. AFCS is based on the assumption of cost minimization by the producers, while SBC argues that firms are insensitive to input prices and tend to have runaway input demands, which is incompatible with cost minimization.[20] Yet the CIA estimates based on

AFCS peacefully coexist with SBC reasoning under the covers of the same textbooks.[21]

Another case of fragmentation concerns empirical matters, and had large practical consequences for the measurement of Soviet productivity growth, which had always been at the center of both the academic and the government research effort. In the 1970s and 1980s, CIA estimates showed an unprecedented sustained decline in the Soviet total factor productivity. Arithmetically, it was the result of slowing gross national product (GNP) growth and the continued rapid growth of capital stock. The CIA derived GNP series by, among other things, removing the so-called concealed inflation from the official Soviet production data. By contrast, the Agency simply reproduced the official Soviet capital stock data without any adjustment for inflation. The Agency (CIA 1982) justified itself by referring to the work of an academic expert on investment (also the Agency consultant) Stanley Cohn, stating that Soviet-supplied data were in constant prices and thus needed no deflation (Cohn 1981). Yet at the same time, a British researcher specializing in Soviet investment argued, in a Cambridge University Press volume, that they were not (Dyker 1983, 188). Cohn's statement was a reversal, without explanation, of his own earlier position (Cohn 1972, 144–45).[22]

These two opposed positions never confronted each other; they just existed side by side, with a drastic effect on the perception of Soviet economic performance stretching to the present day. The conclusion that "the Soviet economic performance conditional on investment and human capital accumulation was the worst in the world from 1960 to 1989" (Easterly and Fisher 1995, 346) was derived using the data mischaracterized by Cohn and accepted as the standard.

Chapters 3–5 will furnish more examples of fragmentation, in which opposing views—on the objectives of planners, motives of industrialization, and the place of military industry in the economy—existed side by side without confronting each other, sometimes within the oeuvre of the same author.

Fragmentation brings to mind prescientific, mercantilist economics, where every writer was free to ignore the contributions of the others and to start reasoning from scratch (Stigler 1983, 530–32). Stigler's description of mercantilism, in turn, appears to be equivalent to the pre-paradigm state of a discipline in terms of Kuhn (1962).

### 1.3.3 Status within economics

The Sovietologists earned their bread as employees of university economics departments. Their field's standing within the larger discipline affected how they went about their business. This section argues that this standing was low.

At any time, there exists a rough informal consensus among academics on the relative prestige ranking of various fields in their discipline. It is a part of tacit knowledge that every student acquires in graduate school. Prestige matters because it influences the choice of specialization by individual scholars and the hiring decisions by the departments, and through these, ultimately, the field's fate. The best way of discovering the ranking would be a contemporary survey of economists. Absent such a survey, I will rely on the opinions of reputable scholars.

A much-quoted pseudo-anthropological article lampooning the mores of the academic economists compared various fields to castes, with mathematical economics ranking above both microeconomics and macroeconomics, and both of the latter outranking development economics (Leijonhufvud 1973, 328–29). Twenty years later, a development economist surveying the state of his field confirmed that its ranking had remained low (Bardhan 1993, 129).

Leading Sovietologists testified that their field was viewed by departmental colleagues as "peripheral," occupying "a lowly position in the internal hierarchy," and being a "low-prestige end of the profession."[23] A prominent "outsider" (the term is explained in section 1.4.1) concurred (Birman 1983b, 226). When the National Council on Foreign Language and International Studies cited "weak responsiveness of economics departments to regional specialization" as a barrier to increasing the number of Sovietologists, they also meant the low regard in which the field was held (US Senate 1982, 65).[24]

Indirect evidence suggests that Sovietology's rank was not just below mathematical economics, but at the bottom of the heap, below that of development. Economic development and Sovietology were Cold War siblings, fields established at about the same time and, in part, for the same reasons. Before World War II, "Western economists ignored the underdeveloped world," though there did exist a field of colonial economics (Arndt 1987, 31). Development did not emerge as a field of economics until the 1950s, its rise motivated, among other things, by the policy need of immunizing poor countries against Soviet advances.[25]

Table 1.1. Number of panels devoted to each of the "Cold
War siblings" at the AEA annual meetings, 1948–1972.

| Subject | Number of panels |
| --- | --- |
| Development economics | 28 |
| Socialist economies | 15 |
| Defense economics | 8 |

Source: Derived from the programs of the annual meetings published in the American Economic Review Papers and Proceedings,
1948–1972. I counted panels with titles, omitting invited disser-
tations and Ely lectures. Classification by field is based on panel
and sometimes paper titles. Panels at the intersection of several
areas were arbitrarily classified as relating to only one of those.

Yet the trajectories of the two fields diverged from the beginning.
Development economists acquired their first American journal, Economic
Development and Cultural Change, in 1952, and by 1977, when the
Sovietologists got theirs, development economists had a number of journals all over the world.[26] At the annual American Economic Association
(AEA) meetings between 1948 and 1972, development had twice as many
panels as did "socialist economies," a broader field including Sovietology
(table 1.1). In the words of one of the founders of development, "the fifties saw a remarkable outpouring of fundamental ideas and models which
were to dominate the new field and to generate controversies that contributed much to its liveliness" (Hirschman 1981, 1). While many of these
ideas were later discarded (Fishlow 1991, 1728–30), others were adopted
by mainstream economics.[27] Sovietology had no comparable period, and
I do not remember ever seeing it characterized as lively. Nor did its contributions ever receive the kind of reviews such as those by Hirschman,
Fishlow, Bardhan, and Krugman, as a comparison with a review by Clarke
(1983) showed.

All this indicates the development field's larger size and, perhaps,
greater productivity compared to Sovietology. This differential does not
seem to be due to higher student demand for development courses. As
table 1.2 shows, at the end of 1970s development lagged in undergraduate
enrollment behind comparative economics, a course a Sovietologist would
typically teach. This lag is even greater if one adds courses on the Soviet
economy proper and on planning. It is natural to assume that the field's

Table 1.2.  Undergraduate enrollment in "Cold War siblings" economics
courses, colleges and universities with economics major, average
of 1978–1979 and 1979–1980.

| Course | Percent of schools offering | Number of sections | Average class size |
|---|---|---|---|
| Economic development | 58.2 | 351 | 21.3 |
| Comparative economics | 63.1 | 367 | 24.5 |
| Economics of the USSR | 11.9 | 58 | 21.6 |
| Planning* | 3.7 | 30 | 34.5 |
| Chinese economics* | 3.5 | 28 | 27.6 |
| Defense economics | 1.8 | 16 | 19.8 |

Source: Siegfried and Wilkinson 1982, 133.

* Planning and Chinese economics are included because they were likely taught by Sovietologists.

prestige is positively correlated with its size and productivity, other things being equal.

Another indirect argument for Sovietology's inferior status relative to development is the anticipation of the former's extinction in the late 1970s. At that time the first generation of Sovietologists, holding positions at top universities, neared retirement, and "economics departments rarely hired more than one Soviet specialist; more than two [was] unheard of" (Millar 1995, 226).[28] It became clear to insiders and the outside observers alike that the high-ranking departments were unlikely to replace their sole, retiring Sovietologists, and thus would lose the capacity to produce new PhDs in the field. In addition to aging, Sovietology also appears to have experienced net outflow of researchers to other fields. I can easily name three prominent émigrés (John M. Montias, Michael Manove, and Martin Weitzman) but only one immigrant (Warren Nutter).

This raised the prospect of the field's withering from the top.[29] A National Endowment for the Humanities–Ford Foundation study of twenty top research universities found East European and Soviet economics to be "on the list of academic endangered species" (Barber and Ilchman 1980, 68). While the development field knew its ups and downs (Diamond and Haurin 1995, 119), it was never an endangered species.[30]

## *1.4  Colleagues and competitors*

Evaluating the performance of academic Sovietology needs to be done relative to some standard. Society's expectations at the time of its founding,
as described earlier in this chapter, provide one such standard, though
rather general and undifferentiated. The success of American academic
Sovietology can also be evaluated through comparison with other groups
writing on the same subject: government analysts, foreign academics, and
various interlopers. These groups, working in different institutional envir-
onments, faced different incentives, and can be expected to have behaved
differently when, say, choosing research topics.

### 1.4.1  The British, outsiders, political scientists, and others

The United States, the main Western player in the Cold War, was home
to by far the largest contingent of Sovietologists, small as it was. Great
Britain was a distant second, with the field arising there at the same time
as in the United States. Courses on the Soviet economy were taught at
the London School of Economics and the universities of Birmingham and
Glasgow since the 1940s and early 1950s (Frank 1964, 91). *Soviet Studies,*
the first periodical devoted to the "systematic study of the society functioning . . . in the Soviet Union," started publication in Glasgow in 1949
("Editorial" 1949, 1).

   However, the motivation for the rise of Sovietology in Britain differed
from that in the United States. In line with the different role of European
countries in the Cold War, strategic considerations had little to do with
the founding of the new field.[31] National security was not mentioned in the
mission statement of *Soviet Studies* ("Editorial" 1949, 1–2). Recounting the
journal's beginnings a quarter-century later, its first coeditor only mentioned the Cold War as a reason for everyone to shun the idea of a new
periodical. Both of the original coeditors were communists, not Cold
Warriors (Miller 1973, 167–68). Canada, Israel, Japan, and the countries
of Western Europe each had a few Sovietologists, some of them with
American doctorates.

   Like the general discipline of economics, American and foreign academic Sovietology were fully integrated. The US government may have
been drawing on the expertise of foreign Sovietologists even more inten-
sively than was the case in the other economic fields, as witnessed by their
participation in the US Senate Joint Economic Committee compendia of

papers. But apparently their professional incentives and constraints differed enough from those of their American colleagues to produce different research outcomes, as will be shown in chapter 3.

Unusually for modern economics, authors who held no academic, think tank, or government job played a significant role in Sovietological literature. Called here "outsiders," they were, by definition, not subject to the constraints and incentives of academic Sovietology. This unconventional group consisted mostly, but not exclusively, of Soviet émigrés, and is best described through a series of examples. Naum Jasny was the earliest and the most prominent outsider, earning both a festschrift and a book-length biography.[32] He started his study of the Soviet economy upon retiring from the US Department of Agriculture (Jasny 1976, 110). Antony Sutton made his important contribution while at the Hoover Institution. He was not trained as a Sovietologist, and prior to Hoover served as a professor of economics at the California State University of Los Angeles, where he did not publish on Soviet matters, or on any other matters as far as I could ascertain. After being fired from Hoover, he does not appear to have held a job, and went on to write volumes with titles like *The Federal Reserve Conspiracy*, *Trilaterals over America*, and *America's Secret Establishment*.[33] Igor Birman, prior to his emigration a well-known Soviet economist, and Dmitri Steinberg, the last of the outsiders, earned their living by doing contract research for the US government.[34]

In a field noted for its lack of public disagreements, British Sovietologists and the outsiders initiated most of the debates. Peter Wiles criticized AFCS in the mid-1950s, and Alec Nove and Philip Hanson raised doubts about the accepted interpretation of the Soviet investment statistics in the 1980s.[35] Jasny (1956) attacked the uses of Soviet statistics. Lee (1977) and Steinberg (1990) disputed the CIA estimates of military expenditures. Most of these controversies and criticisms were also published in the British *Soviet Studies*.

Yet another group of outsiders consisted of the post–World War II Soviet émigrés working for the CIA-financed Munich Institute for the Study of the USSR or teaching at the US Army school in Germany. Often lacking economics training, they published mainly in their in-house periodicals and the Institute volumes, in which they hardly ever referred to the works of the Sovietologists—and the latter reciprocated.

Finally, political scientists, sociologists, geographers, and other non-economists produced literature on some aspects of the Soviet economy.

This natural result of the overlapping interests of various social sciences was perhaps enhanced by the organization of inquiry. The founders of the Soviet studies intended an interdisciplinary approach, hence university centers that brought together all social sciences and humanities concerned with the area (Mosely 1959). This approach succeeded in that Sovietologists attended many of the same conferences, published in the same journals, and contributed to the same joint volumes as the other social scientists more often than was common in mainstream economics. This was also the characteristic of development economics, which, according to Leijonhufvud (1973, 329), earned it its low standing within the discipline. The area-studies approach may be said to have failed in that the disciplinary departments, deciding on hiring, tenure, and promotion, retained their members' primary loyalty. To the degree that the professional agendas and standards differed across social sciences, we may expect to see non-economists' writings deviating from the Sovietological norm.

## 1.4.2 Academics and government analysts

Employees of the federal government, primarily the CIA, and of government-sponsored institutions were the second largest group of experts—after academics—analyzing Soviet and East European economies, or 35%–40% of the total by one estimate (US Senate 1982, 64). Private sector employment of Sovietologists was negligible, though the same estimate puts it at a surprisingly high 5%–10% of the total.

The division of labor between the two groups was similar to that of academic and government economists in the study of the American economy. The government experts' main contribution came in the area in which they had a monopoly: the supply of macroeconomic statistics. The CIA produced annual estimates of the Soviet national income and product accounts, and, in a separate effort, estimated Soviet military expenditures using its clandestine sources (section 2.2.2). Though government experts also worked on a variety of other topics, much of their research dealt with technical issues or was of a short-term nature, looking for quick answers to current questions.[36]

While the academic Sovietologists also did their share of technical and short-term work, they aspired to advance the deep understanding of their subject, perhaps contributing along the way to the knowledge of society in general; to forge new tools of inquiry; and to train specialists to be employed by the government. The net flow of ideas and methods in the study of the Soviet economy went from academia to the government (Engerman 2009, 253), as is also the case for the study of the US economy. The large, visible instances of such transfer included AFCS, developed by Abram Bergson, a professor at Columbia and later at Harvard, forming a base of CIA's national accounting estimates. The large-scale econometric forecasting model used by the CIA was originally developed at the University of Pennsylvania.[37]

Less obviously, but also more importantly, the flow of ideas operated through the government hiring of personnel trained in academia and engaging academics as consultants. General Odom testified on the need to support academic Soviet studies: "The quality of the analysis" in the intelligence community "has its origins in the academic world." Professors "have a tremendous and sometimes greatly underestimated influence in the books they write and in the students they teach. Those people come into the Government, and they bring the insights and the conceptual perspectives of that literature, and our analysis really does not, in its intellectual quality, rise a great deal above that level."[38]

While both tenured Sovietologists and their civil-service colleagues consulted government departments and testified in Congress, the former were the field's public face. They taught college students, published popular books and opinion pieces, appeared on TV when lucky, were consulted by journalists and businessmen, and supplied economic expertise to researchers of Soviet domestic and foreign policy and society. I remember Fen Montaigne, a *Philadelphia Inquirer* correspondent about to go on assignment to the Soviet Union, meeting with Holland Hunter at Haverford College and sitting through a long lecture on the economic problems of the country of his posting.

Academic Sovietologists, with their status as independent experts, enjoyed greater public credibility than CIA analysts. In the late 1970s and early 1980s, the Agency depicted the prospects of the Soviet economy "as more desperate . . . than most specialists consider plausible" (Hanson 1981, 41). At the time, this discrepancy fueled distrust in the work of the CIA. "European officials and private experts . . . are, in general, skeptical about the US intelligence community's bleak forecast of the Soviet economy" (Kaufman 1978, 5). As it happens, the CIA's bleak forecasts turned out to be closer to reality than those of its academic critics (Kontorovich 2001).

The relations between academia and the CIA occasionally went beyond polite scholarly disagreement. *Slavic Review*, the main American journal for Soviet area studies, published a poorly argued piece accusing the Agency of negativity and lack of balance (Moskoff 1981). A college textbook accused the CIA of falsifying the data used to estimate Soviet defense expenditures (Zimbalist and Sherman 1984, 201). This level of distrust and hostility is not found in the relations between the academics studying the American economy and, say, the US Department of Commerce analysts.

The work of the government branch of Sovietology, in developing national income account and defense expenditures estimates, has been subjected to serious scrutiny. The unexpected endgame of the Cold War bolstered the credibility of long-standing critics of the CIA estimates, prompting Congress to conduct a series of inquiries into the agency's work on the Soviet economy. The Senate's Committee on Foreign Relations held hearings, and members of both houses commissioned reports from the then–General Accounting Office and the National Research Council on the estimates of the Soviet economy's size and growth.[39] The House Permanent Select Committee on Intelligence appointed a Review Committee to report on the agency's estimates of the military expenditures (Berkowitz et al. 1993).[40] While the reports were generally favorable to the CIA, the debate continued through the 1990s, with the defenders of the CIA's record responding to its erstwhile "unduly harsh criticism" (Maddison 1998, 307).[41]

Academic Sovietology—the larger, more diversified in terms of topics, more influential, and methodologically the leading part of the field—has so far avoided analytical assessment. Retrospective writings about the study of the Soviet economy tended toward broad general statements unsupported by detailed analysis. Schroeder (1995) offered a blanket apologia, and Wilhelm (2003) an equally undifferentiated condemnation of the field. Engerman's (2009) history of all the branches of Soviet studies is valuable and frequently cited in this book. Yet his evaluation of the performance of economics suffers from the absence of criteria for judging success or failure, as well as the uncritical reproduction of the claims of veteran Sovietologists about the invariably excellent work they believe they did (Kontorovich 2011).

This book does not attempt to provide an assessment of the whole field. It focuses on the work done on just one, though arguably the most important, sector of the Soviet economy.

# *Notes*

1. Millar (1996, 226); Bowen (1953, 212). The scale of pre–World War II work on the Soviet economy in Europe was somewhat larger (Wiles 1964, 69–70).
2. Campbell (1961, 130). See also Gerschenkron (1968, 525); Wiles (1964, 70).
3. Pollak (1996, 40); Friedberg (2000, 35–39); Friedman (2000, 25).
4. Mosely (1959, 20–21) dissents from the commonly accepted view of the Cold War origin of Russian and Soviet studies. Naimark (1998, 2–3) stresses their World War II origins.
5. Also Grossman (1959, 34). This view was shared by the British Sovietologists (Wiles 1961, 88; Zauberman 1963, 455).
6. Accessed November 11, 2004, http://daviscenter.fas.harvard.edu/about_us/history.html (page discontinued).
7. Dallin (1982, 21); Holden (1984, 795); Harris (1997, 451).
8. Dallin (1982, 18); Harris (1997, 454); Engerman (2009, 250–52).
9. US Senate (1982, 48, 72).
10. US Senate (1982, 1, 4, 17, 20, 615–62).
11. References in Bergson (1961, vii–x).
12. Shulman (1970, 585–6); Dallin (1982, 25).
13. Shulman (1970, 585). Also US House (1971, 1433).
14. See Shulman (1970, 586) on funding and section 1.3.3 on the field's extinction.
15. US Senate (1982, 23, 30). Major General William Odom, at the time US Army's assistant chief of staff for intelligence, was a scholar of Soviet affairs.
16. Schultz (1990, 447); Millar (1995, 247–50).
17. *The ACES Bulletin* (previously *The ASTE Bulletin*), published from 1958 to 1984, served as "an informal means of communication among members" rather than a full-blown scholarly journal, as noted by the editors at its conversion to *Comparative Economic Studies* (Brada 1985, iii).
18. Grossman (1963); Bergson (1973).
19. For a critical view of bonus maximization, see Kontorovich (1986).
20. Bergson (1953b, 67); Kornai (1986, 11; 1992, 146, 264–65, 268, 273).
21. CIA estimates: Kornai (1992, 194–5, 200); Gregory and Stuart (2001, 210–15). SBC: Kornai (1992, 140–44); Gregory and Stuart (2001, 116, 186).
22. Cohn (1981) and CIA (1982) were factually wrong and Dyker (1983) correct; see Kontorovich (1989).
23. Herbert Levine in US Senate (1982, 45); Ellman (2009, 14); Millar (1995, 266).
24. Note also this entry at an economics website: http://www.econjobrumors.com/topic/ranking-fields-by-prestige, visited July 15, 2015.
25. Meier (2005, 12–13, 207–8); Backhouse (2002, 301); Arndt (1987, 49).
26. For the other early journals, see Meier (2005, 52).
27. Bardhan (1993); Krugman (1998).

28. A remarkable lack of mobility of Sovietologists across universities, noted by Millar (1995, 228), is also perhaps a sign of the field's low standing. I do not have comparable data on development economists.

29. Millar (1980, 317–18, 327–28); Dallin (1982, 14).

30. All the information on the low prestige of Sovietology used here relates to the 1970s and 1980s, and so do my conclusions. It is possible that in its infancy, the field had higher prestige than in its last two decades.

31. Philip Hanson, personal communication concerning Britain and France.

32. Degras and Nove (1964); Jasny (1976). The latter consists of fragments of a memoir embedded in the biography compiled by the editors.

33. Wikipedia, s.v. "Antony C. Sutton," visited November 18, 2015, https://en.wikipedia.org/wiki/Antony_C._Sutton; Sutton (1995a; 1995b; 2003).

34. On Birman, see Shapiro (2011). An article contrasting Steinberg's work with that of the Soviet statistical apparatus was titled "A Free Economist against All the King's Men" (Sverdlik 1990).

35. The bibliography of the debates is in Bergson (1961, 104) and Kontorovich (1989, 328n2).

36. Dallin (1982, 23); Atkinson (1987, 192).

37. Congress (1982, 11); Green and Higgins (1977); CIA (1979).

38. US Senate (1982, 21–22, 23, 24).

39. US Senate (1991); General Accounting Office (1992); Alexeev and Walker (1991).

40. Further discussed by Holzman (1994) and Millar (1994).

41. Becker (1994); Berkowitz and Richelson (1995); MacEachin (1996); Maddison (1998); Firth and Noren (1998).

## 2

# The Politburo's Holy of Holies

THE CENTRAL THESIS of this book, that Sovietology overlooked the military sector, is only interesting if the latter was worth noticing. It was certainly noteworthy enough to elicit poetic descriptions from high-ranking party officials. "The Holy of Holies" is how General Secretary M. Gorbachev described the task of "strengthening defense" at a high-level party meeting. "Defense is life" are the words of the Politburo member and defense minister D. Ustinov.[1]

In chapter 1 I argued that the Soviet military sector deserved attention because it provided the material underpinnings necessary for the Soviets to wage the Cold War. In this chapter I show that the military sector was a highly unusual part of the Soviet economy which should have interested Sovietologists for its own sake, quite apart from Western security concerns.

## 2.1 A pillar of the system's original design

The Soviet system in its classical form was created in the late 1920s and early 1930s. This is also the time when the military sector acquired its recognizable shape and started on its steep growth trajectory. As with the other important institutions and policies established at that time, such as comprehensive central planning and the strategy of economic growth, the structure of the military sector and its place within the economy lasted the lifetime of the USSR.

The ideas that shaped the creation of the military sector were developed by the military writers of the 1920s, of whom more will be said in section 5.6. Their thinking was based on an analysis of the experience of the major powers in World War I and on the country's reigning Bolshevik ideology. The latter postulated the inevitability of war between the USSR and its capitalist surroundings, that is, the rest of the world.[2] The former showed that fighting such a war would require a continuous supply of very large quantities of technically sophisticated goods—weapons, ammunition, and means of transportation—over a protracted period of time.

Preparing the Soviet economy for the inevitable involved creating the capacity to produce technologically advanced goods in a relatively backward country, where some crucial subsectors, such as tank manufacturing, did not even exist. Once established, military production had to keep up with ever changing weapons technology. While fulfilling the peacetime orders of the armed forces, industry had to be capable of rapidly scaling up production to meet much greater wartime needs, without bankrupting the economy. This scalability requirement applied not just to munitions manufacturers proper, but, equally important, to their upstream suppliers, producers of various metals and chemicals. War against the rest of the world would mean a certain economic blockade, so all this production had to rely solely on domestic inputs.

Much had changed in the world between the 1920s and the 1980s. Nuclear weapons transformed the nature of warfare, making a replay of World War I extremely unlikely. Relatedly, the ideological dogma of inevitable all-out war between socialism and capitalism was retired in the mid-1950s. Still, the military sector preserved the characteristics it acquired at its founding. In 1987, a newly-appointed Foreign Affairs Minister was surprised to hear the Chief of the General Staff expound a Soviet military doctrine which amounted to a plan to "fight practically the entire world" (Belanovsky 1998, 41–42). Even towards the end of Soviet rule, the structure of the economy—and of its specialized military branch—still embodied the principles enunciated by the writers of the 1920s.[3]

## 2.2  A wartime-size peacetime military sector

The magnitude of a nation's military effort is measured by its defense expenditures. The burden of defense, calculated as a percentage share of defense expenditures in the total national spending, such as GNP, for the same period, shows the degree of the economy's militarization and allows for comparisons across economies of different size. Understandably, defense burden varies greatly between periods of peace and war. Burden of defense in the United States went from 1.3% in 1938 to over 40% in 1943 (table 2.1). Our concern here is with the peacetime burden of defense, which was unusually high in the USSR.

**Table 2.1.** Defense burden of the major powers in World War II, 1938–1945, %.

| Year | United States | | UK | Germany | Japan | Italy | USSR |
|------|---------------|---------------|-------------------|-------------------|-------------------|----------------|---------------------|
| | 1958 prices | Current prices | Current prices | Current prices | Current prices | 1938 prices | 1937 factor cost |
| 1938 | 1.3 | 1.2 | 7.4 | 17.0 | 24.0 | 10.0 | — |
| 1939 | 1.4 | 1.3 | 15.3 | 23.0 | 22.0 | 8.0 | — |
| 1940 | 2.4 | 2.2 | 43.8 | 40.0 | 22.0 | 12.0 | 17.0 |
| 1941 | 11.2 | 11.1 | 52.7 | 52.0 | 27.0 | 23.0 | 28.0 |
| 1942 | 31.6 | 31.3 | 55.3 | 64.0 | 33.0 | 22.0 | 61.0 |
| 1943 | 43.1 | 41.6 | — | 70.0 | 43.0 | 21.0 | 61.0 |
| 1944 | 45.0 | 41.6 | 53.4 | — | 76.0 | 17.0 | 53.0 |
| 1945 | 39.0 | 34.7 | — | — | — | 23.0 | — |

*Sources*: United States: share of GNP (Rockoff 1998, 83). United Kingdom: share of net national expenditure (Broadberry and Howlett 1998, 47). Germany: share of GNP (Harrison 1998a, 21). Japan: share of GDP (Hara 1998, 257). Italy: share of GDP (Zamagni 1998, 203). USSR: share of GNP (Harrison 1998a, 21).

For Western countries, the data necessary to calculate the burden of defense are found in the regular government statistical reports. In the case of the Soviet Union and other communist countries, official data were, when available, considered untrustworthy. Hence, the need for independent estimation by foreign experts, who were confronted by the issues of secrecy, peculiar statistical practices, and arbitrary prices when deriving the numerator and, to a lesser degree, the denominator of the burden of defense. There is no single universally accepted estimate for the burden of defense in the USSR, but rather a set of numbers derived by different methods, each with its own serious problems. Some of these are briefly introduced here so as not to give the reader a false sense of certainty in the numbers.

### 2.2.1 Official Soviet data

For decades, defense outlays in the state budget were the only officially reported number concerning the Soviet military sector. It implied a defense burden of 2.3%–2.5% from 1965 to 1988 (Davis 2002, 156). While Western experts initially accepted the state budget allocation as an accurate measure of defense expenditures, by the early 1960s many recognized it as being too low, though some continued to use official Soviet data to the bitter end (Firth and Noren 1998, 175–76). In 1989, the Soviets owned up to deception and issued revised expenditures data. Combined with a few bits of data that filtered into the media in the early 1990s, the new number put the 1987–88 defense burden at 8.3%–8.4%.[4]

The veracity of the new data was undermined by the official pronouncements surrounding their release (Noren 1995, 258–60). It was positively demolished by the orgy of hints and semi-revelations from the top levels of the country's hierarchy.

A former Minister of Finance and Prime Minister stated that military expenditures constituted 34%–36% of Net Material Product (NMP) (Pavlov 1993, 15).[5] A Gorbachev advisor put military expenditures at up to 40% of NMP, and quoted his boss as saying that arms procurement and expenditures on KGB and the Ministry of Internal Affairs together accounted for 20% of the "national income," "the highest military expenditures in the world" (Shakhnazarov 1993, 42, 49).[6] Gorbachev (1995, 334) himself stated that the output of military industry alone—a fraction of military spending—was 20% of Gross Social Product, a broader aggregate than the NMP.[7] Gorbachev (1995, 319) also stated that "for many years, military expenditures were growing at a rate 1.5–2 times higher than national income," implying not just high, but continuously increasing burden of defense. A later and economically literate source repeated Pavlov's number on the military expenditures as a share of NMP, and gave their share of GNP as 20%–25% (Lipsits 1995, 14). The latter is the same as Epstein's (1990, 153) estimate, which included "the cost of empire" in the numerator. One wonders if, in the absence of believable domestic numbers, the ex-Soviet officials were simply recycling the Western ones, as was also suggested by Shlykov (2001).

That Gorbachev and Pavlov, instead of citing the estimates announced by their former subordinates, offered different, much higher ones, probably means that they did not trust the official numbers, and neither should we. However, there is also no reason to trust the numbers cited by the rulers, who supplied no details on their provenance, coverage, or relevant period. All one can conclude is that the rulers, based on their personal experience, believed Soviet defense expenditures to be very high.

Former top officials of the military industry ridiculed Gorbachev's revelations and continued to support low expenditures numbers. In the process, however, they added no details and multiplied confusion. Thus, Shlykov (2002, 166–67) quotes two former heads of the military industry giving military burden at 3% (Baklanov in 1990) or 7% (Masliukov in 1996) "of the country's resources."[8]

The merry-go-round of numbers cited by the Soviet officials suggested that they did not know what total military spending was.[9] This does not mean that the top decisionmakers were negligent or lacked interest in the military sector. Spending on different items of defense was entered on the books of different ministries and administrations, and no one cared to add up all the numbers across bureaucratic boundaries.[10] This was not a specifically Soviet way of doing things. With all the secret archives long open, historians are still arguing about the magnitude of military expenditures in Hitler's Germany, in part due to its "institutional fragmentation of military-economic accountancy" (Abelshauser 1998, 133). Apparently one does not need to know the total expenditures to run a successful military economy. Spending decisions taken at every step are incremental, concerning specific programs, rather than a macroeconomic statistical abstraction of burden of defense.

### 2.2.2 Western estimates

The CIA derived its estimates of Soviet defense expenditures using the "direct costing" method, multiplying physical quantities of goods and services going to the military by their ruble prices (Swain 1990). The quantities were obtained by intelligence means. The prices used were of mixed origin: civilian sector prices for goods and services also used by the military, such as fuel or construction; actual personnel pay rates and prices paid by the military, apparently obtained through intelligence means; and dollar estimates of what it would cost to produce a military item in the United States, converted into rubles using dollar-ruble ratios for different categories of procurement (Noren 1995, 267).

Like the official Soviet reporting on military expenditures, the CIA effort had its own instance of great upward revision. For a time in the 1960s and early 1970s, the CIA estimated the Soviet defense burden at about 6%, roughly the same as that of the United States. In 1976, defense expenditures were revised so as to double the burden of defense. Insufficient and obsolete price information was cited as the main reason for the earlier, low estimates (Firth and Noren 1998, 55, 59–60). The latest numbers produced by the Agency before the estimation project was disconnected put the burden of defense at 14.4%–17.8% in current prices in the 1980s (table 2.2).

The new information that became available with the Soviet collapse did not dispel the uncertainties surrounding these estimates, even according

Table 2.2. Burden of defense in the USSR and the United States,
1950–1990 (% of GNP).

| Year | Soviet Union | | United State | Year | Soviet Union | | United States |
|------|------|------|------|------|------|------|------|
| | 1982 prices | Current prices | Current prices | | 1982 prices | Current prices | Current prices |
| 1951 | 24.2 | — | — | 1971 | 15.1 | — | 6.9 |
| 1952 | 23.4 | — | — | 1972 | 14.9 | — | 6.0 |
| 1953 | 19.4 | — | — | 1973 | 15.2 | — | 5.6 |
| 1954 | 18.3 | — | — | 1974 | 15.4 | — | 5.7 |
| 1955 | 19.5 | — | — | 1975 | 15.5 | — | 5.3 |
| 1956 | 17.1 | — | — | 1976 | 15.0 | 13.6 | 5.0 |
| 1957 | 15.0 | — | — | 1977 | 15.0 | — | 5.0 |
| 1958 | 14.3 | — | — | 1978 | 14.4 | — | 4.8 |
| 1959 | 13.6 | — | — | 1979 | 15.0 | 14.7 | 4.8 |
| 1960 | 14.5 | — | 9.5 | 1980 | 15.3 | — | 5.0 |
| 1961 | 15.3 | — | 9.4 | 1981 | 14.9 | 14.4 | 5.3 |
| 1962 | 16.1 | — | 9.1 | 1982 | 14.8 | 15.0 | 5.9 |
| 1963 | 16.6 | — | 8.7 | 1983 | 14.6 | 14.4 | 6.3 |
| 1964 | 15.7 | — | 7.5 | 1984 | 14.7 | 15.2 | 6.2 |
| 1965 | 16.0 | — | 7.9 | 1985 | 14.9 | 15.9 | 6.4 |
| 1966 | 15.6 | — | 9.0 | 1986 | 14.9 | 16.4 | 6.5 |
| 1967 | 15.8 | — | 9.6 | 1987 | 15.7 | 17.6 | 6.4 |
| 1968 | 16.1 | — | 8.9 | 1988 | 15.5 | 17.8 | 6.1 |
| 1969 | 16.4 | — | 8.3 | 1989 | 14.3 | 15.6 | 5.9 |
| 1970 | 15.4 | 12.2 | 7.5 | 1990 | 13.8 | — | 5.5 |

*Sources*: Firth & Noren 1998, 129–30; US Census 1991, 336.

to their defenders. Thus, it has been suggested that the GNP estimate, the denominator, may have been either on the high side (Bergson 1991, 39), or on the low side because it did not account for the unofficial economy and also was not revised in light of later Soviet statistical revelations (Noren 1995, 245). If the military were paying heavily subsidized prices for goods and services they received from the rest of the economy, as is now acknowledged (Cooper 1998, 245), defense expenditures estimate, the numerator, understated the volume of resources going to the military sector. Correcting for these subsidies proved impossible because of the nature of information available (Firth and Noren 1998, 131–32). Widespread use of different prices for the same goods also undermines the CIA estimates, or at least their economic interpretation according to AFCS, which assumed uniform pricing.

The stocks of some major weapons announced by the Russian officials after 1991 turned out to be significantly greater than the Western estimates at the end of the 1980s. There were one-third more nuclear warheads and twice as much weapons-grade uranium (Broad 1993). The number of tanks was apparently underestimated by more than one-fifth (Shlykov 2001). The chemical and bacteriological weapons program was ten times larger than estimated (Douglass 1995). The exclusion of these items would bias the CIA expenditure estimates—which have not been revised after the fall of the USSR—downward.[11] Finally, much of the CIA work on Soviet military expenditures remains classified, and can only be judged based on the details that the insiders themselves were allowed to disclose.[12]

The CIA effort was by far the most elaborate and costly, relying on the intelligence collection system of a superpower. While no one else could use the "direct costing" method, there were a number of competing Western estimates of Soviet defense expenditures or its components derived by the residual method.[13] These estimates were based on the assumption that in the Soviet statistical system, information was defined, collected, and compiled in a uniform fashion across different sectors and aggregated into national totals which formed a consistent system of national accounts (Treml 1993, 4). Military spending and its component, weapons procurement, were not reported separately, but were included in the total reported government outlays and, in the latter case, the output of machinebuilding. Subtracting all the explicitly identified civilian components from these totals would then yield the residual that had to include the sought-after military magnitude. Alternatively, military components were not included into the totals but could be reconstructed through other, interconnected parts of national accounts.

For such an exercise to be feasible, one needed data on the reasonably complete list of civilian components, a condition more or less satisfied since the early 1960s, when Soviet statistical yearbooks regained their heft. However, even this simple-sounding calculation required additional assumptions about bookkeeping conventions, statisticians' stratagems, and missing magnitudes. Much as the analysts tried to ground these assumptions in what seemed plausible about the Soviet economy, they still came up with widely varying approaches.[14] These, in turn, led to different estimates.

The post-1991 realization that the Soviet statistical system was fragmented, with Ministries of Finance and Defense collecting their own data according to their own definitions and sharing them only sparingly with the Central Statistical Administration, cast doubt on the validity of the residual method. If military expenditures were not added up into a single category, but instead scattered in the accounts of numerous agencies, there is no reason to identify the residual with defense spending.[15] However, it may be premature to completely reject all residual estimates, as Firth and Noren (1998, 191) did, before we know the specific deficiencies of Soviet statistics in greater detail.

The most comprehensive residual estimate, and the only one making use of the additional information released in the final years before the collapse, yielded a defense burden of 18%–19% in current prices for 1980–1988 (Steinberg 1992, 263). While Steinberg's method was based on many vulnerable assumptions, its potential weaknesses appear to be independent from those of the CIA method.[16]

## 2.2.3 Trying to make sense of it all

Revised official Soviet data define the lower bound on possible expenditures, because they exclude military spending by ministries other than Defense, and were calculated in prices that undervalued goods and services purchased by the military (Cooper 1998, 244–45). Still, even the patently low burden of defense these data imply is 1.3 times higher than that of the United States at the time, and two to three times higher than the average for Western Europe in the 1980s (ACDA 1995, 24). The last time the American burden of defense reached such a level was at the height of Vietnam War in 1966–69.

Competing Western estimates were the subject of fierce debates in the last two decades of the Soviet regime. However, much of the past disagreement concerned short-to-medium-run changes in the estimates, which were used as arguments in the debates on the US defense budget, when "every evidence of small acceleration or decline in the rate of growth [of CIA's procurement estimates] was probably taken more seriously than it should have been."[17] These are of no concern for us here, and otherwise, the competing estimates paint a broadly consistent picture of very high defense expenditures.[18] Of course, an 18% burden of defense is 1.5 times greater than a 12% burden. Both, however, are far above what one can observe in a regular peacetime economy.

In the opinion of independent scholars, "in retrospect, the CIA's estimations appear the most plausible"; "14–16% represents a more credible share of GNP in 1988–89."[19] The CIA estimate of the defense burden in the 1980s was 14.4%–17.8%, or 2.5–3 times higher than the American level in the 1970s and 1980s (table 2.2). A burden of defense this high in that period could only be found in the Middle East (17% in 1983 and 12% in 1989), where major wars were actually fought or anticipated (ACDA 1995, 24). It is also comparable to the burden of defense of the United States and United Kingdom in the first year of their respective participation in World War II, of Germany in the years immediately preceding the war, or of Japan the year it invaded China (table 2.3). The Soviet defense burden in 1940 is estimated at 17% (table 2.1). These estimates suggest that the USSR maintained a wartime level of military expenditures during the four decades of peace.

**Table 2.3. Defense burden of major powers in the buildup to World War II, %, 1932–1938.**

| Year | Germany | | | United States | UK | Japan | Italy |
|------|-----|-----|-----|------------------|------------------|------------------|----------------|
| | A | B | C | Current prices | Current prices | Current prices | 1938 prices |
| 1932 | 1.0 | 1.4 | 0.7 | — | — | — | — |
| 1933 | 3.0 | 1.6 | 1.1 | 1.0 | 3.0 | — | 4.0 |
| 1934 | 6.0 | 6.3 | 5.6 | 1.0 | 3.0 | — | 4.0 |
| 1935 | 8.0 | 8.7 | 9.7 | 1.0 | 2.0 | — | 5.0 |
| 1936 | 13.0 | 15.7 | — | 1.0 | 5.0 | — | 11.0 |
| 1937 | 13.0 | 14.7 | — | 1.0 | 7.0 | 15.0 | 11.0 |
| 1938 | 17.0 | 18.9 | — | 1.2 | 8.0 | 24.0 | 10.0 |

*Sources*: Germany A: share of current price GNP (Carrol 1968, 184). Germany B: Military spending (Wehrmacht) as a share of Net National Product at factor cost (Abelshauser 1998, 138). Germany C: Reich military as a share of GDP in 1913 prices (Tooze 2006 63). United States: share of GNP (Carrol 1968, 184). United Kingdom: share of National Income (Carrol 1968, 184). Japan: share of GDP (Hara 1998, 257). Italy: share of GDP (Zamagni 1998, 203).

## 2.3  The defense industry

The defense expenditures discussed in the previous section cover a wide range of activities: paying the armed forces personnel, maintenance and operations, construction, weapons procurement, and research and development.[20] The last two items relate to the most innovative element of the contemporary armed forces. It was the ability to produce large quantities of up-to-date weapons that determined countries' military might in the last century. The sector of the economy that turns out military hardware is called the defense industry. In the USSR, it was the most successful sector of the economy. It owed this success to its unique place in the Soviet economic and political system and its non-standard internal organization.

### 2.3.1  A sector apart

In the last two decades of the Soviet regime, the defense industry comprised nine industrial ministries: shipbuilding, aircraft, radio industry, machinebuilding, general machinebuilding (missiles), medium machinebuilding (nuclear), the defense industry proper (conventional weapons), the electronics industry, and means of communication (Simonov 2015, 482–83).[21] A standard statistical procedure is to assign firms to particular sectors based on the product they turn out. Producers belong to the defense industry if, and as long as, they are supplying military goods. This, however, was not how the Soviet defense industry was defined.

While the nine ministries were responsible for turning out 80% of military hardware, and for nearly 90% of related R&D work, they also produced all civilian aircraft and ships, radio and TV sets, sewing machines, and almost all motorcycles and refrigerators.[22] Altogether, about 40% of the defense industry output consisted of civilian goods (Firth and Noren 1998, 258). The defense industry also included producers of intermediate goods. The Ministry of Aviation Industry ran metallurgical plants making rolled titanium, aluminum, magnesium, and heat-resistant metals. Rare earth metals were also produced mostly inside the defense industry.[23]

At the same time, civilian ministries were important suppliers for the military. Around 1960, more than 800 enterprises of such ministries as agricultural machinery, heavy machinebuilding, and the tractor and automobile industry filled the orders of the military. At a later date, civilian machinebuilding ministries were said to supply 20% of military equipment.[24] This included not just dual-use products but such military-only goods as tanks and armored vehicles. In addition to the institutes of defense industries, military R&D was conducted in the Academy of Science, research institutes of civilian ministries, and higher education institutions (Masliukov and Glubokov 1999, 92). The reason for this mixing of activities will be discussed in section 2.4.

While its output was mixed, the Soviet defense industry had sharply defined administrative borders. It was a separately planned and managed part of the economy, with distinct principles of organization, financing, recruitment, and quality assurance—a veritable "state within a state."[25] It is not unusual for the defense industries to be organized differently from the rest of the economy. In market economies based on private ownership, weapons are often produced in government arsenals or under mixed private-government ownership. Thus, in the United States in the 1970s, about one-third of the plant space and equipment in aircraft industry was government owned, and tanks were built at a government-owned plant operated by the Chrysler Corporation (Gansler 1982, 3, 6). This expanded role of the government reflects the inherent difficulties of market contracting for complex and innovative weapons systems with volatile demand (Williamson 1985, 73).

Soviet industry was fully government owned, so contractual difficulties were irrelevant. It would have been possible to organize ministries along product lines, and then order the aircraft industry to produce some military planes, and the shipbuilding industry to build some ships for the navy. The likely reason for setting up an administratively separate, dedicated military industry was the need to create a technologically advanced sector within the relatively backward economy (Simonov 2015, 46–47). Administrative separation provided a focus for the rulers' attention, an address for preferential treatment and allocation of resources, and a barrier preventing the dissipation of these resources on non-military tasks.

In the hierarchically organized Soviet economy, the military industry was managed by a specialized administrative pyramid organized differently from those of the other sectors. Starting at the very top, military-economic affairs were the preserve of the General Secretary, on which even his high-ranking colleagues dared not encroach (more on this in section 2.3.2). The Defense Council, under the chairmanship of the General Secretary, was the top formal organ making "broad decisions on hardware development and procurement" (Gelman 1992, 2). No other part of the economy had a dedicated formal body at such a high level directing its activity. The operation of the military industry was the sole area of responsibility of one of the Secretaries of the Central Committee (CC) of the Communist Party. The defense department of the CC apparatus closely supervised the work of the industry.[26]

A special body, the Military Industrial Commission (MIC, or *VPK*) at the Council of Ministers (CM), supervised and coordinated military research, development, and innovation, as well as construction projects across the military and civilian ministries and the Academy of Sciences.[27] It consisted of the ministers of military industries, the deputy Minister of Defense, and the heads of the defense departments of the State Planning Committee and the Ministry of Finance, and was chaired by a deputy Chairman of the CM in charge of the military industry (Masliukov and Glubokov 1999, 88). The title "deputy" was misleading in that its bearer did not report to the Chairman, but rather, over his head, to the defense department of the CC and to the CC Secretary for the military industry (Ryzhkov 1992, 102, 104).[28] Again, no other group of ministries had a special permanent body at such a level dedicated to inter-ministerial coordination.

The State Planning Committee had a special department dedicated to planning current production in the military industry, and it appears that the first deputy Chairman of the Committee was in charge of the sector (Baibakov 1998, 168). On the basis of its war plans, the military compiled mobilization requests, detailing the expected materiel needs for a certain period of war. These indicated the production capacity that would be needed in wartime, and served as the basis for investment planning by the Committee (Samuelson 2000b, 4–6). Statistical reporting on the activities of military-industry enterprises went through special channels, bypassing the Central Statistical Administration's normal routes.[29]

The military-industry administrative pyramid differed from the civilian one even at the lower levels. Managers of civilian enterprises in effect had two bosses—their ministry and their regional party committee. A ministry could not appoint a manager without the agreement of the party committee. Military industry ministries were not obligated to obtain such an agreement, though normally the first regional party secretary would be consulted on the appointment (Gorbachev 1995, 122).

Defense industry was not only separate from the rest of industry; it also had different management practices and was home to institutions unseen elsewhere in the economy. Soviet manufacturing turned out low quality output, because users were assigned to particular producers by the planners and thus could not drop a low quality supplier. Quality-control departments of civilian enterprises could be pressured by the enterprise managers, interested in meeting the short-run quantity of output targets, to treat substandard output leniently. The military industry had a different quality-control mechanism. Ministry of Defense personnel stationed at the military plants (military representatives) were responsible for quality assurance. They controlled the complete technological chain of the plant, not just the final product, and had the right to halt production if necessary, a painful sanction for producers whose incentives were tied to reaching the short-run output target. Employees of the office of military representatives were liable under criminal law for problems with product quality and timeliness of completion.[30]

The institutional architecture of the Soviet system was built on the principles of unity of command (*edinonachalie*) and elimination of "wasteful duplication." This tended to promote monopoly and lack of choice in the economy. The defense industry was unique in that sometimes competing design bureaus were ordered to develop new weapons systems. The prototype that performed best in testing would then be chosen for production (Ellman 2014, 115–16).

In civilian industries, R&D establishments and production enterprises were organizationally separate entities, and the latter were averse to product innovations, since these could jeopardize their all-important short-term production targets. In the military industry, at least some production plants were attached to research and design organizations, with the head of the latter in a position of authority (Simonov 1996, 37).

Military industry also gave rise to the unique institution of "closed cities." Home to nuclear weapons plants, missile plants, naval yards, and chemical and bacteriological production facilities, these towns did not appear on the map and did not have a name other than a post office number. The very existence of these cities was not openly acknowledged. Surrounded by an exclusion zone (*kontrol'naia polosa*) and several rows of barbed wire, with entry only permitted at security checkpoints, closed cities were not subordinated to the regions in which they were located either administratively or in terms of public finance. Their residential housing was built to a higher standard than in the regular cities, and they were better supplied with consumer goods. Outsiders needed special permission to visit, and the inhabitants were limited in their contacts with foreigners. Ten formerly closed towns founded in the late 1940s as part of the nuclear weapons program had a combined population of 700,000 in the early 1990s.[31]

Another unique defense-industrial institution was *sharashka*, or a prison-R&D establishment where inmates designed new airplanes, missiles, and other advanced hardware. These were run by the Ministry of Internal Affairs and its precursors from the 1930s until Stalin's death.[32]

The features described in this section did not make for the absolute separation of the defense industry, which depended on the rest of the economy for labor, capital, and most of its intermediate inputs, and was connected to it through the mechanisms of central planning and supply.[33] Nor did the institutions of the defense industry always work as designed. Military representatives occasionally traded lenience for favors from the management of defense plants. After a design competition, both the winning and the losing prototypes would sometimes be ordered into production (Khrushchev 2000a, 634). Still, the defense industry's organization differed in important and interesting ways from that of the rest of industry, which, combined with privileges accorded to the sector, accounted for its superior performance.

## 2.3.2 The most favored sector

In a hierarchical organization, it is the attention of the top levels of the pyramid that confers importance on one activity relative to the others. The military industry was being guided by the highest levels of political authority. "Stalin always paid much attention to armaments and military technology. He often summoned chief designers of aircraft, artillery and tanks and asked detailed questions about the design of these weapons at home and abroad. . . . he had respectable knowledge of the properties of main weapons systems. He personally knew many chief designers and directors of military plants and demanded that they produce . . . on schedule and at the superior technological level."[34] Stalin personally approved designs for new navy ships and ordered them changed as he saw fit and dictated the composition of the navy (aircraft carriers versus battleships), sometimes in opposition to the recommendations of the navy brass.[35]

Similarly, Khrushchev's personal views dictated the prioritization of missiles at the expense of bombers and of submarines at the expense of surface ships (Khrushchev 2000a, 135–36, 321). The accounts of the First Secretary's close contacts with the chief weapons designers and military commanders take up an inordinately large space in his son's memoir, though this must partly reflect the memoirist's occupation at the time. Brezhnev "visited testing grounds and knew well designers and scientists working for defense" (Gorbachev 1995, 206).

The concentration of military-industrial decisionmaking at the very top was reinforced by secrecy that kept even high-level officials in the dark on these matters. Only the High Priest was allowed to enter the Holy of Holies, and the General Secretary was in a similar position in relation to military affairs. Stalin made decisions on military-economic and technical matters by himself, consulting with the other members of the leadership only on the specific topics for which they were responsible (e.g., Malenkov on radars and Beria on missiles). Khrushchev, though Stalin's longtime close associate, had to learn about these issues anew after Stalin's death (Khrushchev 2000b, 246). In the final decades of Soviet rule, decisions on military expenditures and programs were the province of the General Secretary, with Politburo being merely notified. Even the members of Politburo, the secretaries and heads of departments of the CC, and the Chairman of the CM complained, post-1991, of having no access to military-industrial information. High officials were afraid to voice their views on the subject.[36]

The rulers' interest in the sector translated into generous allocations of inputs. The defense industry employed over 8 million people, or about one-fifth of the industrial labor force. About 1.5 million employees of the defense industry were engaged in R&D. They performed 80% of all industrial R&D, almost 70% of which was for military purposes (Cooper 2013, 98–99).

The military industry had the first crack at the higher-quality resources in short supply.[37] In an admittedly difficult to interpret estimate, the sector was receiving 30%–50% of the "most effective types of metal and plastic" (Lipsits 1995, 14). Officials with the experience of visiting both military and civilian plants recalled how much more advanced the former were compared to the latter. However, the average age of equipment installed in the military industry was higher, and the share of imported machinery lower, compared to the total industry.[38]

The military industry attracted higher-quality labor by paying higher wages than civilian industries. Pay differential for employees without scientific degrees was 10% in the 1980s, and greater in the earlier period.[39] The resource-rich sector also offered better in-kind rewards, such as housing and access to other consumer goods and services. Scientists and engineers valued the opportunity to work in laboratories that were "significantly better" equipped than those in civilian establishments (Minaev 1999, 23). Working for the defense industry was prestigious, at least in the earlier decades, as witnessed by the career choices of the top officials. Sergei Beria was a manager of a missile design bureau, and Sergei Khrushchev worked at a similar institution, both when their fathers were in power.[40] The military industry had a freer hand in employing and promoting members of disfavored ethnic groups, allowing it to make better use of the abilities of Jews, and before that, Germans.[41] In the words of a leading Soviet economist, "The best scientists and engineers in the country are concentrated in the military industry" (Iaremenko 1990).

Unreliability of supply was by far the greatest concern of the Soviet industrial managers (Karagedov 1970). The rulers provided the defense industry with a buffer against supply disruptions by affording its enterprises the place at the front of the line of supply recipients. Consider the CM decree on the planned supplies for the Ministry of Medium Machine Building (MMMB) for 1956. It obligates other ministries to accept MMMB's orders for custom-made equipment according to the approved list; to afford MMMB first priority in distribution of resources, up to the full requirement; and to produce, supply, and transport these resources ahead of all other claimants and without regard to the degree of fulfillment of production, supply, and transportation plans for other users (Simonov 1996, 281).

There was a universally known rule on the sequence in which suppliers were to satisfy the users of their products. In this ranking, military industry and export orders came first, followed by heavy industry and then the consumer goods industry (Ericson 1979, 33). (Heavy industry, a concept which will play an important role in this book, includes power generation, coal mining, oil and gas, metallurgy, machinebuilding and metalworking, chemical, and some other sectors.) The same ranking tended to protect military industry input requests in the process of compiling annual plans, as other industries' requests were pared first (Kushnirsky 1982, 135).

### 2.3.3 The most successful sector

The standard test of an industry's success is its ability to attract customers in a competitive market. Soviet civilian manufactured goods found few buyers in hard currency markets, because they were largely obsolete and of low quality (Ericson 1976, 710, 721). Soviet consumers, when given the choice, preferred imported to domestic goods.

By contrast, the Soviet Union was responsible for 28%–45% of international arms transfers in the 1960s and 1980s, and from 1979 to 1988 was their largest source (table 2.4). There was no other broad manufactured

Table 2.4. Global arms deliveries, 1963–1988, four-year averages (% shares).

| Country | 1963–66 | 1967–70 | 1971–74 | 1975–78 | 1979–82 | 1983–86 | 1987–88 |
|---|---|---|---|---|---|---|---|
| USA | 38.5 | 52.0 | 41.9 | 30.4 | 18.9 | 22.0 | 27.8 |
| USSR | 35.1 | 28.0 | 32.4 | 35.7 | 45.0 | 39.5 | 42.5 |
| France | 3.8 | 3.1 | 5.7 | 6.9 | 7.9 | 9.0 | 4.5 |
| Britain | 4.4 | 2.4 | 4.2 | 4.4 | 5.1 | 3.2 | 2.8 |
| West Germany | 2.9 | 2.0 | 1.9 | 3.8 | 3.2 | 3.4 | 2.2 |
| Italy | 0.6 | 0.5 | 1.1 | 2.3 | 2.4 | 2.0 | 0.7 |
| Czechoslovakia | 3.6 | 2.3 | 2.1 | 3.2 | 2.2 | 2.3 | 2.0 |
| Poland | 3.3 | 2.7 | 1.7 | 2.4 | 2.1 | 2.4 | 1.8 |
| Other | 7.8 | 7.0 | 9.0 | 10.9 | 13.2 | 16.2 | 15.7 |
| World | 100.0 | 100.0 | 100.0 | 100.0 | 100.0 | 100.0 | 100.0 |

*Source*: Krauze (1992, 87), derived from the US Arms Control and Disarmament Agency's *World Military Expenditures and Arms Transfers*, various years.

product category where the USSR came close to holding such a share of the world market. Military wares in 1987 constituted 21% of total Soviet export, compared to 7% in the United States (ACDA 1997, 142, 147). This outstanding export performance cannot, however, serve as a clear sign of commercial success, because of the nature of the armaments market. The recipients of Soviet weapons often were not free to choose a supplier, were not charged the market price, or could not be expected to repay the credit used for the purchase. Political motivations were also paramount in American arms transfers (Krause 1992, 110–12, 121–22).

The post-Soviet arms export presents a cleaner economic test of the success of the military industry. The goods that the defense industry had to offer in the 1990s were all developed before the collapse. The end of the Cold War and the loss of clients and satellites destroyed much of the political rationale for arms export, as well as the internal channels through which such political transfers were subsidized. On the buyer side, procurement decisions were no longer associated with choosing a side in the superpower rivalry. Under these circumstances, in 1997–99, Russia was the world's fourth largest arms exporter, with Ukraine and Belarus ranking 10th and 14th, far ahead of these countries' rank in terms of GDP size, 11th, 30th, and 71st.[42] Practically all of Russia's arms transfers in that period were to countries outside of the Commonwealth of Independent States, thus ruling out client-patron considerations (DOS and AVC 2002, table iii). Russia by itself was still the leader in the number of major weapons delivered in 1995–96, responsible for 23% of the world total. It ranked second or third, behind the United States and France, during the rest of the decade, being a prominent supplier of nearly every type of major weapon (DOS and AVC 2002, 14–17).

This is a far better performance than that of any other manufacturing sector of the post-Soviet economies, reflecting the superior Soviet legacy of the defense industry. It may, however, have had some characteristics of a fire sale. Cuts in domestic procurement reduced military production in Russia by an order of magnitude (Cooper 2013, 102), and export at any price presented the only opportunity to keep the defense industry firms afloat.

The greatest success of the defense industry consisted in securing for its main customer, the Soviet rulers, strategic parity "with the USA, NATO, and China" (Minaev 1999, 21). It was this sector that made the Soviet armed forces "the largest in the world . . . in the number of weapons, in varieties of weapons, in mobilization potential, and in the size of their military-industrial base" (Odom 1998, 1). While many categories of weapons lagged in quality behind those of the United States, a few categories were ahead, and several others equal (Odom 1998, 1).

The pre-war achievements of the defense industry were no less impressive. In 1927, the USSR had practically no tank industry and a weak aircraft industry.[43] By the end of the 1930s it had acquired "the largest motorized and mechanized army in the world." "In almost every category of weapon, Soviet-made arms equaled or were better than those manufactured in the West" (Habeck 2002, 104, 106). "The Soviet military was the most modern in the world, at least as measured by the size and technological sophistication of its aviation and tank park" (Stone 2000, 2). While Germany went to war in 1939 with 3,200 tanks, the USSR had more than 20,000 as of May 1940, and by mid-1941 added 1,850 machines "of truly stunning superiority in comparison to the tanks of other powers" (Stone 2000, 215). By 1935, the USSR had the largest bomber force in the world, and by 1937, the strongest submarine force.[44] The military utility of amassing these armadas, which inevitably included early vintage, obsolete models, is open to doubt.[45] The world's largest accumulations of weapons are cited here as evidence of the might of the arms manufacturers, but not necessarily the armed forces.

Soviet rulers recognized the superior effectiveness of the defense industry and attempted to use it to pull up the performance of civilian sectors. Defense industry ministries were routinely ordered to help with the production of civilian equipment when civilian manufacturers could not deliver. In a culmination of this approach, the whole lagging Ministry of Machinebuilding for Light and Food Industries was disbanded in 1988, and its enterprises were transferred to different military-industry ministries (Masliukov and Glubokov 1999, 100–101).

Another approach consisted in spreading the organizational practices of the military sector to the rest of the economy.[46] A large-scale and long-running campaign to introduce automated (computerized) management systems of enterprises and ministries was apparently an attempt to spread the methods of running military systems (Masliukov and Glubokov 1999, 89). An important reorganization of the 1970s, the merging of research and production units into scientific-production associations (Cooper 1982, 456–63), emulated a longstanding military industry practice.

One of Gorbachev's reforms, introduced in 1987, was to make quality-control departments at the enterprises of civilian ministries subordinate to the State Committee for Standards (Hewett 1988, 345). This was explicitly patterned on the institute of military representatives. Another early Gorbachev reform, creation of super-ministries, such as the Bureau of Machinebuilding, was inspired by the MIC's success in inter-ministerial coordination.[47]

## 2.4 Mobilization preparations

During World War I, the demand for arms and munitions quickly exhausted the pre-war stocks and the capacity of existing arms manufacturers. To continue fighting, the belligerents had to convert civilian firms to military production, a slow and difficult process that shifted shortages further up the supply chain to the producers of metals, chemicals, and machines. The post-war Soviet military writers, of whom more will be said in section 5.6, were concerned with peacetime preparations for the gargantuan wartime needs of the armed forces.

In the early 1930s, these concerns prompted the creation of a mobilization-planning bureaucracy that, even in its infancy, numbered tens of thousands of employees. Its units worked at every level of the economic hierarchy, from the enterprise all the way up to the State Planning Commission (later renamed State Planning Committee).[48] The system of mobilization planning covered all enterprises and organizations in the country, both military and civilian.[49] Under the plan, enterprises kept in reserve production equipment, as well as stocks of raw materials, parts, and tools. In the defense industry alone, 20%–40% of capacity was kept in reserve for wartime use (Simonov 2015, 483). This equipment needed to be repaired, maintained, and replaced over time if it were to be ready to produce the latest generation of weapons. Personnel for operating mobilization capacity had to be trained (Burenok 2011, 5). Periodic mobilization drills were conducted. Spare capacity also had to be kept by metallurgical, chemical, machinebuilding, and other plants that were designated as suppliers of the wartime military industry.[50]

An example of mobilization capacity, known only because it was decommissioned, is the secret facility storing a hundred steam locomotives, long ago replaced by other types of traction, for use in "extraordinary circumstances." Employees of the facility maintained the engines and regularly tested them ("Rassekrechen" 1992).

The paradoxical administrative structure under which civilian goods made up much of the output of the defense industry, while tanks and armored personnel carriers were produced in civilian ministries (section 2.3.1), was also an element of the mobilization-preparedness system. In order to reduce the cost of mobilization readiness, military writers proposed "bilateral assimilation," using the excess capacity of the military industry in peacetime to turn out suitable civilian goods, while equipping civilian industry to produce military goods (Ventsov 1928, 64–65). To make this possible, civilian factories had to be designed and built so as to be easily convertible to military production. The design of the production equipment and of the civilian products it was to turn out was also adapted to the needs of mobilization. Thus, American engineers designing the Stalingrad Tractor Plant at first thought that their customers were crazy to demand "tremendous heavy foundations and extra steel all throughout," before figuring out the reason (Melnikova-Raich 2010, 69).

More broadly, the choice of civilian technology was dictated by the ease of converting it to military needs (Shlykov 2002, 150). One example is the General Staff's opposition, apparently unsuccessful, to the introduction of electric traction on the railroads, proposed in 1956. The reasoning was that electric traction would make transportation vulnerable to the enemy attacks at power stations.[51]

Military considerations also shaped the civilian economy outside of the formal system of mobilization planning. Strategic factors left a deep imprint on territorial planning (Pivovarov 1997, 115). The location of a civilian industry that either supplied military plants or was slated for wartime conversion was influenced by considerations of survival in case of hostilities. Industrial dispersion meant building in places that were not only remote from the centers of economic activity, but also colder, and hence more expensive to build and operate in.[52] The development and settlement of a colossal region, the Far East, was dictated by the need to hold onto the territory and to the Pacific naval bases.[53] Military considerations motivated, in whole or in large part, many of the famous, gigantic Soviet construction projects from the late 1920s through the 1980s, such as the White Sea-Baltic canal, the Urals-Kuzbass combine, the Volga-Don canal, and the Baikal-Amur railroad.[54]

A country regarding much of the world as its potential enemies needed to be self-sufficient in strategic materials. This meant developing domestic mineral deposits, however low grade by world standards. These were also frequently located in remote areas with forbidding climates, further adding to the cost of extraction.[55]

Civilian enterprises bore the cost of maintaining their mobilization capacity and stocks (Shlykov 2002, 144).[56] The cost of design modifications and other decisions dictated by the military were borne by the civilian economy in ways undetectable by routine accounting. According to the internationally accepted definitions, expenditures on mobilization preparations and other war-readiness policies described here generally do not count as part of military spending (Ellman 2014, 124–25). While there are good reasons for this approach, it may also be misleading when comparing defense burdens across economies with vastly different extents of mobilization preparedness (Firth and Noren 1998, 147). Informed Russian writers, like Shlykov and Burenok, argued that the mobilization system was very expensive, to the point of blaming it, rather than regular military expenditures, for bankrupting the USSR.

The CIA's estimate of the cost of mobilization preparedness in the USSR in 1983 was four to five times greater than such costs in the United States. It added 10%–13% to the "traditional" narrow estimate of Soviet defense expenditures, and thus "did not greatly alter the general appreciation of defense's impact on the economy. The materials necessary for estimating the costs of the infrastructure supporting defense are not at hand, nor are they likely to be" (Firth and Noren 1998, 133, 148). In the early 1950s, at the height of the Cold War, the US government considered the introduction of a Soviet-scale mobilization program, but shied away because of its high cost, among other reasons (Friedberg 2000, ch. 6). Shlykov (2002, 159) argues that Soviet mobilization planning tried to match intelligence estimates of similar American measures, which were exaggerated by orders of magnitude.

The actual military effectiveness of the mobilization system and other measures described in this section is uncertain. Converting civilian capacities to military production and restarting mothballed reserve equipment may be much more difficult than envisioned in mobilization plans. The military usefulness of Volga-Don canal may be entirely imaginary, and that of the Baikal-Amur railroad doubtful. As with the Soviets having the largest tank fleet in the world by 1941, the point of significance is the magnitude of the military-economic effort, and not the likely strategic outcome.

## 2.5 Importance and impact

One indicator of the importance of the military sector is the impression it made on the informed insiders. According to a top-ranking academic economist of the Soviet era, the organization of the economy was shaped by the unconditional priority of military needs (Iaremenko 1997, 294). Gorbachev, in the words of one of his assistants, described the priorities of his predecessors as having "bankrupted the country, kept the people near starvation, and destroyed agriculture, all to have the missiles" (Shakhnazarov 1993, 49). One of the few Soviet experts on the Western military economy stated that "in the Soviet period, the announced objective of overtaking capitalist countries in labor productivity was actually less important than the objective of creating overwhelming military might" (Kokoshin 1995, 3).

A sector as large and important as the military one must have deeply influenced the rest of the economy. "Nowhere in the developed countries in the post-war period did the military-industrial complex have such an impact on all sides of life and economic development as in the USSR" (Kurnysheva and Petrov 1998, 21).[57] "The priority given to the military industry created a deep gap between the technological levels of military and civilian production; it deformed the sectoral structure of the economy, which lacked a modern consumer goods sector, and forced the economy on an inertial trajectory because of the chronic lack of resources for civilian needs" (Iaremenko 1997, 294).[58] By the early 1980s, the technological gap between the military and civilian sectors became so wide that the latter became unable to absorb technologies transferred from the former.[59]

The economic dominance of the military industry required explanation, and to this end, there emerged in the Soviet intellectual folklore a theory that military-industrial managers were politically more powerful than the party, with Iu. Iaremenko as perhaps its most prominent exponent. Agursky (1983, 9) wrote that the party was becoming a mere executioner of the will of military industry. The theory breaks down in the face of the simple fact that party officials installed and removed industry managers, and not vice versa.[60] Still, its popularity shows how large the military industry loomed in the minds of inside observers in the 1970s and 1980s.

The military sector was also named as the star actor in the final act of the Soviet drama. By the late 1980s, the burden of military expenditures became unbearable (Lipsits 1995, 14). Iaremenko (1997, 274) considered it the main reason for the economic difficulties of the period. Soviet intellectuals spanning the whole political spectrum—from the *etatist* and imperialist Alexander Prokhanov to the liberal westernizer Anatolii Strelianyi—saw Gorbachev's reforms as an attempt to preserve the country's hard-won strategic parity in the face of Western rearmament, renewed assertiveness, and commitment to a technological revolution in military hardware—exemplified by the SDI. The idea that the arms race was the main reason for the Soviet collapse is widely accepted in Russia.[61]

The military sector was the most successful part of the economy, and the most important one from the point of view of its rulers. It was unusually large for peacetime, set apart from the rest of the economy, and governed by special rules. Such a large and privileged claimant on the nation's resources strongly influenced the performance of the civilian sectors. It deserved to be featured prominently in the studies of the Soviet economy for the sake of its role in that economy, quite apart from the security concerns of the Western governments.

## Notes

1. Vorotnikov (1995, 79); Gorbachev (1995, 206).
2. Ellman (2004, 842); Samuelson (2000b, 10); Stone (2000, 3–5).
3. For example, Ventsov (1928; 1931).
4. Cooper (1998, 244). The estimate of GNP was itself a novelty for the Soviet statistics.
5. NMP (national income in Soviet designation) is the final product of non-service sectors of the economy, a narrower concept than the GDP.
6. All translations of Russian-language sources are my own.

7. Gross Social Product is a Soviet term for the sum of outputs of non-service enterprises (i.e., it includes intermediate as well as final products).

8. Oleg Baklanov was the Minister of general machinebuilding (missiles) and Secretary of the Central Committee for defense. Iurii Masliukov was deputy Chairman of the Council of Ministers and chairman of the Military Industrial Commission.

9. Liuboshits and Tsymbal (1992); Treml (1993, 7); Noren (1995, 260–65).

10. As conjectured by Birman (1983a, 59) and hinted at by Hardt in U.S. Congress (1977, 161–62).

11. Rosefielde (2002, 503–4) also makes this point. But see Firth and Noren (1998, 158–59).

12. Rosefielde (2005, 48), the long-time critic of the CIA estimates, accused Firth and Noren (1998) of strategic selectivity in what they disclosed.

13. Briefly reviewed and referenced in Firth and Noren (1998, 173–185) and Harrison (2003, 10–11).

14. Witness the results of the contributors to Jacobsen (1987).

15. Treml (1993, 5–7); Firth and Noren (1998, 191).

16. Noren (1995, 265); Cooper (1998, 244–46); Harrison (2003, 8–12).

17. Firth and Noren (1998, 103). Also the discussion in Rosefielde (2005, ch. 3).

18. Harrison (2003, 9–10) noted the paradoxical closeness of competing estimates.

19. Davis (2002, 155); Cooper (2013, 99).

20. According to the US Defense Department budgetary categories (US Census 1991, 336).

21. For the changing organizational structure of defense industry in the earlier period, see Barber et al. (2000, 10–13).

22. Masliukov and Glubokov (1999, 121). These and other Soviet data in value terms cited in this chapter suffer from the same weaknesses as defense expenditures totals: arbitrary prices, subsidies, uncertain accounting methods.

23. Simonov (1996, 276–77); Masliukov and Glubokov (1999, 120).

24. Simonov (1996, 276–77); Masliukov and Glubokov (1999, 119).

25. Rassadin (1999, 100); Gorbachev (1995, 123).

26. Gorbachev (1995, 231); Ellman and Kontorovich (1998, 46–47).

27. Ellman and Kontorovich (1998, 46); Simonov (2015, 58); Minaev (1999, 33).

28. Ministers of Defense, Internal Affairs, Foreign Affairs, and the Chairman of the State Security Committee similarly did not report to the Chairman of CM (Ryzhkov 1992, 102).

29. Eydelman (1998, 97–98); Simonov (1996, 43–45).

30. Harrison and Simonov (2000); Minaev (1999, 32); Rassadin (1999, 100).

31. Brock (1998); Lappo and Polian (1998, 43–49); Rowland (1996, 435, 441–43). Some of these sources speak of the situation in the 1990s, but it represented no change from the earlier period.

32. Simonov (1996, 113–15); Starkov (2000).
33. Holloway (1982, 277); Barber et al. (2000, 23),
34. Zhukov (1969, 296). Also see Rees (2004, 52).
35. Monakov (1998, 78); Rohwer and Monakov (2001).
36. Dobrynin (1996, 492–93); Gorbachev (1995, 198, 318–19, 334); Medvedev (1998, 96); Ryzhkov (1992, 102, 104). More on secrecy surrounding the military sector in section 6.1.
37. Isaev (1989, 24–25); Ellman and Kontorovich (1998, 54–55).
38. Ellman and Kontorovich (1998, 54–55); Gorbachev (1995, 207); Kuzyk (1999, 58); Simonov (1996, 278–79).
39. Protasov (1990); Minaev (1999, 23).
40. Khrushchev (2000b, 253, 263, 369); Minaev (1999, 24).
41. Cherniaev (2003, 243); Minaev (1999, 22–23).
42. Purchasing power parity terms in 1996 (World Bank 2017).
43. Simonov (1996, 58); Stone (2000, 106).
44. O'Neill (2002, 157); Rohwer and Monakov (2001, 56).
45. Stone (2000, 216); Ellman (2014, 121).
46. See also Harrison and Simonov (2000, 240).
47. Hanson (2003, 187); Pikhoia (1998, 456); Masliukov and Glubokov (1999, 103).
48. Samuelson (2000a, 49); Shlykov (2002, 49, 144).
49. Prime Minister Chernomyrdin quoted in Shlykov (2002, 165).
50. Cooper (2013, 100); Ellman (2014, 106–7).
51. Rodionov (1992); Baibakov (1998, 133) describes L. M. Kaganovich as the only opponent of change.
52. This was due to the shape of isotherms in European Russia (Parshev 2000, 38, 40).
53. Dienes (2002, 452; 1991, 446, 450); Zausaev (1998, 8).
54. Morukov (2003, 105); Davies (1974); Djilas (1962, 156).
55. Humphreys (1994, 9–11); Dienes (2002, 455); Hill and Gaddy (2003, 88–89).
56. After 1991, newly self-financing firms protested the uncompensated impositions and in many cases turned mobilization capacities and stockpiles to private uses (Simakov and Kanka 2002; Burenok 2011).
57. Also Boeva et al. (1992, 269); Ekspertnyi Institut (1996, 6).
58. Also Mozhin (1998, 121).
59. Ozhegov et al. (1991, 62–63); Ellman and Kontorovich (1998, 54–55).
60. Malei (1993); Cherniaev (2003, 135–36).
61. See the memoirs of the former top Soviet officials cited in Ellman and Kontorovich (1997, 262, 267); the views of the former Soviet military brass and military-industrial managers in Ellman and Kontorovich (1998, 41–66) and Shlykov (2001 and 2002); and references in Shlapentokh (2001, 187). Also Burenok (2011, 6).

# PART II

## Soviet Military Power in The Sovietological Mirror

Chapter 2 described the large and uniquely important military sector of the Soviet economy, as it appears today. In this part of the book, I investigate how much notice economists paid to it at the time. An exhaustive survey of books and articles on the Soviet economy in chapter 3 shows that Sovietologists afforded the military sector little attention, both relative to its importance and relative to the attention lavished on the other, lower-priority sectors. This lack of interest in the most successful and important sector of the centrally planned economy is the key finding of the book.

Chapters 4 and 5 focus on the two important aspects of the Soviet economy whose military significance was (uncharacteristically) proclaimed by the Soviets themselves: the objectives of central planners and industrialization. Scholars interested in either one of these topics had no need to peer through the dense secrecy surrounding military matters or to strain their eyes to discern the military industry in between Soviet banking and marketing. Yet I show that, by and large, Sovietologists ignored Soviet-offered military interpretations, and instead constructed their own, inconsistent civilian ones.

# 3

# *The Missing Sector*

## *3.1  How to document an absence*

Sovietological literature was the work of many individuals over almost half a century. Each contribution was tinged with the idiosyncrasy of the author and the professional and political fads of the time. Establishing the place of the military sector in the academic study of the Soviet economy is an exercise in summarizing a large amount of information. For such a summary to be persuasive it needs to rest on a sample of work that is representative of the field, use simple, replicable measures of the attention afforded to the military sector by each publication, and apply explicit standards by which these measures can be judged to be high or low.

The output of academic research on the Soviet economy, like that of the other fields, appeared in two main forms: books and journal articles. I survey all the English-language books published over Sovietology's lifetime that cover the Soviet/socialist/planned economy as a whole, or any aspect thereof for which the military sector played an important role (such as planning, growth, or history). I also consider all articles on the Soviet/socialist economy published in leading economics and Sovietological journals. The reasons for excluding other research products, as well as the details of the survey procedure, are discussed in appendix 3.1.

The highest level of attention authors can afford to a subtopic of their books is to gather all the relevant material in one place, make it a distinct section with its own title, and announce it in the table of contents. For brevity, I will call any entry in a book's table of contents a chapter. Occasionally, a section with its own subtitle will appear in the text but not in the table of contents. I counted such sections when I found them. The number of chapters or index entries on military economy in a book and the number of journal articles with military-economy titles serve as indicators of attention given to the military sector.

Similar measures of attention given to other sectors serve as a standard for comparison. The presence of a chapter on the military sector is more likely, and its omission more telling, in books that have chapters devoted to particular sectors. One can view the military sector both as a sector of origin of the national income, like agriculture and transport, and as a category of expenditures, like consumption and investment. Accordingly, I note the presence of chapters devoted to both types of sectors in the books surveyed. For periodicals, I compare the number of articles about the military sector to the total number of articles on the Soviet economy and to the number of articles on specific sectors.

While some analysis of the substance of the surveyed texts is used to supplement the bibliometric approach and help to interpret its results, the stress in this chapter is on the formal indicators just described. This approach is based on the well-known idea that talk is cheap, and to be credible, a signal needs to be costly to the sender. A sentence announcing the supreme importance of the military sector in the middle of a text that deals exclusively with the civilian economy is not persuasive to the reader, and carries no weight in this investigation. On the other hand, a chapter or a section with a military-related title counts independent of its content, which is addressed separately.

## 3.2 Textbooks and readers

Whatever else they were doing, academic Sovietologists had to teach courses in their field. In the late 1970s, 11.9% of colleges and universities with an economics major offered courses on the economics of the USSR (table 1.2). Textbooks and readers on the Soviet (or socialist, or planned) economy were the most frequently written books in the discipline, with 47 separate editions appearing between 1948 and 1992.[1]

Textbooks are supposed to survey all the aspects of the economy deemed important by their authors. The extent to which a sector or issue is covered may therefore be taken as an indicator of its perceived importance in the big picture. Comprehensive coverage also means that much of a textbook's subject matter lies outside the author's immediate area of competence and thus reflects his reading of the state of knowledge in the discipline. Textbooks also served as the authoritative summary of the field's progress for the public. As the field has grown and developed, "the textbook has become much more important to the non-economist in learning what is going on in the study of the Soviet economy" (Millar 1980, 326).

### 3.2.1 Which sectors merited a chapter

All but one out of 47 textbooks and readers have chapters on at least one civilian sector, for a total of 136 chapters (see table 3.1). Agriculture is by far the leader, with 41 chapters. The typical organization of the textbook material may partially explain this fact. The main exposition usually deals with the standard industry planning and management structure. The planning and organization of agriculture were different from those of industry, thus justifying a separate treatment. But, as has been shown in chapter 2, the planning and organization of the military industry also deviated from the civilian industry standard. Unlike the latter, agriculture was an unsuccessful sector neglected by the Soviet rulers in the first several decades of the planned economy. True, it acquired a higher priority in the eyes of the rulers in the final decades, in part because of its persistent poor performance. Even then, unlike the military sector, agriculture posed no threat to anyone but the Soviets themselves.

There are 27 chapters on foreign trade, which was not a larger part of the economy than the military sector. The arithmetic average of import and export was estimated at 4.1% of GDP in 1970 and may have been 7.6% in 1988 using a different valuation.[2] The burden of defense was estimated by various sources to be in the double digits, as discussed in section 2.2.3. There are also nine chapters on finance, a sector of secondary importance in the economy built on planning and allocation *in natura* (Ericson 2008). Under the most generous definition, I found only eight chapters on the military sector, the same number as chapters on banking, a sector of about the same importance as finance. It is as if, in deciding which sectors to cover, textbook writers reversed the priorities of the Soviet rulers.

In mature sciences, textbooks are the carriers of the reigning paradigm, which accounts for the uniformity of their content (Kuhn 1962, 10, 136–37). Sovietology never reached maturity, so we should expect fragmentation of the subject matter on important issues, in the sense defined in section 1.3.2. Accordingly, the absence of the military sector from the textbooks is not uniform.

The first textbook on the Soviet economy in our sample, Schwartz (1950), published at the height of the Cold War, contains a two-and-a-half-page section on the military sector within a chapter on the growth

Table 3.1. Textbooks, readers, and popular books on Soviet/socialist economy.

| Author, year, edition | Military sector chapter | Chapters on other sectors | Index entries | |
|---|---|---|---|---|
| | | | Number | % of total pages |
| Schwartz, 1950, 1st ed. | Yes | Agriculture + 6 sectors | 20 | 3.5 |
| Schwartz, 1954, 2nd ed. | Yes | Agriculture + 5 sectors | 34 | 5.2 |
| Campbell, 1960, 1st ed. | No | Agriculture, R&D | 0 | 0.0 |
| Nove, 1961, 1st ed. | No | Finance | 5 | 1.6 |
| Wiles, 1962 | No | Heavy and light industry, investment | 1 | 0.3 |
| Spulber, 1962 | No | Agriculture, banking, distribution | 0 | 0.0 |
| Bornstein & Fusfeld, 1962, 1st ed. | No | Agriculture, foreign trade (2) | No index | No index |
| Holzman, 1962 | No | Agriculture, finance, froreign trade | No index | No index |
| Schwartz, 1965 | No | Foreign trade | 12 | 4.9 |
| Ames, 1965 | No | Agriculture, foreign trade | 3 | 1.2 |
| Bornstein & Fusfeld, 1966, 2nd ed. | No | Agriculture (2), banking Consumption, foreign trade | No index | No index |
| Campbell, 1966, 2nd ed. | No | Agriculture, consumer goods | 5 | 2.8 |
| Nove, 1966, rev. ed. | No | Agriculture, banking, foreign trade | 3 | 0.9 |
| Goldman, 1968 | No | Foreign trade | 2 | 1.2 |
| Schwartz, 1968 | No | Agriculture, banking Foreign trade | 6 | 3.7 |
| Sherman, 1969 | No | Agriculture, education, health, housing | 1 | 0.3 |
| Spulber, 1969 | No | Agriculture, finance | 2 | 0.7 |
| Nove, 1969, 2nd rev. ed. | No | Agriculture, banking, foreign trade | 3 | 0.9 |
| Kaser, 1970 | No | None | 11 | 3.4 |
| Wilczynski, 1970, 1st ed. | No | Agriculture, consumption, foreign trade, investment +2 sectors | 1 | 0.5 |

**Table 3.1. Continued**

| Author, year, edition | Military sector chapter | Chapters on other sectors | Index entries | |
|---|---|---|---|---|
| | | | Number | % of total pages |
| Bornstein & Fusfeld, 1970, 3rd ed. | No | Agriculture, banking, consumption | No index | No index |
| Hutchings, 1971, 1st ed. | No | Agriculture Finance Foreign trade | 18 | 5.9 |
| Wilczynski, 1972, 2nd ed. | No | Agriculture, banks, consumption, foreign trade, investment, trade | 1 | 0.4 |
| G&S,[2] 1974, 1st ed. | No | Agriculture, foreign trade | 3 | 0.7 |
| Bornstein & Fusfeld, 1974, 4th ed. | No | Agriculture, consumption, foreign trade, investment +2 sectors | No index | No index |
| Campbell, 1974, 3rd ed. | No | Agriculture, foreign trade, energy | 6 | 2.4 |
| Dyker, 1976 | No | Agriculture | 8 | 4.9 |
| Nove, 1977, 1st ed. | No | Agriculture, finance, foreign trade, investment | 11 | 2.9 |
| Wilczynski, 1977, 3rd ed. | No | Agriculture, consumption, foreign trade, investment +2 sectors | 1 | 0.5 |
| Krylov, 1979 | Yes | Agriculture, finance Trade Supply | 9 | 3.6 |
| Nove, 1980, 2nd ed. | No | Agriculture, investment, trade | 11 | 2.9 |
| Bornstein, 1981, 5th ed. | Yes[1] | Agriculture, foreign trade, energy | 0 | 0.0[1] |
| G&S,[2] 1981, 2nd ed. | Yes | Agriculture, foreign trade, investment | 17 | 4.2 |
| Millar, 1981 | No | Agriculture, natural resources | 18 | 8.9 |
| Hutchings, 1982, 2nd ed. | No | Agriculture, finance, foreign trade | 24 | 7.8 |

(*continued*)

Table 3.1. Continued

| Author, year, edition | Military sector chapter | Chapters on other sectors | Index entries | |
|---|---|---|---|---|
| | | | Number | % of total pages |
| Holzman, 1982 | Yes | Agriculture, petroleum | No index | No index |
| Wilczynski, 1982, 4th ed. | No | Agriculture, banking, consumption, foreign trade, retail +1 sector | 4 | 1.8 |
| Goldman, 1983 | No | Agriculture, foreign trade | 9 | 4.9 |
| Dyker, 1985 | No | Agriculture, construction | 4 | 2.6 |
| G&S,[2] 1986, 3rd ed. | Yes | Agriculture, foreign trade | 12 | 2.8 |
| Nove, 1986, 3rd ed. | No | Agriculture, foreign trade, finance | 3 | 0.8 |
| Buck & Cole, 1987 | No | Investment | 0 | 0.0 |
| Bleaney, 1988 | No | Agriculture | 0 | 0.0 |
| G&S,[2] 1990, 4th ed. | Yes | Agriculture, foreign trade | 14 | 2.9 |
| Jeffries, 1990 | No | Foreign trade | 0 | 0.0 |
| Kornai, 1992 | No | Foreign trade | 5 | 0.9 |
| Dyker, 1992 | No | Agriculture, construction | 5 | 2.4 |

*Sources*: See appendices 3.1 and 3.2.

[1] A chapter on military and economic aid to the less developed countries. Names of particular weapons exported in the index.

[2] Gregory and Stuart.

of industrial production.[3] The section expands to six pages in the second edition (Schwartz 1954). The author of the textbook, an OSS veteran, was an academic economist and a freelance journalist at the time of the first edition. He became a *New York Times* editorial writer in 1951 (Mcfadden 2004). Though the author in the preface thanks all the practitioners of the nascent field for advice, the book, with its detailed recounting of technological information and sector-by-sector structure, belongs to the journalistic, pre-Sovietological era.

No chapter on the military sector appears in the 27 textbooks published over the next quarter of a century, though they have chapters on such low- and medium-priority sectors as housing, light industry, and banking. Schwartz himself dropped the military section from his subsequent textbooks, published in 1965 and 1968. The next textbook to have a military sector chapter was Krylov (1979), a poorly put-together, choppy translation from Russian. The book, written by a lecturer at the US Army Institute in Germany with neither Western nor Soviet economics training, has no references to the Western work, and little connection to the relevant Soviet literature (Birman 1980b).

Textbooks with military chapters written by academics appeared only in the last ten years of the system's existence. Two of them deal with the military sector tangentially in the context of international relations. A reader (Bornstein 1981) reprinted a paper by two CIA analysts on Soviet economic and military aid to foreign countries. The paper deals with the foreign policy effects of military deliveries, rather than the sector that supplied them. Holzman (1982) has a three-page "Military Expenditures" chapter, half of which is devoted to arguing that the CIA exaggerated the burden of defense, and the rest of which deals with international relations.

The first and only textbook written by active academics to incorporate a substantive military chapter was Gregory and Stuart (1981), the second edition of a text that was also published in 1986 and 1990 and is therefore counted thrice in our survey. A four-and-a-half-page section—"Soviet Military Power"—is located in the second of two chapters discussing the economy's performance. The first of these deals with growth, efficiency, equity, consumer welfare, and stability, while the second, in addition to military power, discusses technology and the environment. I will look deeper into the content of the few military chapters found in the textbooks in section 6.3.1.

## 3.2.2 Applying a finer comb: index entries

Textbooks without a military sector chapter still may say something on the subject. I count the number of pages on which, according to the books' indexes, military-economic terms can be found. The procedure is described in detail in appendix 3.2. Out of 41 textbooks with an index, six do not have a single entry on military subjects. Half of the books have four or fewer pages with military entries, while a few books with many such pages pull the average number of pages up to seven (table 3.1).

An index entry usually does not refer to a full-page discussion of the subject, just to a sentence or two, at most a paragraph, where the military sector is mentioned. These snippets are of two kinds. By far the most numerous are casual uses of military terms that are not part of any sustained discussion or description of the sector. There are also one-sentence remarks noting the outstanding characteristics of the military sector, but equally free of follow-up or context. Here, I present examples from six books, four of them from the 1980s, three sharing the highest number of military references, and the other three with about the modal number of references (three to five).

Millar (1981), with the largest share of pages with military terms, mentions military expenditures in the list of budget outlay categories, and military organizations in the list of various other state organs, along with a few more substantive, but brief references. Hutchings (1982) has the second largest number of references among the textbooks—22 pages. Of these, 14 appear in a long and inconclusive analysis of the official state budget data, with defense mentioned as one element of the outlays. There are also passing references to the increase in military expenditures during the Korean War, the secrecy surrounding the military sector, the secrecy of armaments production data, and their impact on economic growth data. Several sentences here and there note that the burden of defense slows down growth, and a footnote debates the existence of a military-industrial complex in the USSR. Most of Kaser's (1970) 11 index entries refer in passing to one of the items of budgetary outlays, as on page 119, where defense is mentioned last among the items of social consumption (health, pensions, education) in Stalin's five-year plans. In a 26-page chapter on public finance, Nove (1986, 246–47) includes a three-paragraph discussion of the official Soviet military expenditures data as announced in the state budget. He considers it improbable that these data are complete but refrains from offering any conclusions about the true magnitude of military expenditures. In the conclusion of the equally long chapter on investment and technical change, there are two paragraphs on why military wares are more advanced than the civilian ones (Nove 1986, 171).

Dyker (1985) has references to four pages in the index, the same number as that for "forestry" or "construction materials." He treats the economy and its planning separately from the military sector, which is introduced as an afterthought in the discussion of the politics of economic reform in the last three pages of the book. There is a sentence about the benefits of central planning to the military-industrial complex, in the context of a discussion of the prospects for the adoption of Hungarian-type reforms by the USSR, and a half-page discussion of the military interests' alleged opposition to economic reform. It is noted that the burden of defense retards economic growth and depresses consumption, which must concern Soviet leadership. Divergent estimates of the burden by the CIA and the Defense Intelligence Agency (DIA) are mentioned. Campbell (1966) indicates five pages with military terms in its index, though I found only three (out of a total of 180 pages). In the section on end-use composition of GNP in the early 1960s, there is a discussion of officially reported military expenditures being too low, with the "informed opinion" of those who had worked on the issue putting it at about 9%–10% of GNP, the same share as in the United States at the time.

Along with these inconsequential references to the military sector, the same authors drop an occasional sentence or two stating the outstanding, unusual, and important characteristics of the sector covered in chapter 2. These appear without explanation, development, or connection to one another, usually in the context of a discussion on some other topic. I will further discuss these substantive references in section 6.3.1.

## 3.3 *Research volumes*

Research volumes are generally more specialized and tightly focused than textbooks. And the military sector is more relevant for some of the topics than for the others. True, in an economy like the Soviet one, military issues cropped up in the most unexpected corners, like farming.[4] However, this connection was peripheral to the workings of agriculture, just as the acute problem of housing for military officers was a peripheral aspect of the housing sector. Here I select eight areas of economics for which the military sector was especially relevant, and survey them for recognition of this relevance.

Unlike textbook writers, authors of scholarly volumes are under no obligation to cover all important aspects of their subject. Thus, the R&D sector may be engaged in predominantly military work, as the Soviet one was, but a researcher still may legitimately choose to write about the civilian side only, as Berliner (1976, 2) does. No judgment is rendered here on the scope of any particular book, only on the profession's collective opinion—as reflected in all the books published during its lifetime—of what is worth its attention. It is unremarkable that there is no mention of the military economy in a book on optimization models in Soviet planning. But if the writing on Soviet planning in the 1970s concentrated on mathematical methods, and in the 1980s on the use of computers, the aggregate result of such decisions is the complete absence of the main features of planning from the literature.

Planning, enterprise management, growth, and national accounting formed the core areas of research into the Soviet economy. Military production and spending were directly relevant to each of these four research areas. The top priority afforded to the military sector meant that it was at the center of the planning process. The military industry was a large component of industry with distinct and apparently effective managerial practices. Some of the prominent innovations in planning and management originated in the military (section 2.3.2). The relationship between the growth of aggregate income and that of its use for consumption, investment, and military expenditures has been a longstanding concern of economists. National income and product accounting (NIPA) had to cover military expenditures as one of the largest items of aggregate spending, alongside consumption and investment.

There is not a single chapter on the military sector in 36 volumes on planning, management, and growth (tables 3.2–3.4). Yet 15 out of 18 books on planning and seven out of 10 books on growth have a total of 31 chapters on particular civilian sectors and end-use aggregates, including 12 chapters on agriculture, nine on foreign economic relations, seven on investment, and—in accordance with the reversed-priorities principle already observed in the textbooks—a chapter each on services, healthcare, and banking.

As far as the literature on planning is concerned, the military sector did not exist. Three-quarters of the books on planning that have an index do not even mention the military sector (table 3.2). Atypically, Kushnirsky (1982) has seven references—all extremely brief—one of which notes the top priority afforded to military needs in the process of planning. The other two books have one and two references, respectively. No mention of the military sector is to be found in five out of eight books on management (table 3.3). The book with the most index entries (12) is by the sole noneconomist among the authors of management volumes (Beissinger, 1988).

The literature on growth is more cognizant of the existence of the military sector, with only a third of the books failing to mention it in the index (table 3.4). Books on national income accounting and statistics also stand out from the core literature, in that four out of 11 have chapters on the military sector, and only one fails to mention it in the index (table 3.5). The unusually high degree of attention to the military sector in this line of research is not a matter of the authors' choice. The accounting system forces anyone trying to estimate the national product or output of industry to include the military sector for the sake of completeness. Similarly, one would expect numerous references to military expenditures in books on

Table 3.2. **Books on Soviet/socialist planning.**

| Author, year | Military sector chapter | Chapters on other sectors | Index entries Number | Index entries % of total pages |
|---|---|---|---|---|
| Grossman, 1960 | No | Agriculture, transport | No index | No index |
| Hirsch, 1961 | No | Investment | 2 | 0.9 |
| Bergson, 1964 | No | Agriculture, consumption, investment | 0 | 0.0 |
| Degras, 1964 | No | Banking | No index | No index |
| Bernard, 1966 | No | Investment | 0 | 0.0 |
| Hardt, 1967 | No | None | 0 | 0.0 |
| Zauberman, 1967 | No | Foreign trade | 0 | 0.0 |
| Ellman, 1971 | No | Wholesale trade | No index | No index |
| Ellman, 1973 | No | None | 0 | 0.0 |
| Marczewski, 1974 | No | Agriculture, foreign trade, services | No index | No index |
| Zauberman, 1976 | No | Investment | No index | No index |
| Cave, 1980 | No | Supply | 0 | 0.0 |
| Kushnirsky, 1982 | No | None | 7 | 4.3 |
| Rutland, 1985 | No | Healthcare | 1 | 0.4 |
| Ellman, 1989 | No | Agriculture, foreign trade | 0 | 0.0 |
| Bennett, 1989 | No | Investment, foreign trade | 0 | 0.0 |
| Eatwell, et al., 1990 | No | Agriculture, foreign trade | No index | No index |
| Hare, 1991 | No | Investment | 0 | 0.0 |

*Sources*: See appendices 3.1 and 3.2.

Soviet public finance (not examined here), as the budgetary system would make it impossible to skip this item.

Books in four additional fields may be expected to address the military sector. Works taking a general view of the Soviet economy should be more likely to mention its most important sector. This includes economic histories dealing with the economy or industry as a whole after 1928, and a diffuse category of general books on Soviet/socialist economics. These are

Table 3.3. Books on industrial enterprise and management.

| Author, year | Military sector chapter | Chapters on other sectors | Index entries | |
|---|---|---|---|---|
| | | | Number | % of total pages |
| Granick, 1954 | No | No | 6 | 2.0 |
| Berliner, 1957 | No | No | 6 | 1.8 |
| Granick, 1960 | No | No | 0 | 0.0 |
| Richman, 1967 | No | No | 0 | 0.0 |
| Conyngham, 1982 | No | No | 0 | 0.0 |
| Guroff & Carstensen, 1983[1] | No | Agriculture | 0 | 0.0 |
| Freris, 1984 | No | No | 0 | 0.0 |
| Beissinger, 1988 | No | No | 12 | 4.0 |

*Sources*: See appendices 3.1 and 3.2.

[1] Part dealing with the Soviet period only.

Table 3.4. Books on growth and development.

| Author, year | Military sector chapter | Chapters on other sectors | Index entries | |
|---|---|---|---|---|
| | | | Number | % of total pages |
| Bergson, 1953a | No | Agriculture, foreign trade, investment, transportation | 11 | 3.0 |
| Bergson & Kuznets, 1963 | No | Agriculture, consumption, foreign trade | 17 | 4.5 |
| Spulber, 1964 | No | No | 0 | 0.0 |
| Treml, 1968 | No | Agriculture | No index | No index |
| Wilber, 1969 | No | Agriculture | 0 | 0.0 |
| Maddison, 1969[1] | No | Agriculture, foreign trade | 10 | 12.5 |
| Cohn, 1970 | No | No | 8 | 6.6 |
| Bergson, 1978 | No | Consumption | 11 | 4.9 |
| Bergson & Levine, 1983 | No | Agriculture, energy, Foreign trade | 24 | 5.4 |
| Bairam, 1988 | No | No | 0 | 0.0 |

*Source*: See appendices 3.1 and 3.2.

[1] Part dealing with the USSR and appendices with comparative data only.

**Table 3.5. Books on NIPA and statistics.**

| Author, year | Military sector chapter | Chapters on other sectors | Index entries | |
| --- | --- | --- | --- | --- |
| | | | Number | % of total pages |
| Jasny, 1951 | Yes | Consumption, investment | 23 | 21.5 |
| Bergson, 1953b | No | No | No index | No index |
| Bergson & Heymann, 1954 | No | No | No index | No index |
| Hoeffding, 1954 | No | Investment | No index | No index |
| Hodgman, 1954 | No | Consumer goods, machinery | 4 | 3.1 |
| Grossman, 1960 | No | No | 0 | 0.0 |
| Bergson, 1961 | Yes | Consumption, investment, government spending | 78 | 17.5 |
| Moorsteen & Powell, 1962 | No | No | 12 | 1.9 |
| Nutter, 1962 | Yes | Machinery & equipment | 19 | 5.8 |
| Becker, 1969 | Yes | Consumption, investment | 75 | 25.5 |
| Treml and Hardt, 1972 | No | Agriculture | 14 | 3.2 |

*Sources*: See appendices 3.1 and 3.2.

mostly books with a generic-sounding title collecting chapters on disparate subjects. The other two categories are books on Gorbachev's reforms and those on research and development, innovation, and technology transfer, called here R&D books for brevity. The reforms were arguably motivated in part by the international strategic rivalry and the heavy burden it imposed on the economy, and led to radical shifts in military-economic policy (Ellman and Kontorovich, 1998 14–16, 20). Some of the reforms consisted in spreading military-sector managerial practices to the civilian economy (section 2.3.3). The R&D sector predominantly served the needs of military industry (section 2.3.2).

Despite this, only one out of 16 books on Gorbachev's reforms has a military chapter, and that by a British political scientist, while 11 books have 24 chapters on various civilian sectors, with agriculture and foreign trade in the lead (table 3.6). Three out of 28 general-focus books have military chapters, while there are a total of 32 chapters on civilian sectors, including 10 on agriculture (table 3.7). History books in table 3.8 have four military chapters, compared to 27 chapters on civilian sectors (seven of them on agriculture).

Even more important than the low number of military chapters in these volumes is the timing of their publication. All but one military chapter appeared after 1988: three in 1989 and another four in 1991–92. By that time, the Cold War was over, conversion of military industry had been officially

**Table 3.6. Books on Gorbachev's reforms and the Soviet collapse.**

| Author, year | Military sector chapter | Chapters on other sectors | Index entries | |
|---|---|---|---|---|
| | | | Number | % of total pages |
| Dyker, 1987 | No | Agriculture, foreign trade | 11[1] | 11.38 |
| Goldman, 1987 | No | High technology | 22 | 8.3 |
| Hewett, 1988 | No | No | 6 | 1.5 |
| Linz & Moskoff, 1988 | No | Agriculture | No index | No index |
| Aslund, 1989 | No | Foreign trade | 21 | 10.7 |
| Desai, 1989 | No | No | 10 | 7.8 |
| Tedstrom, 1990 | No | Agriculture | 6 | 2.6 |
| Roberts & LaFollette, 1990 | No | No | 0 | 0.0 |
| Campbell, 1991 | No | Foreign trade, investment, R&D | 5 | 2.2 |
| Spulber, 1991 | No | Agriculture, foreign trade + 3 sectors | 5 | 1.8 |
| Goldman, 1991 | No | No | 16 | 6.2 |
| Cooper, L., 1991 | Yes | Agriculture, foreign trade | 28 | 15.4 |
| Aslund, 1991 | No | Agriculture, finance, foreign trade, investment, supply | 13 | 5.4 |
| Aslund, 1992 | No | No | 0 | 0.0 |
| Dowlah, 1992 | No | No | 5 | 2.0 |
| Ellman & Kontorovich, 1992 | No | Agriculture, R&D, railroads | 27 | 10.0 |

[1]Not counting 19 entries for the international relations chapter.

Table 3.7. General Soviet/socialist economics books.

| Author, year | Military sector chapter | Chapters on other sectors | Index entries | |
|---|---|---|---|---|
| | | | Number | % of total pages |
| Jasny, 1962 | No | Agriculture + 5 sectors | 7 | 2.5 |
| Nove, 1964 | No | Agriculture | 1 | 0.3 |
| Rosovsky, 1966 | No | Foreign trade | No index | No index |
| Zaleski, 1967 | No | No | 7 | 3.7 |
| Balinky, et al., 1967 | No | No | No index | No index |
| Ward, 1967 | No | No | 0 | 0.0 |
| Keizer, 1971 | No | Consumption | No index | No index |
| Roberts, 1971 | No | No | 0 | 0.0 |
| Eckstein, 1971 | No | No | 1 | 0.3 |
| Fallenbuchl, 1975 | No | Civil aviation, R&D | 5 | 1.5 |
| Fallenbuchl, 1976 | No | Agriculture Foreign trade | 5 | 1.3 |
| Thornton, 1976 | No | Agriculture, foreign trade | 1[3] | 0.3 |
| Abouchar, 1979 | No | Agriculture, cement, transport | 0 | 0.0 |
| Katsenelinboigen, 1978 | No | No | 0 | 0.0 |
| Nove, 1979 | No | Agriculture | 0 | 0.0 |
| Rosefielde, 1981 | No | Foreign trade | 1 | 0.3 |
| Asselain, 1984 | No | No | 7 | 2.8 |
| Hutchings, 1984 | No | Investment | 1 | 0.4 |
| Desai, 1987 | No | Agriculture | 11 | 4.0 |
| Hardt & McMillan, 1988 | No | Natural resources | 0 | 0.0 |
| Berliner, 1988 | No | No | 3 | 1.0 |
| Winiecki, 1988 | No | Foreign trade | 0 | 0.0 |
| Wiles, 1988 | No | Agriculture, investment | 29 | 116 |
| Bergson, 1989 | Yes | Foreign trade | 13 | 4.4 |
| Shtromas & Kaplan, 1989[1] | Yes | Agriculture | 23 | 9.4 |
| Gregory, 1990 | No | Construction | 2 | 1.1 |
| Millar, 1990 | No | Agriculture | 7 | 2.4 |
| Campbell, 1992 | Yes[2] | Energy, water | 15 | 8.4 |

*Sources*: See appendices 3.1 and 3.2.

[1] Economic part of the book only.

[2] Reprint of his 1972 *Soviet Studies* article.

[3] Mentioned in the chapter of the lone Soviet contributor.

Table 3.8. Books on economic history.

| Author, year, edition | Military sector chapter[1] | Chapters on other sectors |
|---|---|---|
| Jasny, 1961 | No | Agriculture, construction, transportation, retail |
| Dobb, 1966 | No | Finance |
| Erlich, 1967 | No | No |
| Carr and Davies, 1969 | Yes | Agriculture, banking, consumption, foreign trad, investment + 2 sectors |
| Nove, 1969, 1st ed. | No | Agriculture, finance |
| Zaleski, 1971 | No | No |
| Zaleski, 1980 | No | Agriculture, consumer goods |
| Dunmore, 1980 | No | No |
| Nove, 1982, 2nd ed. | No | Agriculture, finance |
| Munting, 1982 | No | No |
| Davies, 1989 | Yes | Foreign trade + 4 sectors |
| Nove, 1992, 3rd ed. | No | Finance |
| Edmondson & Waldron, 1992[2] | Yes | Agriculture |
| Hunter & Szyrmer, 1992 | Yes | Agriculture, foreign trade |

*Source*: See appendix 3.1.

[1] Peacetime chapters only.

[2] Chapter by R. W. Davies.

announced in 1988, and the Soviets themselves were speaking openly and critically about their military economy.

Seven books from the general category do not mention the military sector in their indexes, but this may be due to my generous interpretation of how general some of these books are. Two out of 13 economic history books make no mention of the military sector in their indexes, as do two books on Gorbachev's reforms.

Books on growth, planning, and other topics surveyed so far were written predominantly by economists, which made it easier for me to determine which ones belong in this study. The R&D sector is different, in that other social scientists, engineers, and assorted experts wrote about it along with economists. More than half of the entries in table 3.9 are by non-economists. Different disciplines approach the subject from their

Table 3.9.  Books on R&D, innovation, and technology transfer.

| Author, year | Chapter on military sector | Chapter author if different from book author, editor |
|---|---|---|
| Vucinich, 1956 | No | • |
| Zaleski et al., 1961 | No | • |
| The State of Soviet Science, 1965 | No | • |
| Korol, 1965 | Yes | • |
| Sutton, 1968 | Yes | • |
| Sutton, 1971 | Yes | • |
| Harvey et al., 1972 | Yes | • |
| Sutton, 1973a | Yes | • |
| Sutton, 1973b | Yes | • |
| Berliner, 1976 | No | • |
| Hutchings, 1976 | No | • |
| Thomas & Kruse-Vaucienne, 1977 | Yes | D. Holloway |
| Amann, et al., 1977 | Yes | D. Holloway |
| Lewis, 1979 | No | • |
| Holliday, 1979 | No | • |
| Cocks, 1980 | No | • |
| Lubrano & Solomon, 1980 | No | • |
| Amann & Cooper, 1982 | Yes | D. Holloway |
| Hanson, 1981 | No | • |
| Parrott, 1983 | No | • |
| Vucinich, 1984 | No | • |
| Schaffer, 1985 | Yes | D. Holloway |
| Parrott, 1985 | Yes | J. Cooper |
| Fortescue, 1986 | No | • |
| Amann & Cooper, 1986 | Yes | J. Cooper |
| Berry, 1988 | Yes | J. Cooper |
| Balzer, 1989 | Yes | J. Cooper |
| Fortescue, 1990 | Yes | • |
| Scanlan, 1992 | No | • |

*Source*: See appendix 3.1.

own specific, though overlapping perspectives. I included books by non-economists that cover some of the same ground that an economist would have. I have less confidence about the completeness of the list of books in table 3.9, and the appropriateness of including every book, than for the previous tables.

Of all the categories in our sample, literature on R&D stands out in that it has the largest proportion of books with military chapters—more than one-half. Unlike in the other categories, military chapters do not all date from the few final years of the USSR's life, but rather start in 1965 and continue appearing through the 1970s and 1980s (table 3.9). However, no credit for this achievement goes to American Sovietology. Four of the chapters were written by an outsider (Antony Sutton), seven by British Sovietologists associated with University of Birmingham (David Holloway and Julian Cooper), and the remaining four by various non-economists.

## *3.4 Publications on the military sector proper*
### 3.4.1 Journal articles

In the more than 40 years of Sovietology's existence, journals were becoming an increasingly important mode of communicating research results in economics, the number of English language periodicals reaching 200–300 by 1990.[5] Many of these, as well as the numerous journals in the adjacent social science fields, occasionally carried articles on the Soviet economy. It is impractical to try to count all such articles, find those devoted to the military sector, and relate their number to the total. Instead, I limit myself to the periodicals that would have been the most likely or the most prestigious outlets for Sovietologists.

These include 10 general economics journals that existed at the time of Sovietology's birth and that have been among the most prestigious in the profession, according to a ranking by Laband and Piette (1994). I also surveyed five specialist journals: two leading Soviet area-studies journals (*Slavic Review* and *Soviet Studies*) and all three American journals devoted to centrally planned economies (*Journal of Comparative Economics*, *Comparative Economic Studies*, and *Soviet Economy*). The oldest continuously published journal on the subject, *Economics of Planning*, founded in Norway as *Ost Okonomi* in 1962, was also surveyed through 1987. For each periodical, I identified articles on the Soviet/socialist economy and noted if any were related to the military sector by examining their titles. The results are summarized in table 3.10.

Between 1948 and 1991, nine leading general economics journals published 207 articles on the Soviet economy. Of these, only one (Okamura 1991) is devoted to the military sector, and then only indirectly. Over the

Table 3.10. Number of articles on Soviet/socialist economies and their military sectors in general economics and specialized journals, 1948–1991.

| Journal title | Number of articles on Soviet/socialist/ planned economy | Number of articles on military sector |
|---|---|---|
| General economics, American journals | 163 | 1 |
| *American Economic Review*[1] | 49 | 0 |
| *Journal of Political Economy* | 36 | 0 |
| *Quarterly Journal of Economics* | 31 | 0 |
| *Review of Economics and Statistics* | 48 | 1 |
| General economics, five British and international journals[2] | 44 | 0 |
| *American Economic Review* Papers and Proceedings, 1948–1972 | 43 | 1 |
| *Slavic Review* | 126 | 0 |
| *Soviet Studies*, 1949–1991[3] | 582 | 15 |
| *Journal of Comparative Economics*, 1977–1991[4] | n.a.[5] | 1 |
| *Comparative Economic Studies*, 1985–1991 | n.a.[5] | 2 |
| *Soviet Economy*, 1985–1991 | n.a.[5] | 7 |
| *Economics of Planning* (*Ost Okonomi*) 1962–1987 | n.a.[5] | 0 |

*Sources*: For general economics journals, I searched the JSTOR database for articles with "Soviet," "socialist," "socialism," "centrally planned," "central planning," or "planned" in the title. For Papers and Proceedings and specialized journals, I examined the tables of contents, selecting articles by their titles.

[1] Excluding Papers and Proceedings.

[2] *Econometrica, Economica, Economic Journal, Oxford Economic Papers, Review of Economic Studies.*

[3] Articles and notes.

[4] Articles, short communications, discussions.

[5] All articles in this journal are about the Soviet/socialist/planned economy.

years of 1948–1972, 43 papers were published on the Soviet/socialist economies in *Papers and Proceedings* of the AEA's annual meetings, of which one is devoted to the military sector (Kershaw 1951). The leading American area-studies journal, *Slavic Review*, published 126 articles on the Soviet economy between 1948 and 1991—yet none about the military sector. Another American area-studies journal, *Russian Review*, also occasionally published economics articles. I failed to identify a single one devoted to the military sector from 1948 to 1966.

For the planned economies journals, I do not count the total number of articles on the socialist economy, because this includes all their content. The leading periodical on centrally planned economies, *Journal of Comparative Economics,* started publication in 1977 and by 1991 had one article on the military sector in East European countries (Crane 1988).[6] *Comparative Economic Studies* started publication in the same year that Gorbachev came to power, and had two military sector pieces, Kontorovich (1988) and Kushnirsky (1991). Seven pieces appearing in *Soviet Economy* in fact amount to two articles with two short comments for each, plus a 1991 article on conversion.

The paucity of military-sector articles does not reflect the journals' aversion to articles devoted to specific sectors or categories of final expenditures. Table 3.11 shows the number of articles on various sectors found in specialized journals. The usual suspects, agriculture and external economic relations, boast by far the most titles. Across the three journals in the table, articles on investment and those on natural resources/energy/ fuel also outnumber those on the military sector, while articles on consumption are equal in number.

The British-edited *Soviet Studies* accounts for more than half of military articles in our sample. Military sector articles started appearing there after 1972, and were not all concentrated in the few final years of the USSR, as was the case with other publications. A total of 15 articles were published on the subject, compared to 77 on agriculture, 25 on external economic relations, and 23 on investment (table 3.11). One-third of the military articles consist of the exchanges between one economist—the author of a regression model explaining Soviet defense expenditures by Soviet GDP and US defense expenditures (Gregory 1974)—and his critics. There are also three articles on the magnitude of military spending and two on Soviet involvement in the Middle East. An article on the arms trade with the Third World and another on the internal politics of economic reforms are written by political scientists and inclined towards that discipline's problematics.

## 3.4.2 Books

Comparing the number of books on the military sector to that of books on agriculture and external economic relations is subject to the same uncertainties as counting R&D and innovation volumes, discussed in section 3.3.

Table 3.11. **Articles on specific sectors of the Soviet/socialist economies in specialized journals, 1948–1991.**

| Sector | Slavic Review | Soviet Studies[1] 1949–1991 | JCE[2] 1977–1991 | Total |
|---|---|---|---|---|
| Agriculture | 31 | 77 | 9 | 117 |
| Foreign economic relations | 6 | 25 | 14 | 45 |
| Investment | 0 | 23 | 7 | 30 |
| Natural resources, fuel, energy | 3 | 13 | 7 | 23 |
| Consumption, consumer goods | 2 | 10 | 4 | 16 |
| Retail, wholesale, credit, services | 2 | 8 | 4 | 14 |
| Housing | 3 | 6 | 2 | 11 |
| Engineering, machinebuilding | 1 | 5 | 3 | 9 |
| Other industry | 4 | 6 | 1 | 11 |
| Transport | 0 | 6 | 0 | 6 |
| R&D, education | 0 | 4 | 0 | 4 |
| Military sector | 0 | 15 | 1[3] | 16 |
| Total specific sectors | 52 | 198 | 52 | 302 |

*Source*: Tables of contents of the journals.

[1] Articles and notes.

[2] Articles, short communications, discussions.

[3] There is also an article on military expenditures in countries of the Organisation for Economic Co-operation and Development: Smith (1980).

A large share of the volumes devoted to these sectors belong to non-economists, but cover some of the same ground that an economist would. My judgment about which of these books to count may skew the results. To help readers form their own judgment, I supply the bibliographies on which my estimates are based (appendices 3.3–3.6).

The first book on the military sector of the Soviet economy appeared only in 1975, late compared to books on other sectors (appendix 3.3). By that time, there were already three books published on transportation, and one book on each of the following: steel, the chemical industry, oil and gas, and cement. Moreover, books on such low-priority (by Soviet reckoning) sectors as banking, marketing (two books on each), the service sector, and advertising also predated the first military sector volume (appendix 3.4).[7]

So did 23 books on agriculture and 11 books on foreign trade (appendices 3.5 and 3.6).

Books on agriculture and foreign economic relations also outnumbered those on the military sector in the 1970s and 1980s, though by that time diminishing returns for work on the former subjects must have set in.[8] Altogether, 20 books on the Soviet military sector, along with 48 books on agriculture and 37 books on foreign trade were published in the West between 1948 and 1992. While the publication of books on agriculture and external economic relations was spread across several decades, the majority of books on the military sector (11 out of 20) were published between 1987 and 1992, when the Cold War was winding down (appendix 3.3).

Less than half of the books on military sector are authored by academic economists, with those by political scientists being almost as numerous. Their books, while containing valuable chapters on the military sector, are understandably focused elsewhere—on international relations or internal Soviet politics.

## 3.5  The user side

So far, this chapter has focused on the "producer" side of Sovietological research—the low number of chapters, books, articles, and index entries on the military sector, and the insubstantial nature of many of them. Yet what matters is not the number of chapters and articles but their effect on the readers. Given the fragmented nature of the literature, there did appear publications on the military sector, some of them detailed and penetrating (as will be shown in section 6.3.1). Perhaps this sufficed to impress the unique role of the military sector on the public, in which case the number of chapters and all the other indicators cited here are of no consequence. One sophisticated group of users of Sovietological literature, whose understanding of it is well documented, is the fellow economists writing textbooks on comparative economic systems and introductory economics.

### 3.5.1  Comparative economic systems textbooks and readers

Comparative economic systems courses, describing socialism, capitalism, and their variants, were the main channel through which American undergraduates could obtain detailed knowledge about the Soviet economy. In the late 1970s, 63% of all the colleges and universities with an economics major offered classes on the subject, with six times more sections taught than the economics of the USSR (table 1.2). Material on the Soviet economy, though condensed compared to that found in textbooks on the subject proper, constitutes a substantial part of comparative systems texts.

A large number of textbooks were published for this popular course. In table 3.12, I survey those appearing between 1971 and 1992, plus a few random earlier titles. Over 40% of the authors of these books belonged to fields other than the study of planned economies. Their coverage of the Soviet economy reflects their understanding of Sovietological literature. Specialists in the Soviet economy were responsible, individually or as co-authors, for one-third of the entries in table 3.12, and scholars in the closely related fields of East European and other planned economies penned the rest. One would assume that the need to condense familiar material led these authors to concentrate on the most important characteristics of the Soviet economy. The comparative nature of the subject should have also forced the selection of characteristics which set the Soviet economy apart from other cases considered.

It is natural to compare the presence of the military sector in the systems textbooks with its presence in the Soviet economy textbooks. The total number of books is almost the same in each case—46 in table 3.12 versus 47 in table 3.1. On the most generous interpretation, only three comparative systems volumes have sections on the Soviet military economy in their tables of contents, down from the already low number of military sector chapters in Soviet economy textbooks (eight). This was not due to the comparative systems texts' aversion to sectoral analysis, as two-thirds of the books have sections on civilian sectors of the Soviet economy, for a total of 66 civilian-sector sections. There are also eight sections on the military sectors of Western economies in comparative systems textbooks.

The three sections touching on the Soviet military sector do not convey its place in the economy. Gardner (1988, 28) has a one-page description of the statistical difficulties in comparing Soviet and American defense expenditures, presented as an example of the general problems of international comparisons. Wiles (1976), in his idiosyncratic style, makes a few tangential remarks on the Soviet military sector in the chapter on "War and Economic Systems." Zimbalist and Sherman (1984, 198–202) include a highly politicized appendix on US and Soviet defense expenditures,

Table 3.12. Textbooks and readers on comparative economic systems.

| Author, year | Chapter on military sector | | Chapters on other Soviet Sectors | Number of index entries for military sector terms | |
|---|---|---|---|---|---|
| | Soviet | Western | | Soviet | Western |
| Leeman, 1963 | No | No | No | No index | No index |
| Goldman, 1964 | No | No | Agriculture, banking | 0 | 0 |
| Kohler, 1966 | No | No | Agriculture, banking | 0 | 0 |
| Coleman, 1968 | No | No | No | 6 | 5 |
| Goldman, 1971 | No | No | Agriculture, banking | No index | No index |
| Reynolds, 1971 | No | No | Foreign trade, investment | 0 | 0 |
| S&N, 1971 | No | No | Agriculture | 2 | 1 |
| Carson, 1973 | No | No | Foreign trade | 0 | 0 |
| Elliott, 1973 | No | No | No | 0 | 0 |
| Loucks & Whitney, 1973 | No | No | Agriculture | 0 | 0 |
| Bornstein, 1974 | No | No | Foreign trade | No index | No index |
| Dalton, 1974 | No | No | No | 6 | 9 |
| Grossman, 1974 | No | No | Agriculture | 1 | 0 |
| Pickersgill, 1974 | No | No | Agriculture | 0 | 0 |
| Viljoen, 1974 | No | No | No | 0 | 5 |
| Neuberger & Duffy, 1976 | No | No | No | 0 | 0 |
| Wiles, 1976 | Yes | Yes | Agriculture, banking, investment | 3 | 11 |
| Gruchy, 1977 | No | No | Agriculture, finance, foreign trade, investment | 0 | 0 |
| Holesovsky, 1977 | No | Yes | Agriculture, consumption, foreign trade | 1 | 6 |
| Leeman, 1977 | No | No | Agriculture Foreign trade, investment | 0 | 0 |
| S&N, 1977 | No | No | Agriculture, banking | 1 | 0 |

**Table 3.12. Continued**

| Author, year | Chapter on military sector | | Chapters on other Soviet Sectors | Number of index entries for military sector terms | |
| --- | --- | --- | --- | --- | --- |
| | Soviet | Western | | Soviet | Western |
| Viotti & Eidem, 1978 | No | No | No | 0 | 0 |
| Ward, 1979 | No | No | No | 5 | 14 |
| Bornstein, 1979 | No | No | No | No index | No index |
| G&S, 1980 | No | No | Agriculture, trade | 0 | 7 |
| Amuzegar, 1981 | No | No | No | 0 | 0 |
| S&N, 1983 | No | No | Agriculture, banking | 0 | 0 |
| Whynes, 1983 | No | No | No | 3 | 4 |
| Gottlieb, 1984 | No | Yes | No | 0 | 4 |
| Zimbalist & Sherman, 1984 | Yes | Yes | Agriculture, consumption, education, finance, health, housing, investment, trade | 4 | 4 |
| G&S, 1985 | No | Yes | Agriculture, foreign trade | 1 | 13 |
| Bornstein, 1985 | No | No | Foreign trade | No index | No index |
| Elliott, 1985 | No | No | No | 0 | 0 |
| Pryor, 1985 | No | No | Foreign trade, agriculture, consumption | 1 | 1 |
| Haitani, 1986 | No | No | Agriculture | 2 | 1 |
| Schnitzer, 1987 | No | No | Agriculture, banking | 0 | 0 |
| Gardner, 1988 | Yes | Yes | Agriculture | 1 | 1 |
| Agarwal, 1989 | No | Yes | Foreign trade, investment | No index | No index |
| Bornstein, 1989 | No | No | Agriculture, finance, foreign trade, investment | 0 | 0 |

(*continued*)

Table 3.12. **Continued**

| Author, year | Chapter on military sector | | Chapters on other Soviet Sectors | Number of index entries for military sector terms | |
|---|---|---|---|---|---|
| | Soviet | Western | | Soviet | Western |
| G&S, 1989 | No | No | Agriculture, foreign trade, investment | 0 | 5 |
| Kohler, 1989 | No | No | Agriculture, investment | 0 | 2 |
| Carson, 1990 | No | No | No | 0 | 4 |
| Putterman, 1990 | No | No | No | 0 | 0 |
| Schnitzer, 1991 | No | No | Agriculture, banking | 5 | 0 |
| Angresano, 1992 | No | No | No | 0 | 0 |
| G&S, 1992 | No | Yes | Agriculture, foreign trade, investment | 2 | 6 |

S&N = Schnitzer & Nordyke.

G&S = Gregory and Stuart.

accusing the CIA of direct falsification. By contrast, several textbooks provide serious and substantive accounts of the military sector in the American economy.[9]

Among the 41 Soviet economy textbooks with indexes, only six do not have index references to the military sector (table 3.1). By contrast, 24 out of 40 comparative systems books with indexes do not have such references. The majority of comparative systems books do not even mention the Soviet military sector, if their indexes are to be believed.[10]

Some of the indexed references are purely formal, such as a mention of defense expenditures as one of the budget items in a discussion of public spending (Pryor 1985, 221–22). Others are somewhat more substantive, stating that defense outlays in the state budget were understated, and that actual expenditures, as estimated by the CIA, were higher, and put a burden on the economy.[11] Grossman (1974, 119) notes, in one sentence, that "extremely large buildup of military capability" was a characteristic of Soviet growth, without further developing this remarkable point.

Gregory and Stuart (1981; 1986; 1990) are the only Soviet economy textbooks by American academics to include a substantive section on the military sector. There, they argue that "Soviet economic performance . . . cannot be understood without an assessment of the resources devoted to the military and the military might these resources have produced" (Gregory and Stuart 1985, 363). Yet two editions of their comparative systems texts, Gregory and Stuart (1980; 1989), have no index entries on the Soviet military sector. However, there are military economy index entries in 1985 and 1992 editions. This disappearance and reappearance itself shows that the subject was viewed as marginal.

The near-complete omission of the Soviet military sector from the comparative systems textbooks had a perhaps unintended effect of painting the American economy as more militarized than the Soviet one. As with the total number of sections, the total number of pages with Western military sector references in the index is double the number of that for the Soviet military sector (103 vs. 45). The authors of the comparative systems textbooks were not specialists in the military sectors. They were summarizing the existing literature on the two economies. It is natural to surmise that they gave at least twice as much space to the American military sector as they did to the Soviet one, because the American military-industrial complex occupied greater space in the writings on that economy.

The neglect of the military sector in Sovietological literature was not the only cause of its near-total absence from the comparative systems textbooks. Another factor was the lack of appreciation in the discipline of economics for the role of military might in history, and its connection to economic capabilities, discussed in section 7.1.3.

## 3.5.2 Introductory economics textbooks

Introductory economics is the most widely taught and heavily enrolled economics course, required of all economics majors and also taken by non-majors (Siegfried and Wilkinson 1982, 130). The textbooks for the course aspire to cover all fields of economics, and usually include a chapter titled "alternative economic systems," "socialist planning," or "Marxist economies" (see the second column in table 3.13 for title variants). Discussion of the Soviet economy makes up a major part of such chapters. Like the material on other fields of economics in the textbook, this discussion represents the authors' understanding of the special literature.

Because of the large number of introductory textbooks, only those published between 1981 and 1992, as well as a few random older texts, are
surveyed (table 3.13).[12] The final decade of the USSR witnessed an increase
in Sovietological publications on the military sector, as noted earlier in
this chapter. If this greater prominence of the sector was perceived by the

Table 3.13.  Military sector in the introductory economics textbooks.

| Author, year, edition | Title of the chapter addressing Soviet economy | Number of index entries for military sector terms | |
|---|---|---|---|
| | | Soviet | Western |
| Robinson & Eatwell, 1973 | Socialist planning; Socialist states | o | 10 |
| Samuelson, 1976, 10th ed. | Alternative Economic Systems | o | 15 |
| Samuelson, 1980, 11th ed. | Alternative Economic Systems | 3 | 8 |
| McConnell, 1981, 8th ed. | The Economy of the Soviet Union | o | 3 |
| Starr, 1981, 3rd ed. | Socialism, the USSR, and the People's Republic of China | o | 3 |
| Baumol & Blinder, 1982, 2nd ed. | Marxian Economics; Comparative Economic Systems: What are the Choices? | o | 2 |
| Cairncross & Sinclair, 1982, 6th ed. | N/A | o | o |
| Fusfeld, 1982 | Central Planning and Socialism: The Case of the Soviet Union | o | 12 |
| McCarty, 1982, 3rd ed. | N/A | o | o |
| Wonnacott & Wonnacott, 1982, 2nd ed. | Marxism and Marxist Economies | o | 3 |
| Craven, 1984 | N/A | o | o |
| McConnell, 1984, 9th ed. | The Economy of the Soviet Union | o | 2 |
| Miller, 1984 | Comparing Economic Systems | o | 6 |
| Starr, 1984, 4th ed. | Socialism, the USSR, and the People's Republic of China | 2 | 10 |

## Table 3.13.  Continued

| Author, year, edition | Title of the chapter addressing Soviet economy | Number of index entries for military sector terms | |
|---|---|---|---|
| | | Soviet | Western |
| Baumol & Blinder, 1985, 3rd ed. | Marxian Economics; Comparative Economic Systems: What are the Choices? | 0 | 7 |
| Olsen & Hailstones, 1985 | N/A | 0 | 0 |
| Samuelson & Nordhaus, 1985, 12th ed. | Marxism and Alternative Economic Systems | 1 | 1 |
| Mansfield, 1986, 5th ed. | The Communist Countries and Marxism | 0 | 18 |
| Robinson, 1986 | N/A | 0 | 0 |
| Ruffin & Gregory, 1986, 2nd ed. | The Soviet Economy | 1 | 5 |
| Wonnacott & Wonnacott, 1986, 3rd ed. | Marxism and Marxist Economies | 0 | 1 |
| McConnell, 1987, 10th ed. | The Economy of the Soviet Union | 1 | 3 |
| Robinson, 1987 | N/A | 0 | 0 |
| Baumol & Blinder, 1988, 4th ed. | Marxian Economics; Comparative Economic Systems: What are the Choices? | 0 | 3 |
| Clayton & Brown, 1988 | Comparative Economic Systems: Soviet Union | 0 | 2 |
| McCarty, 1988, 5th ed. | N/A | 0 | 1 |
| Reynolds, 1988, 5th ed. | Plan and Market: A Comparison of Systems | 0 | 2 |
| Ruffin & Gregory, 1988, 3rd ed. | Comparative Systems, Marx, and the Soviet Union | 0 | 2 |
| Case & Fair, 1989 | Alternative Economic Systems | 0 | 0 |
| Mansfield, 1989 | Communist Countries & Marxism | 0 | 17 |
| Gregory & Ruffin, 1989 | Allocation of Resources in the United States and the Soviet Union: Comparative Economic Systems | 0 | 0 |

*(continued)*

### Table 3.13. Continued

| Author, year, edition | Title of the chapter addressing Soviet economy | Number of index entries for military sector terms | |
|---|---|---|---|
| | | Soviet | Western |
| Samuelson & Nordhaus, 1989, 13th ed. | The Winds of Change: Alternative Economic Systems | 1 | 2 |
| Gregory, 1990, 2nd ed. | The Soviet Economy | 0 | 0 |
| Thomas & Weber, 1990 | Comparative Economic Systems | 0 | 6 |
| Wonnacott & Wonnacott, 1990, 4th ed. | Marxism & Marxist Economies | 0 | 0 |
| Baumol & Blinder, 1991, 5th ed. | Marxian Economics; Comparative Economic Systems: What Are the Choices? | 0 | 4 |
| Bonstingl, 1991 | N/A | 0 | 7 |
| Mansfield, 1992, 7th ed. | The Communist Countries & Marxism | 0 | 27 |

users, a survey limited to the 1980s may be unrepresentative of 1948–1970 practice by showing a heightened degree of attention to the subject.

Of the 38 introductory economics textbooks in table 3.13, 30 have chapters on the Soviet/socialist economy. However, only six of the latter have index entries for Soviet military-economic subjects. A string of zeros in column three of the table testifies to the widespread lack of awareness among economists of the military sector's place in the Soviet economy. This does not appear to result from a general aversion to military subjects. Most books (28) have index entries on Western, usually American, military matters. Some of them (e.g., various editions of Mansfield) address a variety of military-economic issues, such as the maintenance of industrial base, weapons procurement, and the all-volunteer army recruitment, in addition to the usual discussion of defense expenditures. Fusfeld (1982) even devotes a whole chapter to the military sector of the US economy.

Introductory textbook writers relied on their Sovietological colleagues for information on what was important about the Soviet economy.

Sovietologists failed to persuade other economists that the military sector was important enough to be mentioned in a condensed treatment of their subject.

Among the authors of introductory textbooks, the sole Sovietologist was Paul Gregory, who also co-wrote the only Soviet economy textbook with a chapter on the military sector. Ruffin and Gregory (1986; 1988) have a section on Soviet military power with a three-paragraph substantive discussion. Yet their later books, Gregory and Ruffin (1989) and Gregory (1990), have dropped the section and have no index entries for the subject.[13]

## 3.6 Summary

Brezhnev, the General Secretary from 1964 to 1982, is said to have had two priorities: agriculture and defense (Gorbachev 1995, 206). American Sovietologists displayed much more interest in the former than in the latter, though the latter was central to the concerns of the United States. The military sector, so conspicuous in the Soviet economy's autopsy report, was nearly absent from its regular health check-ups by academic writers.

Literature on Soviet economy contained few chapters, articles, and books on the military sector, compared to other sectors. Disproportionately many of those appeared in the final years of the USSR. And disproportionately few of the military economy publications were produced by American Sovietologists.

Textbooks on the Soviet economy have 136 chapters on civilian sectors, and only eight on the military sector (table 3.14). About one-seventh of the textbooks with indexes do not even mention the military sector there, and most of those that do only reference it in passing. There are no chapters on the military sector in the research volumes devoted to the three core areas of Soviet economics—planning, management, and growth—though these books have 47 chapters on other sectors. Between one-third and three-fourths of books in these categories fail to even mention the military sector in their indexes. Books on economic history, Gorbachev-era reforms, and the general Soviet economy display a similar civilian slant.

There is one article on the military sector among the more than 200 pieces on the Soviet economy published in the top nine general economics journals, and no such articles among the 126 pieces on the Soviet economy in the leading Russian area-studies journal. Books on the military sector are also vastly outnumbered by those on agriculture and foreign trade.

Table 3.14. Summary of military sector coverage in books.

| Category of book | Total books, number | Civilian sector chapters, number | Soviet military sector chapters | | | No military sector index entries/All books with index |
|---|---|---|---|---|---|---|
| | | | Total number | By US Sovietologists | Share published over the period | |
| Textbooks | 47 | 136 | 8 | 4 | 1981–92: 63% | 6/41 |
| Planning | 18 | 31 | 0 | 0 | — | 9/12 |
| Management | 8 | 1 | 0 | 0 | — | 5/8 |
| Growth | 10 | 15 | 0 | 0 | — | 3/9 |
| National income | 11 | 12 | 4 | 2 | 1951–68: 100% | 1/8 |
| Gorbachev reforms | 16 | 24 | 1 | 0 | 1991: 100% | 2/15 |
| General | 28 | 32 | 3 | 2 | 1989–92: 100% | 7/25 |
| History | 14 | 27 | 4 | 1 | 1989–92: 75% | 2/14 |
| R&D | 29 | N/A | 15 | 0 | 1985–92: 40% | N/A |
| Comparative systems | 46 | 65 | 3 | N/A | N/A | 24/40 |
| Principles of economics | 38 | N/A | N/A | N/A | N/A | 24/30 |

*Sources*: See tables 3.1–3.9, 3.12, 3.13.

Five out of eight textbooks with military-sector chapters appeared in the last decade of the Soviet Union (table 3.14). The majority of books on the military sector were published between 1987 and 1992, when the Cold War was winding down, and the Soviets themselves started publicly discussing the subject. American Sovietologists comprised the largest contingent of researchers working on the Soviet economy, yet they authored only about half of the books with military sector chapters (excluding R&D), and about half of the books on the military sector (table 3.14).

It is instructive to examine outliers, categories of books and periodicals paying the most attention to the military sector. Books on R&D, innovation, and technology transfer stand out in the literature in that half of them have chapters on the military sector. There are more such chapters in this category of books (15) than in all other research volumes combined. Yet all of these chapters in R&D volumes were written by outsiders, non-economist social scientists, or British authors. Scholars connected to the University of Birmingham (Robert Davies, Julian Cooper, David Holloway) stand out as major contributors on military economy topics, forming "the Birmingham exception," as suggested by Mark Harrison.[14] *Soviet Studies*, the periodical with the largest number of articles on the military sector, was published in Britain.

Economists drew on Sovietological literature for the content of chapters on the Soviet economy in comparative systems and introductory economics textbooks. More than half of the comparative systems textbooks, and 80% of principles of economics textbooks have no references to the Soviet military sector in their indexes (table 3.14). Sovietologists failed to persuade their colleagues that the military sector was important, or even merited a mention in popular treatments of the Soviet economy.

The post mortem writings on Sovietology have not detected this gap in the scholarship. Schroeder (1995, 221) even counts the analysis of militarization as one of the field's achievements, asserting the existence of a large literature on the subject and the extremely large "amount of resources devoted by Western governments and academics to studying defense-related matters." This statement may be correct, but only with respect to the government's internal efforts. I started documenting the neglect of the military sector soon after the Soviet collapse (Kontorovich 1996). It has also been noted in passing by a retired US Army general, a British Sovietologist, and a long-time insider critic of Sovietology.[15]

## Notes

1. Two or three titles included here may arguably be classified as popular books, rather than textbooks.
2. Pryor (1985, 217); OECD (1993, 68, 71).
3. Not indicated in the extremely concise table of contents.
4. See Kolkowicz (1962) on the use of military manpower in agriculture, and Despres and Khinchuk (1990) on the farms run by the armed forces.
5. Liebowitz & Palmer (1984, 77); Stigler et al. (1995, 333, 335).
6. There was an earlier piece on military spending in the OECD countries (Smith 1980).
7. Almost all books on civilian sectors were authored by the economists.

8. Not all of the agriculture books counted here are about the USSR, while all military books are. But this is just the result of the absence of books on the East European military sector.

9. Holesovsky (1977), Gottlieb (1984), Gregory and Stuart (1985; 1992).

10. On the accuracy of index entry count, see appendix 3.2.

11. Various editions of Schnitzer and Nordyke; Schnitzer (1991); Haitani (1986, 142).

12. As with comparative systems textbooks, no attempt is made to cover all the texts published in this period, just the ones that the interlibrary loan delivered in a timely fashion.

13. Samuelson and Nordhaus (1985; 1989) and Starr (1984) have two sentences on military spending and its burden. McConnell (1987) has one paragraph on the same subject.

14. Personal communication.

15. Odom (1998, 55, 430); Hanson (2003, 31); and Rosefielde (2005).

# 4

# *Civilianizing the Objectives of the Planners*

SIMPLE OMISSION WAS not the only anomaly in Sovietology's treatment of military-economic matters. Another was civilianization, the peaceful reinterpretation of the features of the economy that the Soviets themselves revealed to be of military significance. The objectives of the planners were among the most important aspects of the Soviet economy that underwent civilianization, along with the First Five-Year Plan, discussed in chapter 5.

## *4.1 Objectives and behavior in economics*

At the foundation of the economic approach is the assumption of rationality: actors have stable objectives, which they go after in a consistent, maximizing fashion.[1] Human behavior is explained in terms of the pursuit of these objectives. Microeconomic theory textbooks open with the derivation of an individual consumer's preferences and often include discussions of the plausibility of profit maximization as the objective of a firm.[2] Analysis of macroeconomic policy, with its normative focus, has long assumed that policy makers maximize some version of a social welfare function. Positive analysis of economic policy calls for an objective function derived from the incentives and constraints faced by politicians (Blanchard and Fischer 1989, 567–69).

As economics expanded into new areas of human activity, it had to deal with new classes of actors and their objectives. The field of public choice owes its very existence to the assumption that government officials pursue private rather than public goals, and different specifications of the former have been proposed.[3] The development of law and economics raised the question, "What Do Judges Maximize?" (Posner 1993).

Studying the Soviet economy required discerning the objectives of the actors specific to that economy, usually defined as managers and planners. Berliner (1957) proposed that the enterprise managers under central planning were bonus maximizers. Sovietologists generally accepted this view without a debate, and used it as a foundation for their own analysis of the managers' behavior.

For all the attention devoted to them in the literature, managers played a subordinate role in the Soviet economy, reacting to commands and regulations issued by the planners. The rules for awarding bonuses, which supposedly shaped these reactions, were themselves set by those higher up. In an economy where resources were allocated according to plan, the main actors were those who compiled and enforced that plan, and their objectives are crucial in any analysis of that economy. Thus, it has been proposed that national income in such an economy can be interpreted as a measure of welfare in terms of planners' (rather than consumers') preferences (Bergson 1961, 26).

Sovietological literature never settled on a generally accepted formulation of planners' objectives, and remained fragmented, with a standard and a minority account, plus a number of hard-to-classify individual positions. The Soviets offered their own view of these objectives. In what follows, we show that the standard Sovietological account is at odds with the Soviet one. In particular, it omits an objective of planning that the Soviets emphasized—the strengthening of defense. The standard account also does not make sense in terms of economics. These defects can be remedied by taking Soviet declarations about the objectives of planning seriously while checking them against the evidence on the economy's performance. Adopting this alternative view improves our understanding of several aspects of the Soviet economy.

## 4.2  Who exactly were the planners?

While managers represent a clearly delineated group identifiable in Soviet administrative terms, planners are a more ambiguous grouping. Indeed, Sovietologists used the word "planners" in a variety of contexts to refer to the part of the administrative pyramid above the enterprises, which included, in addition to the planners proper, sectoral ministries and their main administrations, as well as supply, price, financial, and other bodies in charge of particular economic functions.[4] These organizations had different, often conflicting objectives (Nove 1966, 267). They were themselves subordinate to the top leadership. Defining and enforcing the society-wide objectives that the literature ascribes to planners would have been way above their pay grade. That was the exclusive prerogative of the top political leadership, which, in some periods of Soviet history, was co-terminous with the Politburo but, in other periods, included just the top leader, or the top leader and a few close aides (Gregory 2004, 76).

Authors of a more descriptive or historical bent write of the object-ives of political leaders, rather than planners. Some authors also assign objectives to abstract entities, writing of the tasks of the "social engine" (Grossman 1960, 2–3), or the purpose of the system (Nove 1986, 3). Others argue in terms of the personal inclinations of particular politicians (Dyker 1985, 36).

The use of euphemisms such as "planners" or, in the case of Bergson (1964, 338), "the system's directors," presumably reflects the methodolog-ical prejudice of the time—economists' desire to limit their analysis to economic actors to avoid having to deal with politicians who are "outside the economy." Thus, Bennett (1989) disposes of the planners' objectives by postulating a welfare function "that is imposed from outside the model, presumably by politicians."[5] By contrast, he devotes a whole chapter to the motives and behavior of the enterprise managers, supposedly purely eco-nomic actors.

The strictures against the economic study of political behavior, now much relaxed, at least had some justification in the relative separation of the public, political, and private economic spheres in Western societies. This separation never existed in Soviet society, where the leaders of the only political party were also the most important economic actors, and deserve to be studied under a more fitting name. In keeping with the liter-ature, we use the term "planners" in the survey of Sovietological sources, and "rulers" in the subsequent discussion.

## *4.3 The Soviet account of the rulers' objectives*
### 4.3.1 The validity of self-proclaimed objectives

The rulers themselves offered descriptions of their objectives, either di-rectly (the top officials' Party Congress speeches, the party program, and the constitutions) or indirectly (instructions for compiling the five-year plans, higher-education textbooks). What central planning in general, or particular plans, sought to achieve was an ideologically sensitive question. The textbooks could deviate only marginally from the current pronouncements of the rulers and had to be approved at a high level: in all likelihood, within the Central Committee apparatus, in addition to the Ministry of Higher Education and *Glavlit*.

Ever since a mid-1940s survey of business managers produced answers at variance with the profit-maximization assumption, Western economists have been skeptical of using economic actors' self-proclaimed motives to explain their behavior.[6] It has been argued that in economic theory, the assumption of goal-directed behavior is just a modeling strategy. The actors do not have to be aware of the postulated objectives, just to behave as if they pursue them, as has been strikingly demonstrated for animal consumers (Kagel et al. 1981, 13–14).

Yet running a centrally planned economy is not like being an expert billiard player who uses the laws of physics without knowing or being able to articulate them (Friedman 1953a, 21–22). Planning is a deliberate process which is often defined as a specifically goal-oriented activity.[7] The ability to consciously pursue particular objectives has been one of the arguments made in favor of planning. For a plan to be effective, rulers must subscribe to well-defined objectives, which in turn must be explicitly communicated to those who participate in the plan's construction and enforcement. For these reasons, Soviet writings may be, with the usual precautions, used as evidence for the objectives of planning.

## 4.3.2 Constitutions and planning manuals

The 1936 Constitution of the USSR defines the goals of planning as "increasing national wealth, a continuous rise in the material and cultural wellbeing of the working people" and "strengthening the independence and defense capability of the USSR" (*Konstitutsiia* 1960, 6). Later, the "main economic law of socialism" became the most widely quoted statement of economic objectives. It said that the highest purpose of socialist production is the satisfaction of material and cultural needs of all the people (Shafiev et al. 1960, 118). This formulation appeared with slight variations in all textbooks on the political economy of socialism and was also incorporated into the 1961 program of the Communist Party and the 1977 Constitution.[8]

An early planning textbook states that "the first task of socialist planning is to secure the independence of our economy from its capitalist surrounding. Realizing this task is directly connected with the strengthening of defense capability" (Sorokin 1946, 18). This echoes Stalin's blunt statements on the subject (discussed in chapter 5).

Later textbooks on national economic planning reiterate the "main economic law" (e.g., Koval' 1973, 20), but then proceed to list additional "tasks of planning." These vary from ideological (erecting the material-technical base of communism) and systemic (strengthening the socialist economy) to mundane economic tasks (accumulation of reserves, rational location of production), along with growth, military might, and cooperation with other socialist economies. The relationship among these objectives is not often spelled out.[9] Another example of a list of objectives that does not spell out the relations among them is Brezhnev's (1981, 3) summary of the 10th Five-Year Plan's achievements: increasing national wealth and production, scientific and technological potential, strengthening defense capability, and increasing the welfare and cultural level of the people.

A planning textbook that carefully formulates the relationship among objectives by ranking them into a "tree" names satisfying the material needs of consumers and strengthening defense capability as the main national goals of equal importance, their relative weight changing depending on the situation (Berri 1973, 32–4). Similarly, the manual on methods of compiling five-year national plans opens with the proclamation that plans should aim for high rates of growth to improve living standards and strengthen economic and military might (Gosplan 1969, 3).[10] This formula is repeated in the Directives of the 24th Congress of the CPSU (*Materialy* 1972, 129). Ryzhkov (1986, 6) formulates the main goal of the 12th Five-Year Plan (1986–90) as increasing the growth rate and efficiency of the economy as a base for improving the welfare of the people, while maintaining the necessary military might.

According to the textbooks on the political economy of socialism, the two Soviet constitutions, and the 1961 party program, the economic objective of the rulers was always raising the living standards of their subjects. Yet political economy was a purely ideological, scholastic discipline unconcerned with practical aspects of economics (Fomin 2006). Textbooks and manuals on national economic planning, while observing ideological propriety, were written with pragmatic purposes in mind. These, as well as the pronouncements by rulers from Stalin to Ryzhkov, affirm the objectives of consumption and military might with weights fluctuating depending on circumstances. When connections among various objectives of planning are expounded, growth is named as a means for achieving other economic objectives. In shorter or less carefully articulated statements, it is listed as one of several objectives, but not the most important one.

### 4.3.3 Can they be believed?

The Soviet rulers' declaration of consumption as their objective was consistent with the image of themselves that they wanted to project, as evidenced by every conceivable source. But acknowledging the military objective was extraordinary in the context of planning textbooks and manuals, given the virtual blackout in the post-war Soviet economic sources on anything even potentially related to military-economic matters (section 6.1). Apparently the message was important enough to justify breaking the taboo.

Claims identifying military might as the objective are consistent with statistical evidence. The share of the Ministry of Defense expenditures in the Soviet official measure of aggregate income (NMP) took off at about the time that central planning was introduced in the late 1920s. It kept rising steadily even as the aggregate income itself expanded rapidly through the 1930s, and reached 19% before the start of the war.[11] Whole sectors of industry were created from scratch, providing the USSR with the largest stockpile of sophisticated weapons in the world (section 2.3.3). In the post-war period, the military's share of resources remained at the level typical for major powers entering an all-out war, even as the economy's growth rates declined from impressive in the 1950s to anemic in the late 1970s and 1980s (section 2.2.3).

National accounting data rule out the "main economic law of socialism" and consumption as the leading objective. The share of consumption was "lower in the Soviet Union than in most countries, typically by at least ten GNP points" (Ofer 1987, 1790). Between 1928 and 1940, per capita household consumption actually declined by 0.2% per year, even as GNP per capita grew at an average annual rate of 3.6%. While growth of per capita household consumption resumed in later years, the share of consumption in GNP showed no evidence of converging to its Western level.[12]

This is not to say that the rulers gave zero weight to consumption. There exists a minimum level of consumption necessary to create incentives for work and assure social peace, and it has arguably increased after 1953, with the end of mass terror—hence the need to boost consumption.

This would cast consumption as a constraint on the pursuit of military might. However, the nature of consumption growth in the final decades of the USSR, with massive housing construction, introduction of household appliances, and even private cars, suggests to us the rulers' desire to lift consumption above the necessary minimum. For example, 19% of Soviet households owned a car in 1990, up from 10% in 1980 (Goskomstat 1991, 142). If this admittedly impressionistic argument is accepted, consumption was an objective of the rulers, though one with a systematically lower priority than military might.[13]

## 4.4 *The Sovietological account of planners' objectives*
### 4.4.1 Sources: fragmentation in action

Here we survey a subset of the textbooks, and all the books on planning and growth, used in chapter 3 (see appendix 4.1). Only a minority of these make explicit statements on the objectives of the planners supported by some discussion. For the rest, we deduce their views from one-sentence statements made in passing, or a few scattered sentences, or from the listings of investment priorities, historical accounts, or descriptions of the system's achievements. Even with this willingness to impute views to the authors who make no direct statement on the subject, we were unable to discern any specific objectives from many of the books.

Authors who do pronounce on the objectives of planning offer a variety of political, ideological, economic, and technological goals. Objectives vary widely not only across texts, but sometimes within one text. Thus, Granick (1962, 309) lists central planning, industrialization, technological change, motivating managers, and rational factor allocation as objectives, but also mentions "the value system of Soviet planners," under which heavy industry and transport had high priority, while consumer goods and agriculture were treated as secondary sectors. Kornai (1992, 53–54) mentions "the basic promises" made by the Communist Party upon taking power, such as catching up to Western industrialized countries, full employment, and providing basic needs like "food, shelter, healthcare, education, vacations, and cultural goods and services." Catching up serves ideological needs and is also "reinforced by military and defense considerations" (160–61). Yet when writing about investment, Kornai lists the arms industry as seventh among 11 priorities, behind investment goods, domestic production versus import, the "productive sphere," producer goods, industry, and heavy industry (171–74). Elsewhere (179–80), he states that economic growth, as measured by the official statistics, is the objective.

One would expect such divergent views on such an important topic to spark a controversy, but our sources are silent on the alternative formulations of objectives proposed by others. Perhaps the only attempt in the literature on the Soviet economy to systematically contrast different views on the objectives is Ofer (1987, 1798–1801). The only controversy in Sovietological literature is about the role of "building communism" and other ideological imperatives. Some authors take them seriously as a guide for economic policy, while others dismiss them.[14]

Long and sometimes contradictory lists are probably meant to reflect the actual multiplicity of objectives pursued by the country's rulers. However, this attempt at descriptive accuracy undermines the role objectives play in economics—that of a hypothesis to focus an inquiry into the planners' behavior patterns (Bergson 1964, 7). Virtually any behavior can be "explained" by postulating a long enough list of objectives without specifying the weights attached to each one, or the relations among them, but the explanation then becomes tautological.

## 4.4.2 Sovietology's standard view

For all the variation in the individual authors' lists of objectives, most of them include a common element: growth. Among the authors whose views we were able to discern, the overwhelming majority (16 out of 18 textbooks, nine out of 12 books on planning, and six out of seven books on growth) name economic growth as the main, and often the only, objective (tables 4.1–4.3).

The meaning of economic growth here is different from that in the Soviet sources that articulate the relation among objectives, or, as will be shown, in Western usage. It is distinct from, and often opposite to, growth in private and public consumption. When specific components of final product, such as consumption or defense expenditures, are mentioned in the list of objectives alongside growth, they are treated not as the intended results of the latter, but as additional objectives compromising the achievement of rapid growth.[15] Growth means growth for its own sake.

Here are some of the more telling formulations of this view behind the entries in table 4.1. Bergson (1964, 7–8) states that, since the cardinal concern is to assure rapid growth, "in choices between present and future, resource use is supposed to conform to planners' preferences, which favor

Table 4.1. Objectives of the rulers in the textbooks and readers on the Soviet/socialist economy.

| Author/editor, year, pages | Objectives of rulers |
|---|---|
| Schwartz 1954, 102–3, 167 | Military strength, standard of living, growth |
| Granick 1962, 309–11 | Rapid growth |
| Nove 1962, 669 | Heavy industry, weapons, future standard of living |
| Wiles 1962, 253–54 | Growth in pursuit of full Communism |
| Ames 1965, 190–91 | Nothing specific |
| Schwartz 1965, 13–14 | Military under Stalin, later also consumption |
| Goldman 1968, 29, 63 | Growth, heavy industry |
| Sherman 1969 | Nothing specific |
| Spulber 1969, 4 | Industrial growth, military might |
| Kaser 1970, 220 | Cohesion and stability, with growth as a side effect |
| Campbell 1974, 20–21 | "Growth obsession" |
| Dyker 1976, 30–31 | Growth |
| Hutchings 1977, 152 | Heavy industry and defense |
| Wilczynski 1977 | Nothing specific |
| Krylov 1979 | Nothing specific |
| Gregory & Stuart 1981, 3 | Growth, defense capabilities named as achievements |
| Davies 1981, 26 | Investment, producer goods industries, defense |
| Holzman 1982 | Nothing specific |
| Millar 1981, 31, 122 | Heavy industry, military after WWII, also consumption later |
| Goldman 1983 | Nothing specific |
| Dyker 1985, 36 | Growth |
| Nove 1986, 35 | Obsession with the future: high rate of investment, priority of producer goods |
| Buck & Cole 1987 | Nothing specific |
| Jeffries 1990, 4–5 | Catching-up, heavy industry, military power in 1930s |
| Kornai 1992, 160–61, 179–80 | Growth |

*Sources*: See appendix 4.1.

the future as far as seems expedient. Elsewhere . . . the concern is with 'consumer's welfare.'" According to Kornai (1992, 179–80), "The purpose is not maximization of social welfare in the broad sense. . . . The goal is . . . to maximize the growth rate of aggregate output as recorded in the official statistics."[16] Since the official measures of aggregate output for the economy and its main sectors included the value of intermediate product in inter-enterprise transactions, the growth of the latter apparently mattered for the planners as much as that of the final product.[17] The characterization of the growth objective as an "obsession" similarly indicates the perceived irrelevance of final uses.[18]

Other examples come from outside our sample. "Never mind that these were intermediate industrial products, and not an end in themselves. . . . Intermediate industrial products of a traditional kind were for Soviet planners the symbols of modernization; they were what grown up countries had, so the Soviet Union must make more and more of them" (Hanson 2003, 72). Bergson (1961, 16–17) writes of suggestions that "Soviet 'planners' consider some individual commodities, for example, steel, as wholly final." "Because they are growth maximizers, socialist systems consider any increase in the level of consumption associated with the move to the cities as cost rather than as benefit" (Ofer 1976, 223). Gerschenkron (1962a, 577–78) argues that the USSR pursued "investment for the sake of investment." Top priority of investment goods sectors in the allocation of investment, as described by Kornai (1992, 171), also amounts to investment for the sake of investment. Ofer (1987, 1800) states that the objective was growth of the part of GNP other than consumption.[19] Outsiders joined the members of the guild, speaking of "conspicuous production" and "production for production's sake."[20] A theorist trying to explain high rates of investment in Soviet-type economies provides this summary: "The most popular account among students of Socialist economies, perhaps the only one available, appeals to the preferences of the political elite . . . The latter are fond of rapid growth and give first priority to capital goods industries" (Ferrero 1993, 1).

Some of our sources do not mention growth but refer to such objectives as investment, development of heavy industry, creation of a production apparatus, or output of steel and electricity.[21] We consider these statements to be equivalent to the objective of growth for its own sake, since the stress on investment in heavy industry has been understood as the Soviet way of achieving rapid growth (e.g., Gregory 1970, 141).

Growth for the sake of growth as the main objective of the planners was the standard view in Sovietological literature. It has survived the archival revolution. The post-1991 literature on the Soviet economy cannot be surveyed in the same way as earlier work, because the three genres most useful for discerning authors' positions on the rulers' objectives—textbooks,

books on planning, and books on growth—are absent from it. Yet the small volume of recent work makes such a survey unnecessary. The main direction of research into the Soviet economy now is based on the use of newly accessible materials from the Soviet archives, mostly from the Stalin period. In Gregory (2004), one of the leading scholars in this line of study presents the results of a large archival research project focused on the economy. Gregory and Harrison (2005) survey all such work to date, including research focused on politics. These two sources are taken to represent the current state of knowledge in archive-based research.

Gregory (2004, 76) devotes a paragraph to the importance of defining the rulers' objectives and determining the relative weights attached to each objective. He then postulates a list of objectives—"secure power base, maximum growth, investment in heavy industry, and transferring resources out of the countryside"—without specifying their weights or how they relate to one another. Later (82–83), he posits investment maximization as the rulers' main objective. Gregory bases this conclusion on the relationship between investment and growth in Marx's theory of expanded reproduction and in early growth theory, as well as on the actual doubling of the Soviet investment rate between 1928 and 1937. Gregory and Harrison (2005, 723, 731) also name maximization of investment as the economic objective of the rulers.

While the objective of growth for its own sake has been the standard view, a tiny minority of surveyed sources name military power as the main objective. Ellman (1989) states this directly, and Kushnirsky (1982) indirectly by noting that the military industry had top priority in investment allocation. Two editions of a textbook (Schwartz 1954; 1965) name both military might and consumption as the objectives.[22] Like the standard view, the minority view of military power can also be encountered outside the surveyed literature. For example, Grossman (1983, 199): "To surpass America in military power seems to continue to be a prime, if suitably veiled, objective of the Kremlin to this day." A future economics Nobel Prize winner (not a Sovietologist) wondered if in the USSR, the standard concept of national product, with its welfare implications, should be abandoned in favor of "increase in national power as the only substance of final product" (Kuznets 1963, 371). In the post-Soviet literature, Hanson (2003, 31) subscribes to the old minority view. Like its Sovietological precursor, the post-1991 literature remains fragmented and various idiosyncratic combinations of objectives can be found in print (e.g., Hill and Gaddy 2003, 8–89).

## 4.5 Making sense of multiple objectives

One may think of a multilevel hierarchy of objectives, with lower-level ones serving as means for achieving higher-level ones. In economics, every actor is assumed to maximize his personal utility function, which we will call the first-level objective. For the firm owners, under certain conditions, maximizing profit—a second-level objective—also guarantees maximum utility (Mas-Collel et al. 1995, 152). The former objective also turns out to be more helpful in explaining the behavior of firms than the latter. Similarly, budget maximization is used as the second-level objective in the study of bureaucracies. One can also formulate third- and lower-level objectives (e.g., hiring and training employees or assimilating new technology), the achievement of which serves to maximize a firm's profit or a bureau's budget.

Now consider the role that the growth objective plays in market economies. (Like Sovietology, the literature on growth policy in the West for the most part does not explicitly distinguish between the objectives of different levels, so these designations are ours.) Policymakers promote growth, a third-level objective, because it makes citizens more prosperous (a second-level objective). With consumer demand determining the product mix, growth brings about an increase in the quantity of goods that consumers want. This, in turn, increases the politician's chances for reelection by the voters who became better off, and also satisfies his altruistic inclinations, if any—both first-level objectives. It was the search for prosperity that made growth "a primary goal of national policy" in the United States after World War II.[23] This is also how economists motivate their interest in growth.[24] "When we say 'growth,' what we mean is that each person's standard of living should keep increasing" (Easterly 2001, 48).

Economic growth also supplies the means to strengthen a country's military power and its international influence and prestige, recognized as the motives for growth policy in the United States and the United Kingdom.[25] Military power, in turn, is a widely recognized (second-level) objective of the rulers under a variety of political systems, contributing to their survival and glory (first-level objectives). "The [Habsburgs' and Romanovs'] sense of pride, self-image and legitimacy was linked absolutely and inescapably to the great power status of their dynastic empires. . . . To the extent that Habsburg and Romanov rulers could control the political systems, societies and economies of their empires, they subordinated, shaped and manipulated them to meet the overriding priority of military might and great power status" (Lieven 2000, 159).

The objectives of planning, as described by the Soviet sources, are the same as those of rulers elsewhere: military might and popular wellbeing, with growth as the means for achieving those. The only difference is that the Soviets are silent on the first-level objectives, as the rulers were supposed to selflessly pursue the goals of the people and the party.

The objective of planners according to the standard view of Sovietology, growth for the sake of growth, is, to the best of our knowledge, unprecedented in the study of economic policy. A few authors state that growth was the means for achieving higher-level goals, such as building Communism according to Marx's precepts or cohesion and stability, hence, the second-level objective.[26] However, logically, growth for the sake of growth, or anything else for its own sake, can only be the first-level objective, an argument in the rulers' utility function.

Some of the authors who name growth as the objective of the planners also name the additional objectives of consumption and military might. These are the same as the second-level objectives of Western growth policy as discussed in this section. However, instead of representing the results of growth, they appear to be secondary goals of lesser importance alongside growth. Their pursuit detracts from growth rate maximization.[27] Authors united in naming growth as the objective are split on the secondary objectives, with seven textbooks naming military might, and three naming consumption (table 4.1). Among books on planning, consumption is named as the objective three times, and military might once (table 4.2). Three books on growth mention consumption and five books mention military might as a secondary objective if economic self-sufficiency is understood as a strategic objective (table 4.3). And Soviet sources state that it should be so understood: "Strengthening technical and economic self-sufficiency of the Soviet economy from capitalist surroundings is directly related to strengthening defense."[28]

While growth is recognized as the fundamental objective, consumption as an objective is often qualified as applying to the latter part of Soviet rule.[29] Military strength is often limited to the 1930s, explicitly (Schwartz 1965; Jeffries 1990) or implicitly by using quotations from Stalin's speeches, though Millar (1981, 31) limits the priority of defense to the post-war period.

**Table 4.2. Objectives of the rulers in the books on planning.**

| Author/editor, year, page | Objectives of rulers |
| --- | --- |
| Grossman 1960, 1–2 | Rapid industrial growth, military might |
| Ward 1960, 133–34 | Social welfare function, factories before consumer goods |
| Hirsch 1961, 26 | Smelting and machinebuilding, transportation, chemicals, construction were top priority in different periods |
| Bergson 1964, 7–8 | Growth, consumer welfare |
| Hunter 1964, 4, 14 | Electric power & steel |
| Nove 1964, 199 | Growth, consumption |
| Bernard 1966, 96 | Creating a production apparatus |
| Zauberman 1967 | Nothing specific |
| Hardt et. al. 1967 | Nothing specific |
| Ellman 1971 | Nothing specific |
| Ellman 1973 | Nothing specific |
| Marczewski 1974 | Nothing specific |
| Zauberman 1976 | Nothing specific |
| Cave 1980 | Nothing specific |
| Kushnirsky 1982, 90–92 | Military industry's top priority in investment allocation |
| Rutland 1985, 103–9 | Growth in production capacity, consumption |
| Ellman 1989, 12–13 | Catching up in military power |
| Bennett 1989, 1 | Social welfare function imposed by politicians |
| Eatwell et al. 1990 | Nothing specific |
| Hare 1991, 21 | Growth, emphasis on heavy industry |

*Sources*: See appendix 4.1.

**Table 4.3. Objectives of the rulers in the books on growth and development.**

| Author/editor, year, pages | Objectives of rulers |
| --- | --- |
| Grossman 1953, 13 | Growth; also may or may not be consumption or military |
| Bergson & Kuznets 1963 | Nothing specific |
| Spulber 1964, 23 | Catching up and surpassing, building advanced industry and military |
| Vogel 1968, 199 | Raising the standard of living |
| Treml 1968, xi | Growth, self-sufficiency |
| Wilber 1969, 76 | Growth |
| Maddison 1969 | Nothing specific |
| Cohn 1970, 23, 83, 86 | Growth, defense, autarky, consumption |
| Bergson 1978, 3, 34 | Growth, self-sufficiency, consumption |
| Bergson and Levine, 1983 | Nothing specific |
| Bairam, 1988 | Nothing specific |

*Source*: See appendix 4.1.

## 4.6  Problems with the standard view of the rulers' objectives

The standard view diverges from the Soviet pronouncements by introducing growth for its own sake as the supreme objective, and omitting or downgrading the objective of military might. Nowhere in the Soviet writings have we encountered anything suggesting "production for its own sake." On the other hand, the word "defense" occurs on 17 pages of a run-of-the-mill college planning textbook, as the objective of developing military might was reiterated (Berri 1973). Taken together, the 12 Western books on planning listed in table 3.2 refer to military terms only on 10 pages. This displacement of defense by growth constitutes the civilianization of the subject. No explanation is offered for ignoring one strand of evidence in this evidence-starved field.

Several authors who themselves hold growth to be the main objective also call it an "obsession."[30] This is a striking expression of lack of confidence in one's own position, for the rationality of individual actors is the main assumption of the economic approach, and "allegations of irrationality" are viewed as a cover for the economists' lack of understanding (Becker 1988, 11). However, the charge of irrationality is somewhat misplaced. Irrationality would manifest itself in a mismatch of goals and means to achieve them, not in pursuing a particular objective, however strange. Nor can one object to growth for its own sake on the grounds that such an objective is unusual, unique to planned economies (which it is). There is no second-guessing individual preferences.

Instead, if the rulers were maximizing the reported rate of growth, then all of Soviet economic policy becomes irrational, that is, incompatible with the rulers' objective. To maximize growth without regard for the product mix, one should favor the sectors where growth can be generated in the easiest or cheapest possible way. This means avoiding sectors with sophisticated, difficult-to-master technologies, as well as setting up new production in the regions with propitious climate and easy transportation access. Yet the Soviet economic history since the beginning of the plan era, to borrow Naum Jasny's expression, consisted in the push for technological change, setting up new industries, and the development of Siberia and the Far North. The USSR was one of the world leaders in research and development spending. Bear in mind that in Soviet accounting, R&D and education were unproductive activities, and did not count as part of the official aggregate output measure.

If the rulers pursued production for its own sake, then the product itself would be undefined. In economics, the result of a technological transformation is only a product by virtue of consumer demand. The recognition by an independent consumer is what differentiates production from waste or destruction of resources. The mechanism for such recognition by households and especially by firms is weaker in a command economy than in a market economy, even when their demand is well articulated. If the ultimate consumers—the rulers—were only interested in the growth of the official measure of aggregate output, no matter its content, then it is not clear what exactly they were maximizing.

It has been suggested in the literature that high reported rates of economic growth benefited the rulers by making them appear to have fulfilled their promise of an increased standard of living, and by demonstrating the advantages of central planning. For this argument to work, consumers have to derive satisfaction from newspaper reports, rather than from actual goods and services—that is, behave irrationally. True, high reported growth inspired awe in some early Sovietologists (e.g., Wiles 1956a), and the Soviet rulers were interested in high reported growth rates, occasionally falsifying statistics to produce them (Eydelman 1998, 74–75). Like any politician, they preferred good press to bad, which does not elevate publicity itself to the status of policy objective.

## 4.7  Patterns that seem to suggest production for its own sake

Some processes in the Soviet economy reflected the decisions the rulers made in pursuit of their objectives. Others were generated by the structure of the system and proceeded against the wishes of the rulers. The effects of the latter may create the appearance of pursuit of production for its own sake, but have simpler and more plausible explanations.

The rulers and their underlings on all levels of the state and party hierarchy paid an unusually high degree of attention to the production of the intermediate goods, compared to politicians in market economies. As explained in one of the best papers in all of Sovietology (Grossman 1963), the unreliability of the supply system made balancing—that is, securing the continuous flow of inputs to their users—the main task of those running the economy. Its high priority stemmed from the fact that without a tolerable degree of balancing, whole sectors could grind to a halt, and the task was difficult enough to absorb the lion's share of attention of all the levels of the bureaucracy.

The USSR was the world leader in per capita output of many intermediate goods, while lagging in terms of final products. This was the combined result of the comparatively low level of technical efficiency and the enterprises' insatiable demand for inputs fueled by their soft budget constraints, both phenomena deplored by the rulers. The mobilization-motivated hypertrophy of the basic sectors, mentioned in chapter 2, must have contributed to this, as well.

Enterprise managers facing cost-based prices and Gross Value of Output (GVO) success indicators engaged in cost maximization (Kontorovich 1998). While such behavior inflated output, and perhaps the official growth rates, the rulers considered it harmful, as evidenced by the stream of Soviet writings condemning the use of GVO as a success indicator, and reforms aiming at finding substitutes for it.

The rulers and their agents sometimes ordered increases in the output of goods in which the economy had been saturated, as apparently happened with tractors and harvesters in the 1980s. This was generally due to informational constraints on central planning decisions, and in the final decades, perhaps also to the rulers' unwillingness to make difficult decisions necessary to curtail such production (e.g., reallocate labor).

Along with the intermediate goods, it was investment statistics that seemed to support the growth for its own sake thesis. The share of investment in the Soviet GNP from 1928 to 1975 was high "almost without precedent for such long periods" and "very high by international standards" afterward (Ofer 1987, 1784, 1786).[31] In economics, investment has been long considered as the engine of economic growth (Easterly 2001, 47–48). Soviet investment was primarily directed into heavy industry, as if the purpose was to produce ever more producer goods to produce more producer goods.

Stalin himself offered an explanation for this pattern. In his words, Soviet victory in World War II would have been impossible without large quantities of modern armaments, which, in turn, required metal and fuel. "It would have been impossible to defend the country without heavy industry." And the post-war targets for production of pig iron, steel, coal, and petroleum were explained as necessary to protect the country "from any accidents" (Stalin 1946, 10–11, 14–15, 20).

Soviet economics textbooks reiterate these arguments. "The party developed heavy industry, so as to secure the economic independence of the

USSR . . . . . Only the development of heavy industry made the creation of the modern military industry possible" (Sorokin 1946, 18). "The need to possess powerful armed forces . . . requires strong and highly developed industry and, first of all, heavy industry with its heart, machine building. Only an industry with huge production capacity, and, first of all, a formidable stock of machine tools, developed metallurgy, chemical industry, and fuel and power generation sectors, is capable of not just profusely equipping the army with modern weapons, but also of providing a continuous and ever-increasing flow of supplies in the time of war" (Ioffe 1948, 5). "Tasks of sped-up preparation for the defense of the country and further technical reconstruction of the economy made it necessary to develop heavy industry faster than light industry in the Third Five-Year Plan period" (Lokshin 1947, 50).

As was argued in section 2.4 and will be further demonstrated in chapter 5, in the Soviet thinking, preparedness meant not just the amassing of arms and ammunition, but also the creation of an industrial base. The buildup of heavy industry was necessary for the increased production of military hardware, as well as the surge capacity to meet the demands of a total war fought against much of the rest of the world.

The investment/heavy industry/defense connection used to be acknowledged before the standard account evolved to civilianize the objectives of the rulers. In the first book published by Sovietologists, the field's founder notes that "investment in Russian conditions is to a great extent in areas of potential military use, i.e. steel, machinery, etc." The choice between such investment and military outlay is, in effect, the choice "between 'long term' military preparedness in the form of overall economic growth and 'short term' military preparedness in the form of troops, munitions, stockpiles, etc." (Bergson 1953c, 35). In his famous book on growth, Rostow (1961, 103) remarks that "an enormous [Soviet] heavy industry, growing at high rates, is not a goal in itself" and asks "If steel is not to be used for military purposes, what will it be used for?"[32]

## 4.8 Bringing the Soviet rulers back into the fold of rational actors

If we pay attention to the Soviet claims and check them against the data on the structure of the aggregate product, we can formulate the objectives of the rulers consistent with the policies they pursued. The preferences of the

Soviet rulers were not qualitatively different from those of Western politicians, or, for that matter, rulers in other times and places. They valued security, power, prestige, and also, with a lower priority, the well-being of their subjects. These objectives were served by the pursuit of military might and, circumstances permitting, growth of consumption. While I make no claim with respect to the applicability of these results to other Soviet-type economies, Poland pre-1956 seems to fit the pattern (Montias 1962, 57–58, 64).

A different view of the rulers' objectives leads to a different evaluation of the Soviet economy's performance. Post-war Soviet economic history is one of increasing military might and waning growth. If the standard view of the objectives is applied, the rulers must have been deeply frustrated by the economy's performance through the 1970s and early 1980s, and had urgent reasons to seek radical change. And yet economists alarmed by the slowing growth had been sending reform proposals to the rulers since the mid-1970s, to no effect. The view of the rulers' objectives offered here explains why they were satisfied with the country's situation well into the 1980s, even as growth was slowing down.[33]

The argument that rulers/planners pursued military might as their main objective is not entirely new. It existed as a minority view in Sovietological literature, and is widely shared in the authoritative post-Soviet Russian sources cited in section 2.5. However, it was never posed as an alternative to the standard view, which escaped scrutiny and reigned unchallenged in the literature. This chapter confronts the standard view head on, shows that it is untenable, and offers a simple, consistent, and empirically grounded alternative.

## Notes

1. Becker (1988, 5); Sen (1987, 69).
2. Kreps (1990, 18–37, 724–30); Mas-Colell et al. (1995, 41–50, 152–54).
3. Tullock (1987, 1040); Mueller (1989, 247–73).
4. This is implicit in the texts; we have not found a definition of the term "planners."
5. See also Ward (1960, 133).
6. Friedman (1953a, 15–16); Boulier and Goldfarb (1998, 2–3).
7. Spulber (1964, 7); Lindblom (1975, 23); Rutland (1985, 103).
8. Tsagolov (1970, 136); *Konstitutsiia* (1983, 30).
9. Kurskii (1955, 21); Koval' (1973, 20); Kolodnyi and Stepanov (1975, 18); Tsapkin and Pereslegin (1967, 15); Tsapkin (1972, 18).

10. The next edition (Gosplan 1974, 3) listed rapid economic growth, increasing standard of living, strengthening defense, and solving other social-economic problems.
11. Davies (1993); Harrison and Davies (1997).
12. Ofer (1987, 1778); Gregory (1970, 149–56).
13. This paragraph parallels some of the discussion in Ofer (1987, 1800).
14. Take seriously: Nove (1986, 3); Wiles (1962). Dismiss: Schwartz (1954, 101, 103); Campbell (1974, 3); Ellman (1989, 12).
15. Cohn (1970, 86); Hutchings (1977, 153); Millar (1981, 31).
16. Also Rutland (1985, 103–109).
17. The Soviet statistics used Gross Value of Output (GVO) to measure the output of industry and other sectors (Treml and Hardt 1972, 155–57, 247–51). For the national economy, both a GVO measure and a measure net of intermediate consumption, NMP, were reported (73–74).
18. Campbell (1974, 20); Dyker (1985, 2); Nove (1986, 35).
19. Also Hunter (1972, 7).
20. Polanyi (1960); Birman (1983a, 135–39).
21. E.g., Goldman (1968); Hare (1991); Bernard (1966); Hirsch (1961); Hunter (1964).
22. Vogel (1968) names consumption as the only objective, while Bennett (1989) refers to an unspecified "social welfare function."
23. Abramovitz (1989, 11); Arndt (1978, 42–43).
24. Barro and Sala-i-Martin (2004, 6); Helpman (2004, 1); Lucas (1988, 5).
25. Abramovitz (1989, xii, 11, 356); Arndt (1978, 36, 46, 48–51).
26. Wiles (1962) and Nove (1986, 3); Kaser (1970, 220).
27. Cohn (1970, 86); Hutchings (1977, 153); Millar (1981, 31).
28. Kurskii (1945, 8). Also Ioffe (1948, 4–5).
29. For example: Vogel (1968); Cohn (1970); Bergson (1978); Rutland (1985).
30. Campbell (1974, 20); Dyker (1985, 2); Nove (1986, 35).
31. CIA estimates of investment for the latter decades were exaggerated by failure to adjust for price inflation (Kontorovich 1988).
32. See also Berliner (1966, 162).
33. For the alarmed economists and the perceptions at the top, see Ellman and Kontorovich (1997, 260, 262); Zoteev (1998); Khanin (1998).

# 5

# *Civilianizing Industrialization*

FORCED INDUSTRIALIZATION, LAUNCHED under the First Five-Year Plan (1928–32), was a formative event that set the course of the Soviet economy. "Most of the major decisions on the development strategy of the Soviet Union . . . were made in the 1920s and in the early 1930s. . . . their impact can be observed in Soviet patterns of behavior to this day" (Ofer 1987, 1770). Priority of heavy industry was a defining feature of industrialization. After 1945, the industrialization strategy was replicated, at least for a while, in the other Communist countries (Kornai 1992, ch. 9). It also strongly influenced the first generation of development economists, as well as the policymakers of developing countries, in the 1950s.[1]

Unlike the objectives of planners, industrialization has attracted much attention from Sovietologists. Accounts of industrialization feature prominently in economic histories of the USSR, textbooks on the Soviet economy, and even in some cursory treatments of the Soviet experience by non-specialists (e.g., North 2005, 148–9).

## *5.1  The standard account of industrialization*

The literature commonly asserts that a strategy of industrialization was developed over the course of economic debates in the mid-1920s by E. Preobrazhenskii and/or G. Feldman. Its goal was rapid economic growth, which was to be achieved by concentrating investment on heavy industry.[2] This is the standard account of industrialization, drawing on half a century's worth of economists' writings on the subject.

The standard treatment starts with recounting the course of the "Great Debate" (Nove 1992, 115) between the adherents of rapid industrialization from the Left (Trotsky), and the gradualists from the Right (Bukharin).[3]

Each participant in the debate had in mind a growth policy that would promote consumer wellbeing (de Schweinitz 1964, 1137).

Preobrazhenskii was a prominent left-wing contributor to the debate.
He is best known for his ideas about primitive socialist accumulation, the
need to extract resources for industrialization from the peasants (Ellman
1990a). This chapter takes no position on whether these ideas served as
an inspiration for the policy of collectivization. It focuses exclusively on
his views on the rate of industrialization and the role of heavy industry
therein. Preobrazhenskii argued that the production of means of production has to grow faster than the aggregate output to effect the desired acceleration of growth (Erlich 1950, 66).

In the standard account, "the final outcome of the debate was the formidable program of Five Year Plans" (Erlich 1950, 57).[4] In Dobb's (1967,
137–38) words, it has been a widely held view in the West that, while
Preobrazhenskii's position in the debate was officially repudiated, industrialization followed the path he outlined.[5]

Since industrialization has been thought to follow Preobrazhenskii's
blueprint, "his proposals regarding the relative growth rates of heavy industry versus consumer goods industries are likely to have played a similar
role in the formulation of Soviet policy" (Moravcik 1965, 246). "It is not
difficult in this context to understand why Stalin laid such stress on heavy
industry. High rates of growth of national income were viewed partly as an
end in themselves, and partly—certainly by Preobrazhenskii—as a means
of ensuring a rapid increase in employment" (Dyker 1985, 3). "The most
remarkable feature of the 1930s was the extent to which the pro-heavy-
industry bias asserted itself (as Preobrazhenskii said it should)" (Gregory
and Stuart 1986, 93).

Feldman, a Gosplan employee, shares the honor of being considered
the author of the strategy of industrialization.[6] He published a mathematical model of economic growth, according to which, the greater the proportion of new investment in the producer goods sector, the higher the rate
of growth (Ellman, 1990b). Explanations of the observed concentration of
investment in heavy industry by the requirements of "Marxist and Soviet
growth models" (Ofer 1987, 1807) refer to Feldman.[7] In variation on the
standard version, Fallenbuchl (1970, 459, 462) derived the approach to
industrialization directly from Marx's reproduction schema and Lenin's
writings, without the intermediation of contemporary theorists.

According to the standard account, the objective of industrialization
was the acceleration of economic growth.[8] The same point is also made

indirectly when a prominent feature of industrialization—the priority of heavy industry—is interpreted as a policy aimed at growth acceleration, as just quoted. The standard account also sometimes came in an abridged form, in which the priority of heavy industry is interpreted as means for accelerating growth, but without references to Preobrazhenskii or Feldman.[9] And the growth in question is growth for its own sake, familiar from chapter 4: "Economic growth, regardless of its cost, became the absolute value and goal" (Berend 2006, 149).

The standard account has competition—the arguments for industrialization made by the Soviet rulers who actually carried it out. The objectives of industrialization and the need to prioritize heavy industry were discussed in detail in Stalin's speeches and official party documents during the First Five-Year Plan period. Economics tracts and textbooks then repeated the official formulations. The two accounts differed a great deal.

## 5.2 Stalin's account of industrialization

### 5.2.1 Objectives of industrialization

The 15th Party Congress in 1927 adopted a resolution "on the directives for compiling the five-year economic plan." The very first directive said, "It is necessary in the Five-Year Plan to pay maximum attention to the fastest possible development of those sectors of the economy and of industry which play the main role in supplying defense and in the economic stability of the country in wartime. Not only planning and economic organs, but, most importantly, the whole party must pay unflagging attention to the issues of defense in connection with compiling the Five-Year Plan" (Voronetskaia 1969, 42). All other directives for the future plan—on the tradeoff between consumption and investment, the growth rate, foreign economic relations, and the relative development of agriculture versus industry and various sectors thereof—followed the directive to concentrate on defense.

Stalin (1928, 247–53) gave three reasons for the accelerated development of industry. The first was the need to complement the most advanced social system with the most advanced technology, so as to achieve the final victory of socialism in the country. The second reason was that "it is impossible to stay independent without a sufficient industrial base for defense. It is impossible to create such an industrial base without the most advanced industrial technology."[10]

Later on, Stalin (1931, 38–39) gave a colorful, often quoted, justification for the rapid pace of industrialization as the need to avoid reliving Russia's long history of military defeat at the hands of its stronger neighbors.

In his speech on the results of the First Five-Year Plan, Stalin (1933, 172–73) named six main tasks of the plan: (1) equip the country with modern technology, (2) turn it into a powerful, self-sufficient industrial country independent of the whims of world capitalism, (3) increase the share of socialist institutions in the economy, (4) create an industry capable of re-equipping all sectors of the economy, (5) collectivize agriculture, and (6) create all the technical and economic conditions necessary to maximize the increase in defense capability. Tasks 1 and 4 refer to means rather than final objectives (modern technology for what?). Tasks 3 and 5 concern building socialism; tasks 2 and 6—defense.

Stalin then named the four accomplishments of the plan in industry: the extinction of capitalist economic institutions, turning an agrarian country into an industrial one, reaching 93.7% of the five-year target for industrial production in four years, and turning a weak and militarily unprepared country into one capable of mass-producing any modern weapon (Stalin 1933, 179–81). On the last point, one of Stalin's harshest critics concurred: "Undoubtedly the most important successes . . . have been achieved in the war industries" (Trotsky [1937] 2004, 10). Again, the second and the third accomplishments listed by Stalin are means to some greater goal. The first achievement concerned building socialism and the fourth—defense. In justifying the break-neck rate of change during the First Five-Year Plan, Stalin only briefly mentioned the need for a new technological base, speaking mainly of the mortal danger facing the country, the threat of military intervention, and the need to overcome military weakness (Trotsky [1937] 2004, 183–84).

The official party history summarized the expected benefits of industrialization as seen in 1925: "Industrialization would secure economic independence for the country, strengthen its defense capability, and create the conditions necessary for the victory of socialism in the USSR" (*Istoriia* [1938] 1997, 264).[11]

## 5.2.2 The role of heavy industry

The official reasons for the stress on heavy industry were the same as for industrialization itself—building socialism, providing for defense, and preserving the country's independence. In some pronouncements, independence could be interpreted as the inoculation of the USSR against boycotts and other politically motivated trade disruptions, or against the danger of becoming a "raw material appendage" of capitalist economies.[12] However, on other occasions the country's economic independence was clearly cast in strategic terms.

The 15th Party Congress resolution "on the directives for compiling the Five-Year Economic Plan" demanded that first priority be given to the production of means of production, so as to satisfy the demands of all sectors of the economy from domestic sources. "The sectors of heavy industry that should grow the fastest are those that, in the shortest time, increase the economic and military might of the USSR, guarantee development in case of an economic blockade, weaken our dependence on the capitalist world" (Voronetskaia 1969, 285). The resolution of the 16th Party Conference "On the Five-Year Economic Plan" stated, "Based on the general idea of the country's industrialization, strengthening its defense, and freeing it from its dependence on capitalist countries, industrial investment is directed primarily into the sectors making means of production" (IMELS 1953, 450).

Speaking on the results of the First Five-Year Plan, Stalin (1933, 182–83) listed what would have happened if heavy industry had not been favored at the expense of consumer goods production. The country would have been left unarmed in the face of a technologically advanced capitalist world; agriculture would have been deprived of equipment, and hence the country of food supplies; capitalist elements would have been left intact, thereby "unbelievably increasing the chances of capitalist restoration"; and the country would have been deprived of means of defense, making it vulnerable to external enemies. The overall result would have been a bloody, unequal battle to the death against better-armed enemies. The introduction to a collection of documents on industrialization states that "the threat of imperialist aggression . . . demanded the accelerated development of machine building in general, and especially the defense industry" (Khlusov 1971, 5).

## 5.3 *How the standard account developed*

The standard account omits defense and socialism, the main motives of industrialization cited in the original sources, and substitutes growth as the sole motive. In the 1950s and 1960s, a large share of primary materials for the study of the Soviet economy dated back to the 1920s and early 1930s, as few statistics and little research was published from the mid-1930s to the mid-1950s (section 6.1.2). The first generation of Sovietologists knew their Stalin, if only because there was little else yet to know in their field. The writings from this period acknowledged the official pronouncements on the military and the socialist motivations for industrialization, often quoting Stalin's speeches or Party Congress resolutions. Yet from the beginning, growth received most of the attention.

The first three book-length economic histories of the USSR, appearing in the 1960s, pronounced the official defense explanation of industrialization to be false. Erlich (1960, 167–69) disagreed with the "widely accepted line of explanation" ascribing defense motivation to the actually adopted industrialization strategy. "It is very far from being true, as some have asserted, that military considerations were major motives for industrialization" (Dobb 1966, 13). "Industrialization was not simply the principal initial aim of the Drive; it was the only aim. Contrary to official and semi-official assertions, 'defense' was not a problem at the birth of the Great Industrialization Drive" (Jasny 1961, 4). Without mentioning his name, these three scholars implied that Stalin was mistaken or intentionally misleading in his repeated characterizations of his own policies. Dobb and Jasny did not explain their claims. Erlich's reasoning is discussed in section 7.3.3.

Other major volumes considered both defense and building socialism as valid goals, but strongly emphasized growth. The central goal of "catching up with" the most advanced countries was in the case of the USSR tied to a number of other aims: (a) the construction of an advanced industrial and military establishment, and (b) the liquidation, in the process of industrialization, of all "pre-capitalist and capitalist forms of production" (Spulber 1964, 23). The volume from which these words are taken is titled *Soviet Strategy for Economic Growth*, not *Soviet Strategy for Military Might*. Nove (1969, 121–22) acknowledges national security as one of the motives for industrialization and discusses it, but later in the book he sounds uncertain on the military strength as the objective (Nove 1969, 187–88, 226). One had to go to the writings of outsiders to find formulations like "Soviet industrialization has been preeminently Soviet militarization" (Sutton 1973b, 17).

In most of the literature, the security motive receives only a short, perfunctory mention disconnected from the main thrust of the work. The extremely detailed index of Zaleski (1971) lists many dozens of industrial products, including, for example, macaroni and sausages—hardly the focus of the First Five-Year Plan—but has no entries for defense, military, or armaments. He mentions in passing that the development of the defense industry was urged by the resolutions of the 15th and 16th Party Congresses, and that the increase in military might was a result of industrialization (Zaleski 1971, 56, 107, 300). Swianiewicz (1965, 74, 180–81) mentions briefly the "building up of military power" as one of the two objectives of policy without developing the point or connecting it to the rest of the discussion. The chapter on the end of the NEP and the beginning of industrialization in Munting (1982, ch. 3) does not even contain the words "defense" or "military," though it speaks of heavy industry implying strength and independence, and makes several mentions of the international situation (Munting 1982, 67, 74). Campbell (1966, ch. 2) and Spulber (1969, ch. 12) barely mention defense in the chapters devoted to the choice of strategy in the late 1920s. Note that support for the standard account is different from the general lack of attention to the military side of the economy, as documented in chapter 3. Some of the scholars cited as supporting the standard account also did significant work on the Soviet military sector.

Later economics writers, roughly from the 1980s to the present, less frequently quote the original sources, but rather build on the findings of their predecessors. Through this process, the standard account achieves its pure form, described in the opening section of this chapter, as military motivation disappears, along with "building socialism." Defense is absent from Davies' (1994, 137–38) section on "industrial plans and objectives" and from Gregory's (2004, 29, 76) lists of "four core values" and "four main economic objectives" of the Politburo at the time. If this is so in the detailed, book-length economic histories of industrialization, it is unsurprising that the defense motive is missing altogether in the more concise treatments.[13] Western textbooks on the Soviet economy and comparative systems from the 1980s discuss industrialization but do not mention its military motivation.[14]

Similarly, extended treatments of the priority of heavy industry take the official political economy of socialism seriously. They discuss the derivation of the law of faster growth of the output of producer goods from Marx's schemes of reproduction, and its relation to the rate of economic growth, but do not mention Stalin's explanations.[15]

Writings on industrialization are characterized by the usual fragmentation (section 1.3.2). One can find one-sentence remarks in the writings of Sovietologists affirming the military motivation of industrialization and the military significance of the priority of heavy industry.[16] Outsiders were even more outspoken. At about the same time that the economic histories of the USSR (Erlich, Jasny, Dobb) outright denied the military motivation of the First Five-Year Plan, a military historian wrote that the plan was about developing "an industrial-armaments base. Thus, the only consumer interest considered was that of the armed forces."[17] Perhaps uniquely, Temin (1991, 587) confronts the standard version, noting that viewing production as an end in itself, as Sovietological literature did, was "unusual in economics," and that it must have been a means to some other goal, namely, in the 1930s, military might.[18]

The displacement of Soviet military explanations by the Western civilian ones has not been limited to the overall strategy of industrialization discussed so far. It can also be seen in the analysis of the particular projects and policies of industrialization, a period when the Soviets were more open about military-economic issues. Thus, the Soviet war minister, in a Party Congress speech reviewing the state of defense preparedness, spoke of the tractor industry as being of equal importance for agriculture and the military, and specifically lamented the delays in construction of the Stalingrad tractor plant (Voroshilov [1927b] 1936, 202). American engineers who designed the plant and participated in its construction knew back in 1932 that they were building a tank factory (Melnikova-Raich 2010, 68). And the wartime tank production at Stalingrad was publicized by the Soviets. Yet a 1966 article on the Stalingrad tractor plant construction, with one of the co-authors just having completed a dissertation on Soviet tractor industry, discusses it exclusively in terms of its contribution to agriculture and the timing of collectivization (Dodge and Dalrymple 1966).

The Urals-Kuznetsk combine, one of the largest projects of the First Five-Year Plan, has been used as a case study of the Soviet investment efficiency criteria.[19] In a unique occurrence for Sovietological literature, this peaceful usage was challenged by scholars citing Soviet sources on the defense motivation of the project.[20]

## 5.4 Problems with the standard account

Creating and enlarging the economic basis of military power served both as the motivation for industrialization and as the objective of planners in the day-to-day running of the economy. Both got civilianized in a similar way, by dropping defense and inventing growth for its own sake. The standard account of industrialization thus shares the weaknesses of that of the planners' objectives.

In a centrally planned economy, the proclamations of the "system's directors" (Bergson 1964, 7) about the direction of the system, while certainly not conclusive, cannot be simply ignored or glossed over. Yet the omission of the defense motivation for the First Five-Year Plan is not even acknowledged, let alone explained in the standard account. This is especially hard to justify because Stalin's pronouncements cited here breached the Soviet norm of not discussing military economic matters publicly. A forceful call for a military-industrial buildup was what lawyers call a statement against interest, which bolstered its credibility. Indeed, later Soviet accounts of industrialization were significantly more peaceful, in keeping with the usual strictures against mentioning military matters. Thus, priority of heavy industry came to be explained by the "law of the faster growth of output of producer goods," which purportedly reflected the nature of modern technological change (Notkin 1984, 145–55).

There exists a textual basis for considering growth the objective of industrialization, such as the numerous statements by Stalin about catching up with the leading capitalist economies. These pronouncements freely mixed means and ends. Economic growth is a means to an end—the increase in the magnitude of specific components of the final product, guns and butter. The former, in turn, contributes to the achievement of the rulers' objectives—holding onto power and amassing more power, as argued in chapter 4. But in the standard account, in which consumption as the end of growth is rightly dismissed, and defense de-emphasized, denied, or simply dropped, growth becomes its own objective. It is "the process of producing producer goods in order to produce producer goods in order to produce even more producer goods" (Fallenbuchl 1970, 463). Yet, as shown in section 4.6, growth for its own sake is ill-defined, and the actual policies of the First Five-Year Plan would be irrational if this were the objective.

The standard account of industrialization also has its own specific weaknesses. There exists no direct evidence of Preobrazhenskii's or Feldman's authorship of the industrialization strategy, such as their work being cited by Soviet rulers, or their being mentioned by V. Molotov in conversations with F. Chuev. To the contrary, according to a contemporary observer, "G. A. Feldman played a microscopic role in the literature on the Soviet strategy for economic growth" (Jasny 1964, 214). The standard account rests entirely on the strength of the perceived similarities between their writings and the actual policies adopted, such as the high rate of transformation and promotion of heavy industry.

These similarities need to be weighed against the differences. Preobrazhenskii and Feldman were interested in maximizing consumption over the long run, yet the economy built in 1928–1932 had a permanently depressed share of consumption in the national product (Ofer 1987, 1790). Preobrazhenskii was critical of "overinvestment" in the First Five-Year Plan (Ellman 1990a, 216–17), and was himself attacked "for his theory of "production for consumption's sake," which conflicted with the official theory of developing heavy industry at all costs" (Filtzer 1979, 66). Allen (2003, 63) inverts this argument. If Stalin followed the policy prescriptions of the Feldman model, as Allen believes he did, "this precludes a common argument" that he only cared about heavy industry.

Chronology rules out Feldman's authorship. The principle of the faster growth of production of means of production was proclaimed at the 15th Party Congress in December of 1927 (quoted in section 5.2.2). The 14th Party Congress in December of 1925 and the 15th Party Conference in October of 1926 made somewhat less emphatic statements to the same effect (IMELS 1953, 75–77, 185). Feldman ([1928] 1964) appeared only in November, 1928. Preobrazhenskii's piece in which he elaborated on the priority of heavy industry came out in 1927 (Erlich 1950, 66, 79n2). Taking into account usual policy lag, this makes Preobrazhenskii's authorship unlikely, as well.

The broader context of policymaking at the time also casts doubt on Preobrazhenskii's and Feldman's authorship. With the onset of industrialization, the economic discussion was shut down. The economists were jailed, fell silent, or started toeing the official line. In the course of the First Five-Year Plan, Stalin dictated to Gosplan instead of taking expert advice. After the plan was adopted, its targets were repeatedly revised upward (Davies 1989b, 170–88). These were all actions of a ruler who was self-assured, trusted in simple solutions, and did not seek complex advice from the economists. In Leontieff's (1960, 262) words, the Soviet rulers of the time "were their own economists."

Difficulties in the interpretation of industrialization disappear if we just take Stalin at his word. Military might as the (second level) objective of industrialization is consistent with the observed patterns of the Soviet development during the First Five-Year Plan described in sections 2.3.3

and 4.3.3. It puts Stalin and his followers back into the company of rational economic actors, a fundamental requirement of economic analysis. Complicated, tenuous connections between the policy of industrialization and the writings of Feldman and Preobrazhenskii become unnecessary.

## 5.5 *The banality of military industrialization*

The motives for industrialization and the issue of authorship of its strategy are interrelated. If the First Five-Year Plan pursued historically unprecedented objectives—achieving rapid economic growth while building a new, socialist economy—then it is naturally of interest who came up with the route across these uncharted waters. If, however, the First Five-Year Plan pursued objectives common to governments throughout the ages, using tried-and-true means, the issue of the authorship becomes less intriguing.

Stalin (1928, 248) compared his efforts to those of Peter the Great, who "feverishly constructed plants and factories to supply the army and strengthen the defense." The emperor concentrated his industrial efforts on "production and working of metals . . . uniforms for the army, sails, ropes, and timber for the ships, and powder for the guns" (Gerschenkron 1970, 78).[21] In that, he followed the then-common policy of mercantilism, which, from the sixteenth through the eighteenth century, "was . . . primarily a system for forcing economic policy into the service of power as an end in itself." In this school of thought, "The end was war" (Heckscher 1935, 17). In pursuit of power, governments across Europe concerned themselves with supplies of saltpeter, copper alloys, timber, and tar, the heavy industry of the period (Heckscher 1935, 32–33, 39). They adopted policies familiar to students of Soviet industrialization, such as the promotion of economic self-sufficiency and the creation of mobilization reserves by ordering "the building of private ships which could be adapted in time of war" (34–35, 40–46).

More recently, "some Chinese officials [in the nineteenth century] came to see, reluctantly, the unbreakable chain that led from firearms and ships to coal mines, iron foundries, and railroads; from military technology to industrialization. . . . The beginnings of China's industrialization and Westernization can be traced to the same late-19th century military concern." (Hacker 1977, 52–53). In Japan, the Meiji oligarchy "wanted to create a strong country, and for such a purpose a modern army and navy was a necessity. They could not be created without establishing, in turn, strategic industries to support the military institutions. . . . Heavy industry was developed, in effect, before light industry, and almost exclusively for military purposes" (Vayrynen 1992, 40–41).

In the early twentieth century, Brazilian army officers believed, based on the example of Germany, France, Japan, and the United States, that "national greatness was linked to military preparedness, which in turn depended upon the country's economic development." In their publications, they argued for the need to develop the national coal and steel industries (McCann 1984, 37, 760–61).[22]

In the then Soviet rulers' lifetimes, Russian industrialization of the 1890s was motivated by similar militarily concerns.[23] "Russia's integrity as a great power was a primary consideration in . . . the state's promotion of industrialization. This motive was reflected in the type of industry which the state encouraged—heavy over light" (Siegelbaum 1983, 26). "The very [Soviet] insistence on heavy versus light industry . . . is of Russian origin. It simply reflects the controversies of Witte's days [i.e., the 1890s]" (Wiles 1967, 5n4).

At the time of Soviet industrialization, World War I had happened just yesterday. The general belief was that economic weakness, as manifested in the shortage of shells, guns, rifles, and other hardware, was "the main cause for the relatively undistinguished performance of the Tsarist army."[24] The expansion of the production of armaments was, in turn, constrained by the weakness of heavy industry, as manifested in the shortages of non-ferrous metals, iron ore and coking coal, machine tools and precision instruments (Gatrell 2005, ch. 5).

Only a few years after the onset of Soviet industrialization, the strategy was adopted by two major economies. In Japan in the 1930s, "it was chiefly the metallurgical, machinery, and chemical industries . . . which mushroomed under the stimulus of armament spending and industrial construction. Consumer goods production in Japanese industry advanced only 33% from 1930 to 1936. By contrast, the output of producer goods jumped 83%" (Lockwood 1954, 71).

At the time of the second and third Soviet Five-Year Plans, the Nazi economy showed signs of following the Preobrazhenskii-Feldman growth strategy: high rate of investment, which was directed towards producer goods sectors; production of producer goods greatly outpacing that of consumer goods; and depressed consumption. Contemporary observers saw these as manifestations of a massive military buildup.[25] Half a century later, Temin (1991, 584–86) noted that both Soviet and German economies in the 1930s had stagnant consumption, rapidly increasing capital investment and government expenditures, and rapid growth in steel production. At the time, Germany was engaged in a military buildup, and Temin argued that the Soviets were doing the same. It is a testament to the entrenchment of the standard version that he is the only one, to my knowledge, to point out the similarity of the two cases.

Throughout recent history, rulers in pursuit of power sought to build up their armaments industries to equip their armed forces. They understood, without resorting to sophisticated economic analysis, that this required the development of upstream sectors (i.e., heavy industry). The standard version unnecessarily intellectualizes the Soviet episode of military industrialization.

## 5.6 The real industrialization debate

The 1920s saw an outpouring of writings on military-economic topics in the USSR. Top army commanders discussed the modern economy in their military theory treatises (e.g., Tukhachevskii 1928). Volumes with titles like *National Economy and Defense* and *Economics of War* discussed in detail the military significance of specific sectors of the economy (e.g., Ventsov 1928). Western works on the subject were being translated. So massive was this stream of publications, that there was even a bibliographic guide issued (Pugacheva et al. 1927).[26]

The writers analyzed the events of World War I and the Russian Civil War to determine the course of the future inevitable war and the best ways to prepare for it. They agreed that the future war would be fought not only by armies, but by whole societies, and that the state of the belligerents' economies would be the decisive factor in the conflict's outcome. For this reason, military and economic planning had to be thoroughly integrated, and civilian industry had to prepare in peacetime to switch to military production at a short notice. The writers recognized the relative backwardness of the Soviet economy and enumerated sectors (most of them branches of heavy industry) that had to be expanded or created from scratch in order to provide the armed forces with the tools necessary for fighting the next war.

The contributors to this discussion included the Chief of Red Army Staff, M. Tukhachevskii, and the People's Commissar (i.e. Minister)

for War, M. Frunze, who had access to Stalin and the Politburo, unlike Preobrazhenskii, an opposition member, and Feldman, a minor
functionary.

Echoes of the military economic discussion are clearly heard in the
pronouncements of the top officials, such as the speech of Kliment
Voroshilov—People's Commissar of War, member of Politburo, and
Stalin's crony—at the 15th Party Congress (Voroshilov [1927b] 1936). It
briefly reviewed the writings of Western experts, quoting a French general who wrote that "the future war will be predominantly the war of factories" (Voroshilov [1927b] 1936, 190). There followed a lengthy account of
the legislative and administrative measures taken by the Western countries to ready their economies for war (191–95). Thus, "Poland develops
its metallurgy, constructs machine-building plants, pays a lot of attention
to chemical industry, especially the artificial silk factories which, in case
of need, can produce explosives. Poles take a serious approach to, and ev-
idently resolve the problems of, building tanks, engines, aircraft, and so
on, and so forth" (195). Both the attention to Western thought on industrial mobilization, and the confusion of policy proclamations with actual
developments—evident above—characterized the literature of the 1920s
(Samuelson 2000b, 16, 19). Voroshilov also described the development of
Soviet mobilization bodies within the economic administration of sectors,
regions, and factories (196).

Most relevant for our purposes is the sector-by-sector discussion of
the need for new ferrous and non-ferrous metallurgical plants, a chemical industry, an automobile industry, the production of tractors, and
an aircraft industry, followed by the war industry proper, transport, and
agriculture (Voroshilov [1927b] 1936, 199–209). Voroshilov's speech
at the Fourth Congress of the Soviets earlier the same year contained
the same elements, including a list of industries that needed to be created or strengthened (123–25, 129–132). These lists represented a condensed program of heavy-industry-led industrialization, built not from
Preobrazhenskii's theorizing, but from the armed forces' mobilization
requests.

The Soviet military-economic writings of the 1920s appeared in open-
circulation, generally accessible journals and books. To the best of my
knowledge, they were never mentioned by Western scholars in the literature on the "Great Debate," and were first discussed in an economic (as
distinct from a military) context by an outsider writing in a non-economics
periodical (Checinski 1985).

## 5.7 *Taking socialism too seriously*

The official pronouncements just quoted named building socialism the primary objective of industrialization, followed by strengthening defense. The standard account, as it developed, shed both socialism and defense in favor of growth for the sake of growth. Yet given the fragmentation of the field, some scholars kept affirming socialism as a full-fledged objective of industrialization on equal footing with growth. Lenin's heirs "were bound to regard the ultimate achievement of socialism as the one possible justification for their being in power" (Nove 1969, 120–21).[27] "The purpose of the [First Five-Year] Plan was not just to expand the economy but to 'build socialism'" (Harrison 2006, 1098).[28] The Sovietologist to most consistently oppose this view was Gerschenkron (1962b, 150; 1970, 115–16), arguing that the rhetoric of Marxism and socialism was mere window-dressing "to blur and to disguise the actual motivation and aims" of industrialization policy.

Historians, for whom the concept of economic growth has no professional importance, may be even more inclined to name building socialism as the primary motive of industrialization. Thus, according to Malia (1994, 209), the goal "clearly was to put industrial and proletarian 'base' under the existing 'superstructure' of the Party, and thereby to make the Party viable within the country as the vehicle for building socialism."

The analysis of the objectives of industrialization should not be limited to restating the pronouncements of the actors in their own terms, but should look into the real meaning of ideological terms. Socialism was not a concept with a fixed, predefined meaning. For all the formidable rhetoric about building a new society, much of that construction was indistinguishable from the creation of the military-industrial base, and some represented relatively simple police measures.[29]

Building socialism meant first and foremost getting rid of "capitalist elements" and non-state economic activity (Pavlova 2001, 126–30). The extinction of capitalist institutions in industry, the first of the four accomplishments of industrialization named by Stalin, was realized through a combination of police action and defining socialism down. Private industry accounted for less than 10% of total industrial production in 1927, and government repression quickly drove down this share, as well as that of private trade. The remaining individual artisans working on their own account were reclassified as being part of the socialist sector.[30]

More redefining concerned the allocation of labor and consumer goods. In the USSR in the 1920s and the early 1930s, as in standard Marxist doctrine, socialism was understood as a moneyless, in-kind economy in which product exchange replaced the market, everyone was employed by the state, and labor was centrally planned. "The postponement of these goals eventually led the party leadership to abandon the daunting assumption that socialism would not be established until they were achieved, in favor of the more restricted notion that socialism simply required the social ownership of the means of production. . . . It eventually proved possible to achieve the first, socialist, phase of communism by 1937 only by making drastic changes in its definition, so as to incorporate socialised trade, the *kolkhoz* market and the money economy within the first phase of communism" (Davies 1989b, 170–73). Building socialism was something Stalin himself defined; it was his choice when to declare victory in this battle.

Parts of what was billed as socialist construction were equivalent to the elements of military-economic buildup. Thus, creating a proletarian base for the party superstructure (Malia 1994, 209) meant, in economic terms, recruiting, training, and breaking in the workforce for the industrial sectors supporting the production of aircraft engines and tank turrets.

Military objectives were more exigent and less malleable than the construction of socialism, and thus more pressing. The level of expertise required to, say, build aircraft engines was much higher than that needed for rounding up private traders or adjusting ideological definitions. Unlike socialism, military preparedness had clear quantitative dimensions, which could be assessed by experts and compared to those of other countries. It was subject to the potential test of the battlefield, where unilateral declarations of victory carry no weight. As far as economic policy was concerned, building up defense industry was the real objective, building socialism in industry a largely rhetorical one. This argument does not apply to the collectivization of agriculture, an extremely large-scale police operation with wide-ranging unanticipated consequences that, in Stalin's own words, turned out to be very difficult (Ellman 2006, 969).

## 5.8  Summary

This chapter, like the previous one, does the double duty of confronting the long-accepted view of the formative events of Soviet economic history, and also documenting Sovietology's tendency to civilianize all things military.

The notion that Soviet industrialization was motivated by military considerations, advanced here, is not new. It was stated in the Soviet sources at the time and received the occasional mention in Sovietological writings. Post-1991 archival research illuminated the central place of defense in the First Five-Year Plan.[31] The military objectives of industrialization are also broadly accepted in Russian literature.[32] Yet none of the newly available information has made a dent in the acceptance of the standard, civilianized account, by now enshrined in the *Oxford Encyclopedia of Economic History* and the *New Palgrave Dictionary of Economics*.

Ellman (2004, 842) briefly cast doubt on the elements of the standard version and, together with Temin (1991), inspired this chapter. What is new here is the critical examination of the standard account as a whole and its comparison with Stalin's version.

Also like the previous one, this chapter deals with an aspect of the Soviet economy that the Soviets themselves explained in military terms, yet that the Sovietologists (with all the exceptions mentioned earlier) sought to civilianize. The most striking manifestation of this flight from the evidence is Erlich's, Dobb's, and Jasny's unreasoned (in the case of the latter two authors) but categorical denial of the military objectives of industrialization. Over time, the elaborate standard account has developed in place of these blunt denials. It disregards or glosses over contradictory Soviet sources, violates the basics of the economic approach by posing growth for the sake of growth as the objective, and fails to draw connections to similar policies in other countries and periods.

The near absence of the military sector from the literature on the Soviet economy, documented in chapter 3, could be explained by Soviet secrecy, the Sovietologists' lack of interest in military-economic matters, or their general views on the relative importance of military and civilian factors in economic life. Yet active civilianizing of the military-related aspects of the economy in chapters 4 and 5 reveals a different, more complex scholarly strategy to which these explanations would not apply.

# Notes

1. World Bank (1991, 34); Easterly (2001, 30–32).
2. The most recent references are Spulber (2003, 181); Gregory (2004, 29–31, 76–77, 82–83); Berend (2006, 146, 149); Ofer (2008, 722).
3. Campbell (1966, 12–21); Spulber (1969, 219–23); Nove (1969; 1992); Millar (1981, 11–16); Munting (1982); Gregory and Stuart (1986, ch. 4; 2001, 59–61); Ofer (2003, 422–23); Allen (2003, 51–64).
4. Also Spulber (1964, 62); Ofer (1976, 219); Boettke (1990, 148–49); Ofer (2008, 722).

5. Indeed, this was the view of Erlich (1950, 58); Jasny (1964, 214); Spulber (1964, 66; 1969, 223); Prybyla (1965; 69); Moravcik (1965, 246); Kaser (1970, 83; with qualifications); Dyker (1985, 3); Gregory and Stuart (1986, 93); Allen (2003, 63); and Gregory (2004, 31). Miller (1965, 835) disagreed and Dobb himself had reservations.

6. Erlich (1978, 203); Unsal (1991, 391); Allen (2003, 63); Gregory (2004, 83); Ofer (2008, 722).

7. "The first mathematical growth model by a Russian economist, P. [sic] A. Feldman, supported an investment maximizing strategy" (Gregory 2004, 83; also Erlich 1978, 203).

8. Spulber (1964, 54; 1969, ch. 12); Campbell (1966, 25–26); Dyker (1985, 2–3); Hunter and Szyrmer (1992, 24); Davies (1994, 137–38); Gregory (2004, 76).

9. Kershaw (1961, 8–9); Wilczynski (1970, 69).

10. The third reason was the need to provide agriculture with modern equipment.

11. Leontiev (1946, 11–13) lists the same three reasons in reverse order.

12. Stalin (1925a, 298–99; 1925b, 354–56; 1926, 120–21); IMELS (1954, 196–97).

13. Rutland (1985, 73–97); North (2005, 14–19).

14. Millar (1981, 21–33); Dyker (1985, 3); Gregory and Stuart (1985, 234–35); Gregory and Stuart (1986, 68–105).

15. Dobb (1955); Moravcik (1965); Wiles (1964, chs. 14 and 15); Dyker (1983, 109–113).

16. Schwartz (1954, 276); Grossman (1958, 17); Berliner (1966, 161–2); Nove (1969, 122, 227–29; with some hesitation); Kaser 1970, 201.

17. Erickson (1962, 322) and the rest of chapter 10.

18. Also Rostow (1961, 99, 103) and Sutton (1968, 1971) at great length.

19. Clark (1956); Holzman (1957); Hunter (1957); Abouchar (1979).

20. Davies (1974); Koropeckyj (1967, 234–42).

21. Paul Bushkovitch, a historian of the period, argues that Stalin overstated the actual extent of Peter's military industrialization (personal communication). What is important for our purposes is the monarch's image.

22. Sen (1984) and Vayrynen (1992) attempted to generalize over these and similar cases of military industrialization.

23. Gerschenkron (1962b, 131); Gatrell (1994, 4). Goldstein (1971, 78–79) sees the need to highly qualify such statements. Again, it is the perception by posterity that matters for us.

24. Stone (1976, 108–9); Samuelson (2000b, 15).

25. Balogh (1939, 488, 496); Cole (1939, 60); Grebler (1937b, 516–17); Hutton (1939, 525–26); Mendershausen (1943, 87). More on German rearmament in the 1930s in section 8.1.1.

26. For surveys of some of this literature, see Samuelson (2000b, ch. 1) and Stone (2000, 16–18).

27. Also: Dobb (1966, 1); Zaleski (1971, 290); Davies (1994, 136–37).

28. However, Harrison (1985, 625–26) gave a detailed account of the defense motivation of industrialization.
29. More on socialist essentialism in section 7.2.
30. Davies (1989b, 76–79); Davies (1994, 137).
31. Davies (1993); Stone (2000, ch. 5); Samuelson (2000b); Harrison (2008); Ellman (2008b, 105).
32. Gaidar (2003, 23); Pavlova (2001, 110, 442); Zhuravlev (2009).

# PART III

# *Why Government Money Could not Buy Economists' Love*

When I shared the findings of chapter 3 with veteran Sovietologists, most of them cited the secrecy that shrouded the military sector as the reason for its omission from the literature. Let us call it a secrecy hypothesis. The second most common reaction of the field's veterans to early drafts has been to ascribe the neglect of the military sector not to an external constraint, but to the internal workings of Sovietology (e.g., "[Maurice] Dobb was a Communist").

Secrecy is commonly cited in the literature to explain gaps in the understanding of the Soviet economy during its lifetime. By 1991, "our lack of knowledge about this economy remained considerable. This ignorance was not due to the lack of acumen or effort but to the veil of secrecy that had been erected by Soviet leaders" (Gregory 2004, ix). Secrecy is doubly plausible as an explanation for the neglect of military matters: "research on the economic history of the USSR in the 1930s has had a surprisingly 'civilian' character. . . . The secretiveness of the Soviet system was, of course, a fundamental reason for this" (Samuelson 2000b, 1).

A detailed study of Western views on the role of defense in the First Five-Year Plan (Davies 1993) shows that, while Soviet secrecy and falsification certainly played a role, they were not the whole story. There were also early sources that went unused, overlooked revelations in the official pronouncements, and a flood of information that arrived too late, after the Western interpretation of the First Five-Year Plan had already congealed. Practices internal to Sovietology mattered for the state of knowledge as much as did external constraints.

In this part, I investigate both secrecy and the internal workings of Sovietology, both political and professional, in order to understand why an academic field created and maintained to help parry a strategic challenge tended to ignore the very part of its subject that made the challenge possible.

# 6

# The Secrecy Hypothesis

LITERATURE ON THE Soviet economy was fragmented; while most scholars ignored the military sector, a small number did write about it, as shown in chapter 3. This is enough to reject the secrecy hypothesis in its strong form, "secrecy made work on the military sector impossible," yet not enough to dismiss the impact of the informational embargo on scholarship. This chapter describes the extent and function of secrecy in the Soviet society, economy, and military sector, explores how Sovietologists responded to secrecy in their work, and demonstrates how much a scholar who bothered to look at the military sector managed to uncover, secrecy notwithstanding.

## 6.1 The shape of the constraint
### 6.1.1 Secrecy in Soviet society

Secrecy surrounding the military sector was a part of the general Soviet information-control regime. For Western researchers of the USSR, it posed problems of similar kind, if not degree, across disciplines and subjects of study. Outside observers were primarily concerned with Soviet restrictions on the publication of information of the type that was routinely available in other countries. Yet this was but one aspect of an elaborate system that also regulated insiders' access to information already in government possession (e.g., through security clearances) and restricted the acquisition of new information (e.g., by defining permissible topics for social science research) (Shlapentokh 2001, 57–59).

While national security considerations and propaganda abroad played a role in motivating the secrecy regime, the main reasons for it were domestic.[1] Many of the secrets were of no interest for foreigners, such as the goings on in local party and government organs. Other secrets were widely known abroad. These included world events that were kept from the Soviet public, as well as the blacked-out pages of Soviet history, such as the details of intra-party struggle in the 1920s. Much information was beyond the reach of even top Soviet officials (see section 2.3.2). Diplomats negotiating arms control treaties with US representatives were kept in the dark about assets their side possessed. At one such negotiation, the head of the Soviet delegation asked Americans not to present their estimates of the Soviet missile deployment in front of the civilian members of his delegation.[2]

The main function of secrecy was to shield the officials on all levels from public scrutiny. Since the early years of the Soviet regime, the decisionmaking process in the party and government was one of the most closely guarded secrets (Pavlova 1993, 71, 130–31). Since the party aspired to direct an extremely broad range of social processes, practically any information could be seen as casting its activity in the wrong light, and thus unfit to print, including such seemingly innocent examples as news of natural disasters and industrial and transportation accidents, and the names of the spouses of political figures.[3] Secrecy surrounding government and party proceedings made the work of Western political scientists difficult, but did not have the silencing effect that secrecy surrounding the military sector is alleged to have had on economists, as I show in section 6.2.2.

### 6.1.2 Economic information: civilian and military sectors

The extent of secrecy concerning the economy changed over the course of the regime's life. The 1920s were the period of greatest informational openness, curiously coinciding with the period of the greatest military weakness in Soviet history. Statistical reporting on both the economy and its military sector started to shrink in 1927, as military-industrial buildup revved up.[4] A virtual blackout set in after 1939, when no statistical yearbooks were published, and the data on economic performance appearing in the press were meager. While the publication of economics books and journals continued, practically the only numbers they contained were those of the pages, as the joke went.[5]

The publication of statistical yearbooks resumed in 1956, and after a few slim volumes they regained the heft they had in about 1936.[6] Researchers and journalists again occasionally cited useful data in print. This greater degree of openness prevailed, with some variation, until the final years of the USSR and also coincided with most of Sovietology's lifespan. Still, the publications in this period omitted a wealth of data that were collected by Soviet statistics and were routinely published in the other countries.

For example, data on the money supply, the gold and hard currency reserves, the balance of payments, and anything concerning the non-ferrous metals sector never appeared in print.[7] Information on government revenues and outlays, national financial flows, earnings by industry and occupation, pensions, the employment breakdown by sector of industry, input-output tables, foreign trade, and finance were revealed with significant omissions. Economists using the published fragments of information were unable to restore the full statistical picture—the state budget, the national income accounts, the distribution of personal incomes—without massive additional guesswork. From time to time, previously available data would stop being published, such as input-output tables, wholesale price indices, and much data on imports and exports in the early 1980s. Documentation of published statistics was often inadequate, making their definition and coverage unclear.

The increase in the availability of economic information since the mid-1950s did not involve the military industry. The very existence of this sector was almost never mentioned in print. Some of the military-industry ministries bore euphemistic names, such as the Ministry of Intermediate Machinebuilding for nuclear technology. A Western scholar had to piece together five different Soviet sources to suggest that the Ministry of General Machinebuilding may be in charge of rocket technology (Korol 1965, 356–67). Even the euphemistic names were mentioned in print extremely rarely, on such occasions as the unveiling of the composition of the CM at the session of the Supreme Soviet. The *VPK* and the defense department of the State Planning Committee, the coordinating organs of the industry, were practically never mentioned in published sources. An extremely thorough researcher noted: "Little is known of this body, except that it is called the Military-Industrial Commission" (Holloway 1982, 298).

Sovietologists derived much of their understanding of the microeconomic problems in the civilian economy from newspaper reporting. Yet military firms could not be mentioned or identified in the media (Simonov 2015, 13). Precautions went so far that a college graduate assigned a job at a military sector establishment would be directed to a "post office box" with a particular number in a particular city—no street address.[8] G. I. Khanin, one of the most profound insider students of the Soviet economy and a voracious reader, recalls that he never saw anything on the post–World War II military industry in Soviet economic literature (personal communication).

The only number on the military economy which was regularly published was labeled, without explanation, "defense expenditures of the state
budget" (discussed in section 2.2.1).[9] Data on the production of civilian
goods in the military industry, such as ships, aircraft, and electronics, were
kept secret. Much of the secrecy in reporting on the civilian economy, as
described in this section, was presumably motivated by the desire to shield
military-industry information. Data on the non-ferrous metals industry
were kept under wraps because the industry's main customers were the
military ministries. The breakdown of employment by sector of industry,
disaggregated data on machinery production, elements of the state budget,
national income accounting, foreign trade, and input-output tables were
withheld, in all likelihood, to thwart any attempts to indirectly estimate
military sector magnitudes by the residual methods described in section
2.2.2. These are exactly the data that open societies withhold in wartime.[10]
This is yet another reason, in addition to those given in chapter 2, to think
of the USSR as having a peacetime war economy.

Consider, for comparison, the data available in a national economy statistical yearbook for a civilian sector of industry, such as ferrous metals or
construction materials. Just leafing through a randomly chosen edition
(TsSU, 1981), one can find several dozen numbers for a particular year,
including the output of the sector's main products in physical terms; the
rate of growth of total output in value terms; the number of enterprises;
the sector's share in the total industrial output; the growth rates of labor
productivity, fixed assets and working capital, and fixed assets alone; percentage shares of structures, equipment, and other elements in the fixed
assets; the rate of change of the capital/labor ratio; the share of fixed assets
in all assets; the share of fixed assets commissioned in the last 10 years in
the total fixed assets; the commissioning and decommissioning of fixed
assets by type, as share of the total; the cost structure; the number of pieces
of automated and other advanced equipment installed; the structure of investment; and the volume of construction in progress.

Some of these data would be reported consistently enough to provide
time series spanning several decades. Even more data on a civilian sector
could be dug up in economic and technical publications, and in specialized statistical publications. If, instead of a sector of industry, one looked
at a sector of the economy (e.g., agriculture or transportation), data availability would be even greater. This was still meager by international standards, but much more than the single number on defense.

One would expect the lack of publications on the military sector to suppress Western research on the subject by denying it necessary inputs. Secrecy also played a more direct role in restraining budding Sovietologists' choice of specialization. In 1958, a US-Soviet agreement established an exchange program for graduate students and young scholars. On the US side, it was initially run by the Inter-University Committee on Travel Grants, later transformed into the International Research and Exchange Board.[11]Applicants to the program had to specify their areas of interest, and their visits were subject to hosts' approval. Needless to say, research into the military sector by the visiting Western students and scholars was not allowed.

For an aspiring country specialist, studying and doing research in one's country of interest is an important step in professional development, as well as a valuable credential. To be granted this opportunity, Sovietologists had to specialize in civilian topics. In the words of the original head of the Inter-University Committee, the exchange program "has given the Soviet authorities an unwelcome influence over the direction of our research. Their refusal to countenance work on the Communist party and on the central government has forced scholars to work on peripheral subjects. Soviet control of American research in Moscow and Leningrad into the Soviet economy may also distort the direction of our study in that discipline as well."[12]

## 6.1.3 Breaches in the wall

Despite continuous, massive, and costly Soviet efforts to keep the military sector hidden, knowledge on the subject was accumulated in the West, as will be shown in section 6.3. Some information was extracted by foreign spying, estimates of the Soviet defense burden discussed in section 2.2.2 being an example. Westerners who had worked in the country and Soviet citizens who ended up abroad served as another conduit. Surprisingly, in the light of the strictures described in the previous section, much information about the military sector was supplied by the Soviets themselves. Two such instances of candor—late 1920s and early 1930s rulers' pronouncements on the motivation of industrialization and the textbooks' insistence on defense as the goal of planning—were documented in chapters 4 and 5.

Other revelations were allowed at different times and for a variety of reasons. World War II occupied an exceptional place in Soviet ideology, with its story being continually retold. This included the story of the structure and functioning of the wartime military economy, from which a great deal could be learned about its peacetime version.

While weapons factories could not be publicly named, their products were broadly publicized. Twice a year at military parades in Moscow, foreign military attachés saw samples of equipment driving or flying by. Space launches were officially announced, as were nuclear and ballistic missile tests. Navy ships made officially arranged calls at foreign ports. Soviet rulers bragged about the quantity and capabilities of their weapons in their published speeches and interviews.

Consider some of the revelations of the first postwar decade, when Soviet secretiveness was at an all-time high. The first jet-propelled military planes were exhibited at an air show in August, 1946 and discussed in *Pravda*. In 1947, the Soviet government officially announced "breaking the secret of the atomic bomb," and in 1949 announced its first nuclear test. In 1951, Stalin discussed the past and future nuclear tests in an interview to *Pravda*. An official announcement followed the test of the multi-stage intercontinental ballistic missile in 1957 and a concurrent series of nuclear and thermonuclear tests. ICBMs were carted through Moscow during the November 7, 1957 parade. Also, it was revealed "during the air parade of May 1, 1954 that the Soviet Union was building giant intercontinental jet bombers."[13]

This seemingly contradictory treatment of the products of the secret sector was due to the fact that much of the utility of military hardware derives not from its battlefield use, but from the impression it makes on the adversary before battle. Completely withholding information about military production would have sacrificed this effect. Thus, German plans of invasion in 1941 were based on "severe underestimation" of both the stock of advanced weapons and the mobilization potential of the Soviet industry, and one may speculate that greater openness could have deterred the attack (Samuelson 2000b, 198–99). Absolute secrecy in the Soviet Union was reserved for the phenomena the very existence of which was denied, like riots, strikes, and official privileges. Soviet rulers were far from denying the existence of their arsenal.

Soviet rulers routinely made general statements unsupported by additional evidence concerning other secret subjects, with uncertain effects. Thus, the state budget was said not to be in deficit (Garbuzov 1984, 168), though much of the data necessary to verify this claim were not published. The deliberations within the party organs were kept secret, but were routinely said to exhibit monolithic unity. The claim about the state budget was false, at least towards the end of the Soviet era, though mostly taken at face value in the West.[14] The claim about unity within the party leadership mostly was not believed in the West, even for the periods for which it was correct (Khlevniuk 1996, 6–8). For the adversary to be definitely overawed by the Soviet military might, general statements were not enough. The main products of the secret sector had to be shown with some specificity (Hutchings 1987, 72–74, 197).

It remains to be demonstrated whether these disparate information disclosures, both forced and voluntary, added up to a coherent picture useful for an economist.

## 6.2  The constraint was not binding

Secrecy surrounding the military sector only mattered for our subject if it prevented Sovietologists from realizing their research plans. If that was indeed the case, there must be a record of complaints about secrecy and discussions of the gaps in knowledge it produced. We should be able to observe researchers making repeated attempts to overcome secrecy by roundabout means. The work of those who claim to have found anything new about the military sector should have attracted attention and emulation in the profession. We consider evidence for each of these three patterns of behavior in turn.

### 6.2.1  Concern about secrecy and the recognition of gaps in knowledge

Sovietology was born in the late 1940s, when the availability of data on the economy was at its lowest. At that time, complaints about secrecy as a barrier to understanding the Soviet economy (and not just its military sector) were not uncommon. The preface to the first major book published by the new discipline spoke of "the enormous difficulties posed for this discipline by the information policy of the Soviet government, especially the extreme secrecy," and asked the readers to bear it in mind when examining the often tentative conclusions that left many gaps (Bergson 1953a, iii). The need to overcome secrecy and the ability to do so were viewed as defining characteristics of the new discipline at its inception. "Even more important was to learn how to combine statistical data so as to obtain information which never was intended to be divulged by the compilers and publishers of Soviet statistics" (Gerschenkron 1968, 528). "The necessity of creating its own data has left a definite stamp on the character of this branch of economics. Because the data were otherwise not readily available, or where available, not reliable, or at least had to be checked, the economist has had to dig up the basic figures and to combine them into assimilable and digestible aggregates" (Grossman 1959, 36).

However, the general concern with secrecy would soon abate. In the late 1950s and early 1960s, some of the new discipline's founders published surveys of the field to mark its tenth anniversary. Their overall assessment was upbeat, with no more talk of tentative conclusions or gaps in knowledge: "the facts are now known, the concepts forged"; "at the mere level of quantitative factology we are well informed about the Soviet and indeed most European communist countries; certainly better than about underdeveloped countries" (Wiles 1961, 87; 1964, 71).[15] Grossman (1959, 41–43) in his survey mentioned secrecy once as an obstacle to research into labor compensation, but suggested that a non-quantitative study still could be done. Lack of data on the defense industry output was mentioned as a barrier for accurate measurement of economic aggregates, but not as a problem in its own right.[16]

As is common in anniversary surveys, the papers identified the areas where knowledge remained deficient and more work was required. Among the latter, they listed steel, coal, and petroleum industries, construction technology, obsolescence, collective farm management, finance, foreign trade, labor, and wages.[17] Even water transportation was named as "a big enough activity to justify treatment of itself alone" at the time (in 1960) when internal waterways carried 5.2% of freight shipped by common carriers in the USSR, and merchant marine carried 1.9%.[18] The defense industry was not deemed worthy of such a treatment.

Many of the leading Sovietologists participated in the collective volume aimed at the "assessment of availability, reliability, and credibility of Soviet economic statistics" (Treml and Hardt 1972, v). The introduction to the book mentions "defense-related producing sectors" as one of three "vast areas of relative silence," and suggests, in one sentence, that this hurts the Soviets themselves by preventing them from analyzing policy tradeoffs. This is followed by an extended argument about the Soviet economy's need for better statistics on agriculture, consumption, and services. There is no comment on what, if anything, the "silence" on military production did to the Western understanding of the economy's tradeoffs. Secrecy had an easy explanation in "longstanding Russian tradition" and was "understandable, given Soviet experience" (Hunter 1972, 5).

Later surveys of the field (Clarke 1983; Millar 1980) focused exclusively on achievements and did not name any areas where knowledge was still deficient. There was also no longer any need to deal with Soviet secrecy. If the earlier generations of Sovietologists had "to comb through large masses of publications for individual numbers, for descriptions of institutions, and for hints about problems and conflicts," in the 1970s, one could rely either on the official Soviet data or on the CIA (Millar 1980, 324–25).

In the introduction to his textbook on the Soviet economy, Millar (1981, xv) proclaims that "we have developed the basis for a full and reliable description and analysis of the Soviet economic system." The only issues worth mentioning on which there was still little information were the World War II period and its immediate aftermath, and "how political decisions are taken and get translated into economic directives." Otherwise, however, enough was known to "visualize the overall pattern and much of its detailed complexity" (Millar 1981, xvi). It is only in retrospect that considerable gaps in knowledge of the Soviet economy were acknowledged and blamed on secrecy (Gregory 2004, ix).

A formal approach to documenting the degree of concern for secrecy on the part of researchers is to look for the words "secrecy" and "secret" in the books' indexes. Table 6.1 presents a result of such an exercise for

**Table 6.1. Secrecy in books on the Soviet/socialist economy, by category.**

| Category of books | Books with index: | |
|---|---|---|
| | Total | With "secrecy" or "secret" in the index |
| Textbooks and readers | 41 | 2 |
| Planning | 12 | 0 |
| Enterprise management | 8 | 1 |
| Growth | 9 | 0 |
| National accounting, statistics | 8 | 1 |
| General Soviet/socialist | 25 | 3 |
| Gorbachev, collapse | 15 | 0 |
| Economic history | 14 | 0 |
| R&D, innovation | 11 | 4 |
| TOTAL | 143 | 11 |

*Sources*: All books with index included in tables 3.1–3.5, 3.7, 3.8; most books included in 3.6; and selected books from 3.9.

*Note*: Entries for "commercial secrecy" and "secret police" were not counted.

143 books on the main aspects of the Soviet economy, which we surveyed in chapter 3. The terms are present in the indexes of only 11 books, including two out of 41 textbooks. Secrecy does not make it into the indexes of most books on the national income accounting, the studies undertaken in large part to overcome Soviet secrecy. It is not mentioned in the books on planning, though some aspects of plan construction have always remained secret. It does not appear in the indexes of books on Gorbachev's reforms, of which the relaxation of secrecy (*glasnost'*) was a major plank.

The absence of the word "secrecy" from the indexes of Sovietological books reflects not only the authors' lack of concern for the phenomenon, but also the tendency not to call it by its real name, substituting euphemisms like "areas of relative silence" or "data availability" problem.[19] This is further discussed in section 7.1.2.

The neglect of Soviet secrecy and its effects was not specific to economic literature. Hutchings (1987, 6) searched for the word "secrecy" in the indexes of books about the USSR from different disciplines, and then followed up on the entries he found to see if there was a substantive discussion of it in the text.[20] He found no discussion of secrecy in the general histories, and no extended discussion in other fields. The two most extensive treatments of the subject that he found were in books written by journalists, not social scientists.

## 6.2.2 The use of roundabout means to overcome secrecy

Secrecy surrounding a subject does not necessarily result in the absence of publications about it; the effect may well be the opposite. Withholding information itself supplies a motive to find out what is being hidden: "Given that such enormous trouble, in so many dimensions and at such expense, is taken to preserve secrecy, what is kept secret must be considered to be of great importance" (Hutchings 1987, 264). In the case of the Soviet military sector, while information on its workings was being hidden, its output was shown off around the world, practically teasing the experts to find out more about its origins, as will be demonstrated in section 6.3.1.[21] A dearth of information need not prevent publications about a subject deemed interesting and important. It may actually lead to an excess of publications, as authors use fragmentary, secondary, and otherwise deficient evidence in support of hypotheses some of which would have been rejected with higher-quality information.

The Western study of top-level Soviet politics provides an example of massive published output in the face of unavailable primary data. In a tightly centralized system, all important national decisions and a great many unimportant ones were made at the Politburo level (Khlevniuk 1996, 3). The operation of that body was, therefore, key to explaining the country's policies. Yet the internal workings of the ruling circle—procedures for arriving at decisions, positions of particular personalities, their alliances, or even the scope of the agenda—were among the jealously guarded secrets. As with the military sector, only a part of the Politburo's output, published party decisions and official speeches, was visible. This was true even with respect to a relatively distant past. A historian writing about the sources available for the study of the Politburo in the 1930s during the late Soviet period speaks of "absolutely closed . . . archives and, to put it mildly, tight-lipped politicians," "falsified official documents, unpersuasive memoirs, and cleaned-up archives" (Khlevniuk 1996, 4, 259). Millar (1981, xvi), while claiming that Sovietologists more or less possessed the full knowledge of how the Soviet economy works, concedes that "how political decisions are taken" remained an important unanswered question.

Yet this did not prevent the emergence of a voluminous scholarly literature on the politics of the Soviet ruling circle. Commensurate with its importance in the system, political scientists directed the lion's share of their attention to the "question of leadership. Much effort was expended on scrutinizing Politburo politics and second-guessing the moves of the general secretary" (Rutland 1993, 118).[22] Absent direct evidence, scholars analyzed in detail the short official biographies of Politburo members and their published speeches, or retreated into pure theorizing (Rutland 1993, 115). When dealing with the high politics of the 1930s, they used sources such as hints in Khrushchev's 1956 speech and Nikolaevsky's purported conversation with Bukharin (Khlevnyuk 1996, 258–59). These efforts did not necessarily produce valid results; indeed, Rutland and Khlevnyuk are highly critical of the fruits of this research. But this only strengthens my point: when a subject is considered important and interesting, the lack of reliable information about it is not necessarily a barrier for research publications. Evidence of any sort will be used to produce studies on the burning topic.

There was an approach to the study of the military sector analogous to Kremlinology: the estimation of secret economic magnitudes as residuals, described in section 2.2.2. One could expect a proliferation of residual studies in the 1960s through the 1980s, as researchers explored the consequences of different assumptions for the important and hotly contested question of the size of the military sector. Unlike the CIA's building block method, residual estimation was well within the capabilities of individual researchers. Yet I found only four such studies published in the books and journals I surveyed: Lee (1977), Jacobsen (1987), and Steinberg (1990) on military spending, and Kontorovich (1988) on new product prototypes. Three of them came out towards the very end of the Soviet rule, and two more appeared right after its fall, illustrating the belated peak of interest in the topic (Kushnirsky 1993; Steinberg 1992). The main practitioners of this approach were outsiders (William Lee, Dmitri Steinberg), rather than established academic Sovietologists. The actual effort at residual estimation of military sector magnitudes was greater than the first four publications just cited indicate, reflecting Western governments' interest in finding out about the subject. Yet the results of this work appeared as research reports for the project sponsors, and thus remained outside the main flow of professional information in the field.

Secrecy is a strategic denial of information, and one can try to understand its purpose and play it back. In the words of a British pioneer in the development of national income accountings who also did some early work on the Soviet economy, "The real connoisseur of Soviet statistics . . . can frequently draw his most interesting conclusions from the statistics that are *not* published" (Clark 1956, 11). This was echoed by a British non-academic and the author of the only book on Soviet secrecy: "What we do not know about the Soviet Union because information is withheld is potentially, and in the most literal sense, of vital importance. As far as possible, it must be taken into account in any evaluation or study of the USSR" (Hutchings 1987, 1). An example of this approach can be found in Grossman (1974, 106): "The Soviets have published almost no systematic information on income distribution . . . of course, this official reticence is itself suggestive of considerable inequality."

Yet such an approach was hardly ever attempted, for reasons discussed in section 7.1.2. An appraisal of the Soviet wage and income statistics noted, "Why this relative statistical silence on the part of a government that has long proclaimed among its major purposes the abolition of inequality . . . One can only speculate" (Schroeder 1972, 287). A thorough review of everything known on inequality notes that "those are matters on which socialist countries have not always been especially forthcoming. This is an interesting fact in itself, but it necessarily obstructs accurate appraisal of income inequality" (Bergson 1984, 1052). The interesting fact is not pursued further, however. A book in which the alleged low level of income inequality in the USSR is an important argument discusses it without even mentioning secrecy (Hewett 1988, 2–3, 48–49). A leading textbook suggests that the lack of published data on income distribution was "more likely the result of the relatively low priority attached to the gathering of such information than to any official policy of secrecy" (Gregory and Stuart 1986, 343). In fact, both were the case, as the publications of the late 1980s have revealed (Alexeev and Gaddy, 1993). Secrecy and lack of good data were not independent phenomena in this system, as can be seen from the discussion of Soviet military expenditures in section 2.2.1. Soviets guarded their secrets not just from Sovietologists, but first and foremost from domestic officials, researchers and statisticians. With access limited or denied to qualified personnel, no wonder collection and compilation of the data was poor.

### 6.2.3 Response to the writings on the military sector

One would expect researchers frustrated by secrecy to be alert to any breakthroughs in the informational blockade. Publications purporting to have things to say on the important yet obscure subject would be noticed and receive careful scrutiny, their results, if found valid, would be cited, and their methods would be imitated by other researchers. To see if this was the case, I turn to the reviews of the few books that contain substantial material on the military sector (none of them by American Sovietologists).

Krylov (1979) was the first textbook in a quarter of a century to include a chapter on "Militarization of the Economy." The only reviewer to have mentioned the chapter complained that it was very short (Gay 1980, 507), as if there had been textbook chapters of any length on this topic before.[23]

One of the first works on science and technology to include a discussion of the military sector was Sutton's three-volume "monumental study" (Ofer 1984, 138). It uses the US Department of State and Western company sources to document, sector by sector, the transfer of technology to the USSR, and concludes that the Soviet economy was incapable of generating innovation, relying instead on the West for practically all civilian advances. Sutton's important secondary thesis is that, since the Soviet economy was focused on the buildup of defense industries, Western technology export ended up strengthening the declared adversary's military. Sutton (1968) has a chapter on the technology transfers as a result of the Soviet-German military cooperation, and Sutton (1971) has chapters on aircraft and on tanks, guns, and explosives. Sutton (1973a) has chapters on atomic energy and on space and aircraft technology, as well as an extended argument about dual-use technologies such as automotive and marine transport, a discussion of the relation between the industrial base and the military industry, and a section on the innovativeness of the weapons industry compared to the rest of the economy. Unprecedented in the economics literature, the three volumes document in meticulous detail the military orientation of Soviet development in general, and its import policy, in particular.

Out of 17 book reviews of Sutton written by economists (predominantly Sovietologists), 14 take no note of the military economy part of Sutton's argument. Hunter (1974) touches on it in passing, in a noncommittal way. Cameron (1975) notes that the concentration of resources and comparatively better innovation record in priority areas, such as the military, was familiar from other contexts. Grayson (1975) complains that the book defines strategic goods too broadly, to include engines for merchant marine ships and automobiles. Incidentally, the commander of the Soviet Navy sides with Sutton on the strategic value of the merchant marine (Gorshkov 1979, 47–73).

The landmark survey of the level of Soviet technology (Amann et al. 1977) includes an 80-page chapter on military technology by David Holloway, with detailed case studies of tanks and ICBMs, and a shorter chapter on space technology. Several reviews call these chapters interesting or very interesting and relate their argument in a sentence or two, without further comment.[24]

The follow-up volume (Amann and Cooper 1982) contains a 90-page chapter with a remarkably detailed general account of the military industry (Holloway 1982), to be discussed in the next section. There is also a chapter with a case study of innovation in tanks and ICBMs. Each one of the eight reviews which I read notice the military chapters, but no one express surprise at the author's ability to learn that much about a secret sector, or discuss his sources of information. Two reviews (both by economists) start their retellings of the military chapters with the words "Not surprisingly . . ." (Schroeder 1983, 46) and "Western observers have long noted . . ." (Hunter 1983a, 1027).[25]

Holloway (1983) contains a section on industrialization and military power, a chapter titled "The Defence Economy," and another one on "Military Technology." The 16 reviews of the book that I located were published in political science, international relations, history, and Russian studies journals, and even in the *Washington Post*. Not a single one appeared in an economics journal or was written by an economist.

## 6.3 Direct test of the secrecy hypothesis

The previous section documents Sovietologists' lack of interest in the military sector, but does not disprove the proposition that secrecy made work on the subject impossible. Indeed, the lack of interest itself could be induced by the dearth of information. A simple and direct way of debunking the secrecy hypothesis is to show how much was known in the pre-1991 West about the military sector. A complete survey of Western publications, those by government, think tanks, and scholars of military affairs, would be too long and repetitive. My account is limited to a major newspaper, fragmentary references in Sovietological writings, and an outstanding chapter in a volume on R&D from table 3.9.

### 6.3.1 Sovietologists versus the *New York Times*

From 1950 to 1987, the *New York Times* featured 40 front page articles about Soviet weapons or about one front page headline per year (table 6.2). The coverage was more frequent in the 1960s (14 articles) and 1970s (12). Most of the articles reported testing or deployment of new, more capable models of hardware, followed by a discussion of how American weapons measured up and what the news meant for the balance of forces. Western intelligence reports served as the most frequent source for these articles.

News reporting on the output was occasionally followed by a discussion of the sector that produced it. "The Russian challenge affects all factors of military power: industrial-economic power; maritime power; aero-space power; all types of weapons from assault rifles to multi megaton bombs. . . . Experts agree that Russia is the world's second military power—first in some aspects and making a determined effort to achieve superiority in all. . . . The Soviet economy has major weaknesses, not the least agriculture. Its computer, chemical, electronic, automotive and transportation industries and its mass production techniques—all of basic military importance—appear behind those of the United States. But the Soviet Union has a tremendous capability for the production of arms of all types."[26]

Coverage in the *New York Times* can be taken as a challenge to Sovietology, and also as a benchmark against which to measure the performance of the

**Table 6.2. Soviet military hardware in the front page headlines of the**
*New York Times*, 1946–1991.

| Date | Weapons | Source | Substance |
|------|---------|--------|-----------|
| Oct. 4, 1950 | Tanks, planes | American in East Germany | New models |
| Feb. 22, 1951 | Tanks, artillery | Unspecified | Arming East Germany |
| May 2, 1954 | Jet aircraft, artillery | May Day parade | New models |
| Dec. 10, 1955 | Missile, nuclear test | Soviet announcement & unspecified | New models |
| Feb. 6, 1956 | Missiles | US | New models |
| May 26, 1956 | Bomber | US | New models |
| Nov. 12, 1956 | Various | British | Arming Arab countries |
| July 7, 1957 | Various | US Army | Military balance |
| Feb. 2, 1958 | Missiles, planes, nuclear | Western | Military balance |
| Dec. 11, 1958 | Missiles | Khrushchev interview | New models |
| Dec. 18, 1958 | Bomber | Jane's Aircraft | New models |
| Dec. 8, 1961 | Nuclear | US | New models |
| July 18, 1964 | Missile | US | New models |
| Nov. 8, 1964 | Missiles | Nov. 7 parade | New models |
| Nov. 8, 1965 | Missiles | Nov. 7 parade | New models |
| Dec. 8, 1966 | Missile defense | US | New construction |
| Feb. 5, 1967 | Missile defense | US | Military balance |
| Oct. 30, 1967 | Various | US | Military balance |
| Feb. 19, 1968 | Missiles | US | Growing number, new models |
| Dec. 11, 1968 | Defense spending | Supreme Soviet | Increase in budget allocation |
| Feb. 21, 1969 | Missile defense | US | New models |
| June 9, 1969 | Missiles | US | New models |
| Oct. 28, 1969 | Missiles, planes, etc. | US | Growing number, new models |
| Dec. 17, 1969 | Defense spending | Supreme Soviet | Increase in budget allocation |
| April 28, 1970 | Missiles, ABM | US | Military balance |
| Sep. 5, 1971 | Bomber | US | New model |
| Oct. 11, 1971 | Missile silos, subs | US | New construction |

**Table 6.2. Continued**

| Date | Weapons | Source | Substance |
|------|---------|--------|-----------|
| Aug. 18, 1973 | Missile | US | New model |
| Oct. 8, 1973 | Tanks, aircraft | British | Growing number in Europe |
| Jan. 15, 1975 | Missiles | US | New models deployment |
| June 21, 1975 | Missile | US | Growing deployment |
| Dec. 26, 1976 | Cruise missiles, etc. | US | Military balance |
| Feb. 2, 1979 | Cruise missile | US | New model |
| Apr. 24, 1979 | Missile | US | New deployment |
| Sep. 21, 1980 | Various | US | Military balance |
| Dec. 7, 1980 | Various | US | Military balance |
| Dec. 8, 1980 | Arms technology | US | Military balance |
| Sept. 27, 1981 | Various | US | Military balance |
| Apr. 15, 1982 | Missile | US | Accuracy |
| July 12, 1987 | Tanks | US | New armor |

*Source*: Front page headlines of the *New York Times* from 1946–1991 searched for words "Soviet" (or "Russian") and one of the following: arms; weapons; missiles; rockets; tanks; nuclear. Articles focusing solely on Sputnik and space exploration were not counted.

field. Front page articles signal the public's interest in the subject, which the experts could help satisfy by supplying more information and a deeper analysis. Let us see if the textbooks on the Soviet economy rose to the challenge and exceeded this benchmark.

As shown in chapter 3, many textbooks fall below the newspaper benchmark, staying silent about the military sector or mentioning it in a perfunctory way (e.g., as an item of state budget expenditures). The minimal substantive level of attention consists of a few sentences noting an important aspect of the military sector. Thus, Kaser (1970, 191, 201) mentions in passing the economy's success in establishing a massive defense industry according to the rulers' wishes, and the buildup of heavy industry as a foundation for military parity with richer countries. Campbell (1966) has two sentences about the military program being the fastest growing GNP end-use category between 1928 and the early 1960s. Dyker (1985) mentions superior quality control in and effectiveness of the military industry, and Hutchings (1982) devotes three sentences to the subject.

These statements do not rise above our benchmark, and also pose a puzzle. If the military sector was a success, the fastest growing part of the economy, with distinct, effective management practices, then it is interesting and deserves extended exposition and analysis. Instead, the coverage of this important subject in a several-hundred-page book is limited to one sentence proclaiming its importance.

The next level up, perhaps exceeding the *New York Times* benchmark, is represented by Millar's (1981) remarks on the pervasiveness of military considerations in planning, the priority accorded to the production of military output, military considerations limiting reliance on foreign trade and contributing to autarky in natural resources, heavy military claims on output, and the status of the USSR as the second-ranking military power. These outstanding features are mentioned in the context of a discussion of other topics and are scattered throughout the text without connection to one another. In two terse paragraphs tucked in the end of a long chapter on technical change, Nove (1986, 171) explains why military hardware is more technically advanced than civilian goods by pointing to the attention military production receives from high officials, access to the best resources, having the state as the customer, and competition with the United States. Both authors hint at a good understanding of the workings of the military sector and its connections with the rest of the economy, which they neglect to flesh out and communicate effectively.

The latter task required devoting a chapter to the subject. Table 3.1 indicates eight textbooks with chapters dealing with some military economic matters, yet only six of those, addressed here, can be considered as treatments of the military sector.

Schwartz (1950 and 1954) notes the high technical level of Soviet weapons, discusses the progress of the nuclear program, and has several pages filled with Western estimates of the changing output of the military industry. Krylov's (1979) one-and-a-half-page chapter titled "Militarization of the Economy" precedes the chapters on all other sectors. It opens with the statement that the whole Soviet system is "more adaptable to solving the problems of war than those of peace." The importance of the military sector stems from the "enormous" attention paid to it by the top leaders. Military production enjoyed this status since the very beginning of the five-year plans, having doubled in three years of the Second Five-Year Plan. The author presents the usual argument that if Soviet military production is as large as that in the United States, the Soviet military burden must be 2–2.5 times greater than that in the United States. Much of the chapter details preparations for mobilization. It states that the peacetime economy is geared towards wartime requirements. This imposes a heavy burden on the economy, but should not be expected to change, given the Soviet military doctrine. Economic and defense planning are done jointly, with all economic decisions evaluated from a military point of view. Military needs dictate the specifications of civilian machinery, civilian construction projects are designed to accommodate potential military needs, and civilian enterprises incorporate military shops.

Gregory and Stuart (1981, 1986, 1990) state that postwar Soviet economic development cannot be understood without considering military expenditures, and compare the military might of the United States and the USSR in terms of selected physical indicators and of spending. The section discusses the difficulty of deriving estimates of the Soviet defense expenditures that would be comparable to those of the United States, using the literature that accumulated in the debate around the CIA calculations. It concludes that the Soviet Union at least matches the United States in terms of military might. It further states that the burden of defense has been "too large," with the military industry attracting the best labor and enjoying preferential access to scarce resources, while being responsible for one-third of machine building output (Gregory and Stuart, 1986, 364–69). Elsewhere in the text, a paragraph describes the institution of military representatives at the defense enterprises and states (erroneously) that the Ministry of Defense is in charge of planning and supplying these enterprises (10–11).

Notice also that the authors cited in this section address different aspects of the subject, with minimal overlap. Viewed in combination, they show that a great deal of important information was available, enough to fill a book chapter. But these findings still pale beside what comes next.

## 6.3.2 What an interested scholar found in Soviet publications

Amann and Cooper (1982) is a weighty interdisciplinary volume produced by a team of scholars centered on the University of Birmingham (United Kingdom). It explores the reasons that Soviet industrial technology lagged behind that of the West. This is a legitimate economics question, and indeed, several economists participated in the book. David Holloway, at the time a lecturer in politics at the University of Edinburgh, contributed a chapter titled "Innovation in the Defence Sector" (Holloway 1982), also a topic within the range of the economists' interests.

To demonstrate how much was known about the secret sector, I list the main topics addressed in the chapter, giving the number of pages devoted to each in parentheses, followed by a list of sources used.

The core of the chapter is its account of coordination and incentives in the military sector. It describes the structure of central policy-making bodies in military research and production in the 1930s and during the war, and traces their post-war evolution (2). This is followed by a discussion of how military industry was planned (3), its structure, its interpenetration with civilian industry, and the maintenance of reserve production capacity (4). Also described are the differences and the similarities between the military and civilian sectors, and the interactions between them, the meaning of priority of military industry, how much it sets the sector apart from the rest of the economy (3).

Turning to the chapter's narrow topic of weapons R&D, Holloway describes the categories of military R&D establishments, their subordination, their internal structure and functioning, the weapons acquisition process, the system of military representatives at the defense plants, and the relationship between customer and producer (13). Military and civilian research-production cycles are compared (3), and the weaknesses in the military innovation process are analyzed (6). There is also an inquiry into the impact of the science policy agencies on military R&D (4) and the role of secret police, prison design bureaus, and secrecy (6). An appendix on the estimates of military R&D expenditures is based exclusively on Western sources (10).

There is also a five-page account of the origin of the military sector. Industrialization is said to have included a "major, if not dominant, military element." It was realized that the defense industry could flourish only if supported by a strong industrial base, one that included metallurgy, fuel, machine tools, electrical, and chemical industries. Self-sufficiency in the strategic materials was pursued. New civilian plants were designed with military production in view. Special shops were set up in most of the civilian machinebuilding plants to smooth the way for arms production. The pattern of investment, the organization of production, and the choice of industrial location in the late 1930s were shaped by the needs of defense. The priority given to the defense sector, which shielded it from shortages, was built into the whole system of economic planning and administration. Soviet policy emphasized both quantity and quality of armaments. The organization of the military sector set up in the 1930s persisted through the succeeding decades.

The chapter refers to 80 Soviet sources. These include memoirs of Marshals, prominent scientists and weapons designers, and a former People's Commissar of Defense Industry; biographies of leading scientists; publications signed by the active duty top brass; histories of World War II and the Great Patriotic War (the Soviet-German portion of the former); a history of the wartime Soviet economy; various war memoirs and war histories; publications in the main party (*Pravda*) and the Ministry of Defense (*Krasnaia Zvezda*) newspapers; articles in half a dozen military-historical and military journals; entries in the Great Soviet and Military encyclopedias; textbooks on economics and the organization of the electronics and aircraft industries; collections of Marxist-Leninist and Communist party writings on military affairs; proceedings of Party Congresses; books on party ("political") work in the armed forces; publications on history of branches of science and technology (cybernetics; radio location); constitution and the compendium of laws; publications on military-economic issues; general economics books and periodicals; and books on the Academy of Sciences.

A special category of sources included English-language publications by defectors and emigres (Kravchenko, Checinski, Agursky), underground writings (*samizdat*), and Khrushchev's memoirs.

Western sources included the materials of the US Congress hearings, Rand Corp. reports, the work of A. Sutton described earlier in this chapter, and the writings of specialists on the Soviet military. Soviet references outnumbered the Western ones, and many of the latter, such as the remarkable, unpublished Cooper (1976) and the historical work of E. H. Carr, were in turn based on the Soviet sources.

Holloway's references by no means exhaust Soviet sources with information on the military sector. And there are whole additional categories that have not been tapped by the Sovietologists. Thus, Davies (1993) mentions Western journalists, diplomats, and engineers working in the USSR as reporting the military direction of the First Five-Year Plan, yet this evidence was not used in the writings on industrialization recounted in chapter 5. Thus, the Moscow correspondent of the *Christian Science Monitor* noted the military value of many industrialization projects. The new factories built in West Siberia and the Urals "possess definite potential war utility" and would be secure from the hostile air raids (Chamberlin 1935, 48). The experience of World War I showed "with what ease steel plants [like that in Magnitogorsk] may be utilized for the manufacture of shells and munitions," while the Cheliabinsk tractor plant "on short notice could be set to making tanks." He reported a Soviet engineer at a Sverdlovsk machinebuilding plant boasting of producing "everything that Krupp ever made, for war as well as for peace," and a foreign expert explaining that a fertilizer plant at Berezniki could become a producer of explosives in time of war. Industrial projects in the Ukraine would provide the Soviet Union with "a new, powerful, industrial-military base" (Chamberlin 1935, 53–55). In conclusion, "With all its shortcomings and failures in other fields, the first Five-Year Plan unmistakably and considerably increased the military preparedness of the Soviet Union" (Chamberlin 1935, 199).

Former Soviet citizens, arriving in the West *en masse* after 1945 and again in the 1970s, carried first-hand knowledge of the secret sector. The post-war displaced persons were interviewed under the massive Harvard Interview Project. A foundational Sovietological text based on these interviews mentions in passing reports covering the basic characteristics of the military sector, such as the top priority accorded to military orders, the heightened requirements for input quality, the special system of quality control for output, and the ample supplies (Berliner 1957, 127, 151–52, 204). However, these indications were not pursued further.

The information on the military sector carried by the 1970s Soviet immigrants also had no perceptible impact on Sovietological literature. The treatment of the mobilization system provides an example. To the degree that Sovietologists wrote about the military sector, they tended to focus on defense spending. The unique system of mobilization preparedness went unmentioned, except by the outsiders such as Krylov (1979) and the University of Birmingham scholars (broadly understood). An informative article on the subject by a former leading Soviet economist (Katsenelinboigen 1978) went unnoticed in the literature.

## 6.4 Conclusion

Secrecy surrounding the military sector was a mixed affair, strict along some dimensions and in some periods, and hole-ridden in others. Unsurprisingly, Western governments used their intelligence means to pry some of the secrets, and make public parts of what they found out. More surprisingly, the Soviets themselves revealed significant information about the part of their economy that they generally tried to hide. Emigres, defectors, underground writers, and returning foreigners supplemented these two streams of information.

Sovietologists did not point to secrecy as a barrier to studying the military sector, and expressed no surprise at or appreciation for colleagues who managed to do such work. There was enough information to support such work, and it was done, but mostly by the political scientists, think tank employees, and British scholars, not by the largest division of experts on the Soviet economy—American academics.

Secrecy did block some types of research. For example, it would have been impossible to estimate a production function of the military sector, an exercise that was done for other sectors. However, the bulk of publications on the Soviet economy were descriptive in nature (Ellman 2009, 5). The sources listed here were more than adequate for work of this kind. Sovietology neglected the military sector by choice, not out of necessity.

Holloway's (1982) references list shows that information on the military sector was highly dispersed. Collecting it involved combing "through large masses of publications," an effort Sovietologists of the 1970s did not see as being of intrinsic scholarly interest (Millar 1980, 324–25). One would presume that the higher cost of data collection should have been counterbalanced by the strategic value of the work, as well as the novelty of treating a successful, advanced sector in place of over-studied agriculture, but this did not turn out to be the case.

## Notes

1. Herman (1963, 6–7, 11); Hutchings (1987, 264); Holloway (1982, 340–41).
2. Dobrynin (1996, 492–93); Graham (2002, 55).
3. Hutchings (1987) has a detailed discussion of the matters kept secret at various times.
4. Herman (1963, 5–8); Simonov (1996, 42–43).
5. Hutchings (1987, 138–39); Kaser (1972, 47–50).
6. Herman (1963, 9); Kaser (1972, 56–60).
7. See Nove (1986, 363–66) and Hutchings (1987, 77–90 and elsewhere) for a more detailed discussion.
8. Kuratov (2004, 163) reports being also given the name and telephone number of a personnel officer.
9. E.g., Goskomstat 1988, 588. A number for "national income used for defense," published for a few years in the 1970s, was identical to the state budget defense allocation (Nove 1987, 177–78).
10. Hutchings (1987); Herman (1963, 11).
11. Byrnes (1962, 213–14); Engerman (2009, 179).
12. Byrnes (1964, 65); also see Engerman (2009, 171–72, 247).

13. Babakov (1987, 40, 45–46, 94–95); Schwartz (1954, 125).

14. Birman (1980a, 95–97); Hanson (2003, 188).

15. But, cf. Grossman (1959, 49): "We still know little about what makes the Soviet economy and its components tick."

16. Wiles (1964, 71); Grossman (1959, 38).

17. Campbell (1961, 140); Gerschenkron (1968, 532).

18. Campbell (1961, 140); Goskomstat (1988, 306).

19. Hunter (1972); Nove (1986, 363).

20. Hutchings (1987) does not say how the books were selected and how many were covered.

21. See Hutchings (1987, 28–29) on the importance of keeping a secret inconspicuous in order to safeguard it.

22. On the centrality of "high politics" for the field of Soviet political studies, see also Unger (1998, 19).

23. Other reviews were Birman (1980), Thornton (1980), and "The Soviet Economy" (1979).

24. Bailes (1979); Campbell (1979); McKay (1979); Solo (1978); "The Gap in Technology" (1978).

25. The other six reviews referred to here are: Beissinger (1984); Erickson (1983); Hutchings (1984); Ofer (1984); Parrott (1983); and Rabkin (1984).

26. Baldwin (1967). See also Middleton (1980).

# 7

# *Beating Soviet Swords into Sovietological Ploughshares*

SOVIETOLOGY WAS A sparsely populated, inbred field with few opportunities for independent critical examination of new findings, and so was likely to accumulate unreliable results in its knowledge base (chapter 1). But why the specific deformation described in chapters 3–5, presenting a pacific picture of a militarized economy? This chapter describes the influences that inclined scholars in the field to recast their subject in civilian terms. These include the general norms of academic economics, of which Sovietology was a tiny part; the professional specifics of dealing with the Soviet case; and political sensitivities associated with the subject of study.

## *7.1 The norms of the economics profession*

Scholars' individual interests are not necessarily aligned with the demands of producing new knowledge. In terms of professional advancement and recognition, it pays for a researcher in a marginal field to pursue problems and use techniques that are highly prized by the larger discipline. If the problems important to the larger discipline are also important to the field, and the techniques fit its subject, this serves to advance knowledge. If not, the understanding of the field's subject suffers. This argument is developed here for economics, Sovietology, and the latter's neglect of the military sector. However, it is general enough to apply to the research strategies of scholars in marginal fields of other disciplines, as will be demonstrated in chapter 8.

### 7.1.1 How scholars choose research topics

Sovietologists ignored the military sector by choice. In order to understand this particular choice, we need to establish how scientists, in general, make their professional decisions.

The traditional way of thinking about science is that it is an especially noble activity, with its practitioners interested solely in attaining the truth. The secrecy-as-the-only-constraint explanation of the failures of Sovietology, recounted in the beginning of chapter 6, is compatible with this view. The alternative, post-Kuhn (1962) approach is that scientists are no different from the rest of mortals, pursuing their individual interests while subject to their cognitive limitations and the social relations in which they are embedded.[1] The economics of science approach, used here, is congruent with this modern view. It postulates that scientists, in addition to satisfying their curiosity, pursue remuneration and recognition.[2]

This does not necessarily mean that graduate students choose their thesis topics, and professors their research projects, with the thought of maximizing income. The economic model is a device for predicting a subject's behavior, not for describing his thought processes. The latter are most likely governed by considerations of "things economists do and don't do," that is, the prevailing professional norms.

As is the case with informal norms more generally, these unwritten rules of professional conduct are absorbed by graduate students in the process of socialization in their discipline. Internalized norms are reinforced by the fact that, in academia, scientists are evaluated and accorded recognition and remuneration by other scientists who review publication submissions and grant applications and decide on hiring, tenure, and promotion. And some disciplines have been known to sanction violators of norms in more drastic ways (Freeman 1999, 209).

A rational scientist will choose a research topic or a technique of investigation that will enhance his standing with his colleagues. This creates a pressure for conformity, necessary for upholding scientific standards but potentially stifling innovation.[3] Several formal studies have shown that, under different simple assumptions, such behavior may either advance or retard the acquisition of new knowledge.[4]

At any given time, there exists within the profession an understanding of which topics and methods are hot, which ones are acceptable, and which ones are beyond the pale. To the degree that topics and methods are specific to particular fields, this understanding overlaps with the ranking of the fields discussed in section 1.3.3. "The things economists do" are a mix of technical topics dictated by the internal logic of development of the subject; fundamental, persistent problems of social organization; and the problems currently considered important for the society (such as unemployment in the 1930s and inflation and the energy crisis in the 1970s).[5]

There is also a broad consensus on the topics and methods unfit for economics investigation. As mentioned in the previous chapters, the list of taboos at one time included topics smacking of political science or sociology, and asking subjects about their motives. While the limits of what economists do expanded greatly since the 1960s, pushed by the pioneering work of "economic imperialists," they still remained binding at any particular moment in the course of a normal career.

The ascription of either prestige or stigma to certain topics or methods serves as a means of directing research efforts towards new, promising areas, or well-established ones with proven productivity. Like all such mechanisms, it is not precise, and may inefficiently distort behavior, as when too much effort is devoted to a fashionable topic, or a new method is used beyond its range of productive applicability. The neglect and civilianization of military aspects of the Soviet economy is one such distortion.

## 7.1.2  How Sovietology fit in

Sovietologists belonged to a small, low-prestige, precariously established field of economics (section 1.3). They were hired and promoted by their departmental colleagues working in the other fields of economics, and stood a higher chance of being noticed, understood, and treated favorably if their research could be seen as dealing with the issues of interest for, and using the methods current with, the larger discipline.

Finding a common language with general economics was not easy. The subject Sovietologists studied was very different from that with which their colleagues dealt, even apart from the hypertrophied military sector, which is our concern here. The defining feature of Soviet-type economies was the substitution of administrative distribution for market transactions among firms. Within the core of these economies, money, prices, cost, and profit did not exist, though there were objects that, misleadingly, bore those names. Yet the tools of economics had been developed, over a long period, to analyze the problems of markets. The demands placed on Sovietology illustrated the proposition that, unlike natural scientists who can concentrate on the problems they believe they can solve, social scientists are forced to attack socially important research problems for which they may be ill equipped (Kuhn 1962, 164).

In David Kreps' telling, the post–World War II adoption of mathematical techniques, often imported from price theory, unified the language of economics but led to a "contraction of topical concerns." "The newly dominant dialect of mathematical modeling lacked some topically important vocabulary; rather than speak in an unfashionable dialect, some things were just not discussed." This concerned, in particular, the study of economic institutions (Kreps 1997, 65–66). Development economics once entertained the idea that "a wholly different theory was needed to understand correctly the developing countries" (Fishlow 1991, 1728). It got "marginalized in the process" (Bardhan 1993, 129) and eventually came around to adopting the framework of mainstream economics. In what Kreps called "Romer's hourglass," the narrowing of topical concerns in economics was followed, since 1975, by its broadening, as new techniques were being developed and applied to new areas. Still, the lifetime of Sovietology coincided with the period when the hourglass was at its narrowest.

This left a Sovietologist with three choices. A researcher could focus on the specific, defining features of the planned economy and try to develop new economic tools and concepts adequate for analyzing them. This is a task with uncertain chances of success; it could take a long time, perhaps generations, to come to fruition if successful, and it is beyond the ability of most researchers. Alternatively, a Sovietologist could apply the not-quite-adequate models of the larger discipline to the unique features of the Soviet economy, perhaps a productive approach for some problems but one yielding misleading answers to others. The final alternative was to use existing methods to study features that were similar across market and planned economies, but not necessarily central to the latter.

Not surprisingly, the last two strategies predominated. An influential survey of the field confirmed this tendency: "The Soviet economy is treated as much less of an exotic type of economy today than it used to be, and much of what the fourth generation [of researchers] is discovering is the extent to which the Soviet economy exhibits traits common to all developed, industrialized economies" (Millar 1980, 326). This is mirror-imaging, a common error in intelligence analysis, in this case born not out of ignorance or lack of imagination but induced by the incentive structure of the profession.

To take examples from among the subjects already discussed (in 6.2.1), the de-emphasis and euphemization of secrecy was an attempt to treat the Soviet economy as just another industrialized economy. Any economy may suffer from "data availability" problems, but one with wartime levels of secrecy in peacetime must be an exotic type indeed. Similar motivation underlay the refusal to draw conclusions from the fact of secrecy, which would have been unscientific, smacking of Kremlinology or intelligence analysis, thus confirming one's departmental colleagues' worst suspicions.

In another example, the most fundamental (391-page) volume on Gorbachev's economics argues that the main dilemma of reform was "equality versus efficiency" (Hewett 1988). The USSR had succeeded in promoting income equality, yet had not done well in terms of efficiency, and improving the latter would require sacrificing some of the former (Hewett 1988, 2–3). The Soviet situation was thus portrayed as a neat mirror image of the Western one. The central place of this tradeoff in American society is the thesis of a classic book by Hewett's Brookings Institution colleague (Okun 1975).[6] It was certainly easier for a mainstream economist to accept than, say, the tradeoff between efficiency and the maintenance of "the permanent readiness for large-scale war and surge production capacity" (Blank 1995, 691).

Presenting the Soviet economy in familiar Western terms was not costless. For Hewett's argument to work, the USSR should have had something substantial on the equality side to trade for extra efficiency, and to show this, the book has to contradict the only empirical study on the subject in question. While Bergson (1984, 1065) writes of "a rather striking similarity in [wage] inequality" between the USSR and Western countries, Hewett (1988, 2) cites an "egalitarian wage system" as one of the Soviet achievements. In the end, there was not that much to trade for the badly needed efficiency gains, with income distribution in the USSR being "probably somewhat more equal than in most Western countries" (48). Even this is somewhat stronger than Bergson's (1984, 1073) conclusion that Soviet income inequality "is possibly as great or greater than that in Sweden, and not much less than that in some other Western countries such as Norway and the United Kingdom."

### 7.1.3 Military topics out of favor with economists

Military and economic matters are closely intertwined. In the late 1980s, the nations of the world were spending an average of 5% of their gross domestic product on defense (Sandler and Hartley 1995, 1). Some large and important countries spent an even greater (and at the time of crises much greater) share (tables 2.1 and 2.2). Historically, economic policies in many countries around the world have been designed to attain military power (section 5.5). In the twentieth century, the relative economic potential of the combatants decided the outcomes of two world wars.[7]

Despite all that, "since about 1800 economists have left the war out" (Wiles 1976, 491). In a book surveying the interaction of economics and national security, Goodwin (1991, 1–2) notes the disengagement of modern economics from the military problems.

Comparative systems textbooks surveyed in section 3.5.1 illustrate the lack of interest in the military-economy relationship. Most of the texts devote a section to the discussion of the objectives or desirable outcomes of economic activity by which different economic systems should be compared. With slight variation, these include consumer welfare, economic growth, static and dynamic efficiency, income equality, unemployment, and inflation. Some authors add economic freedoms, economic sovereignty, environmental protection, alienation, and worker and citizen sovereignty.[8] The majority of the textbooks, though written by the citizens of Great Powers, do not even mention military might or national power as a criterion of performance or a desirable outcome of economic activity.

In the minority of books that do mention national security, it is afforded all the space of one sentence. Thus, Gruchy (1977, 17) and Gregory and Stuart (1980, 360) present militarization and survival of the system as a Soviet (but not general) goal. In the most extensive treatment of the subject in my sample, Gregory and Stuart (1985, 33, 42) acknowledge military power as a performance criterion that is "important to some observers," but prefer a "continuation of national existence," which includes only defensive aspects of military power. Several other books mention national prestige and power or national security, but do not actually use these criteria to compare different economic systems.

Defense economics, a Cold War sibling of Sovietology also born at Rand, enjoyed a brief spike of interest in the United States in the early 1960s, but remained a small and obscure specialization within academia.[9] It lagged behind Sovietology in institutional development, not getting its first journal until 1990. There were only eight panels on defense economics at the AEA meetings between 1948 and 1972, as compared to 15 on socialist economics (table 1.2). And as table 1.1 shows, undergraduate enrollments, and thus demand for specialists to teach defense economics courses, were negligible around 1980.

Other fields of economics that could legitimately deal with military-economic matters also neglected them. Thus, of the 10 textbooks of

American economic history published between 1972 and 1990, not one has a chapter or a section on the Cold War economy, and only two have any discussion of military spending (Higgs 1994, 283).

Goodwin (1991, 1–2) suggests the low status of the military in the scholarly culture and the politicization of national security issues, which scared off middle-of-the-road researchers, as possible reasons for the avoidance of national security problems. Evidence on how other social sciences deal with military topics, presented in chapter 8, supports this suggestion.

Professional incentives inclined Sovietologists, as members of a peripheral field, to follow the priorities of their discipline, which were exclusively civilian.

There is positive evidence, independent from the neglect of the military sector documented in chapter 3, that the ranking of research areas in Sovietology broadly aligned with that in general economics. A 1973 survey asked American specialists in Soviet and East European economies about the desired allocation of research effort across 51 topics/specialties/subfields (Bahry and Millar 1975). For each topic, the number of responses saying it deserved less attention was subtracted from the number of those saying more work was needed, and the topics were ranked according to this difference.[10] The respondents were also asked about the specializations that they would encourage graduate students to enter, with the responses ranked in the same way.

Defense economics came in 32nd in terms of need for more effort, sharing this rank with the history of economic thought and the economics of property rights, the practically non-existent subfields of Sovietology, and far behind such a burning issue for a highly centralized economy as regional and local finance (ranked ninth). The rank of defense economics in terms of desirability for graduate students was even lower at 42nd.

Topics thought to deserve greater research effort included well established, important areas of research in general economics: money, credit, and banking (ranked fourth), fiscal policy (fifth), and monetary theory and policy (ninth). However, these subfields were of marginal importance for the Soviet economy, where, outside the consumer sector, money played a passive role (Ericson 2008). The authors of the survey themselves explain the high ranking of "human resource economics" (eighth) and "health, education, and welfare" (14th) by them being "currently fashionable" (Bahry and Millar 1975, 91). The ranking of topics was governed by their standing within the larger discipline, even if they were of little relevance for the subject at hand.

The already well-researched agriculture and foreign trade ranked substantially higher than defense, as could be expected based on the findings of chapter 3.

## 7.1.4 Dressing military buildup in fashionable civvies

In a highly militarized economy, much of what one touches turns out to be either motivated by or related to defense. A researcher looking for topics to write about, but uninterested in defense, keeps stumbling on it all the same, as in a Soviet joke about a retiring sewing machine factory worker who is asked what gift he would like to receive on the occasion, and answers, "a sewing machine." "Come on, in all your years at this factory, you must have pilfered enough parts to assemble a dozen of those!" "Yeah, I tried, but every time I got a machine gun." Some military-related subjects, such as industrialization and the objectives of planners, were just too large and important for the understanding of the Soviet economy to be simply ignored. These topics got civilianized, dressed up as high-prestige, non-defense issues of interest to general economics.

The experience of building a semi-autarkic economy with the largest stockpile of weapons in the world (industrialization) and maintaining its status as such (the objective of the planners) was irrelevant for the other countries after World War II and inspired no interest among economists. Repackaging it as a matter of economic growth provided a ground on which Sovietologists could address their departmental colleagues and hope to be understood. I should perhaps clarify that the study of Soviet growth was an important and instructive effort both from a general economics and a national interest point of view. What I address here is a rhetorical use of growth that obscured rather than clarified the Soviet economy.

The resurgence of interest in growth among Western governments and economists after World War II was motivated chiefly by internal concerns.[11] For one of the founders of growth theory, growth was to be a remedy for the economic depression that was widely expected to set in once the stimulus of war spending was removed (Domar 1957, 5).

High reported Soviet rates of growth in the 1930s and 1950s were "a subject of almost universal interest" (Bergson and Kuznets 1963, vi), as well as concern and sometimes panic in the West.[12] The influential, ostensibly general theory of stages of economic growth (Rostow 1961) aimed, to a large degree, to size up the challenge of Soviet growth. This made the subject of Western growth all the more important, as it could provide additional resources needed to parry the Soviet challenge it (Abramowitz 1989, xii).

In the 1950s, the period of the greatest Western concern about Soviet growth, linking industrialization and objectives of planners to growth would not accomplish much in terms of their civilianization. At that time, Soviet growth was widely recognized outside of Sovietology as "a version of the common growth experience, abnormally centered in heavy industry and military potential" (Rostow 1961, 104).[13] This recognition soon faded from the economics literature, as chapter 3 has shown, and growth has since become a generic civilian achievement.

The related topic of fostering growth in poor countries provided another plausible civilian costume for Soviet industrialization. The field of economic development was outgrowing and outranking Sovietology (section 1.3.3). In the words of an old Soviet hand, "Study of growth, balanced or unbalanced, development and dynamic equilibria are all the rage; and it is academically fashionable to conduct empirical studies of "underdevelopment" (Dobb 1967, 126). In the 1950s, the governments of poor countries, impressed by what was understood as successful Soviet industrialization, were inclined to emulate its strategy of high rate of investment, priority of heavy industry, and semi-autarkic development.[14]

Linking Soviet industrialization to economic development immediately overshadowed its origins and its goal of defense buildup, even if that was mentioned in passing, as in Dodge and Wilber (1970, 333). Using Soviet industrialization as a lesson for the developing countries, which were not interested in building the world's largest fleet of tanks and warplanes, reduced it to non-military, general economic issues. Thus, the problems faced by the Soviet economy in the 1920s "have a significance far beyond the period and location in which they took place. Many developing countries today face similar problems: the financing of capital accumulation, the strategy of economic growth in industrialization . . . politicians and economists first became conscious of such problems in the Soviet Union" (Nove 1969, 117, 120–121).

This substitution of what is interesting to one's broader discipline for what was important for the society under study can also be seen in Spulber (1964, 23): "The Soviet policy makers' goal of expanding the country's productive capacity, of raising its productivity, and of increasing sharply the level of per capita income recognized the need, now familiar in many underdeveloped areas, to cut through the vicious circle of low total income, low savings, and slow growth, and to secure . . . revolutionary technological changes." If Soviet industrialization was about economic development, then one could use later development theories to analyze it. Thus, the allocation of a very large share of investment to heavy industry under the First Five-Year Plan was a "historical example of unbalanced growth strategy advocated by economists such as Hirschman [in the 1950s]" (Wilber 1969, 76–86).

The same impulse to adapt to the priorities of the larger discipline dictated the assignment of Preobrazhenskii and Feldman as the authors of the industrialization strategy in the standard account. Both were looking for ways to accelerate economic growth, as understood in the West, and both were original economists whose work was interesting to other economists. Feldman's economic growth model was a pioneering effort in the field that became prominent in the 1950s and earned recognition from Western theorists.[15] The debate in which Preobrazhenskii and Feldman participated, while constrained by the obligatory use of the Marxist framework and loyalty to socialism, was freer than any in Soviet history (with the exception of the one in 1987–91), and incomparably more original (Domar 1957, 223–24). It was still inspiring Western economic theorists 60 years later.[16] By contrast, the military-economic writings of the 1920s did not contain anything of interest for economists, though the DNA of these writings matched that of industrialization most closely.

Other themes of interest to the general economic audience were also used to frame the discussion of industrialization, which was presented as a solution to the problem of underutilization of resources, a means of increasing employment in the same league as the New Deal and the Keynesian revolution (Swianiewicz 1965, 68–69). Erlich (1950) is said to have distorted Preobrazhenskii's thought by casting it in terms of Keynesianism, the *dernier cri* at the time (Millar 1976, 51–52). The existence of fluctuations was the chief concern of a study on Soviet planning and growth through 1932, motivated by the importance of business cycles for market economies, and the socialists' contention that planning would smooth out the cycles (Zaleski 1971, xx–xxi, 300–304).

## 7.2 Looking for the essence of socialism

Investigating the claims made on behalf of socialism leads us to another set of factors that inclined Sovietologists away from considering the military sector. The Soviets claimed that theirs was a socialist economy, the likes of which had never existed before, a realization of a grand theory with noble lineage stretching to German philosophy, classical political economy, and French socialist writings. Government policies were automatically christened "socialist," as reflected in the titles of economics volumes containing the phrases "socialist accumulation," "socialist planning," "socialist industrialization," "socialist location of production," "socialist division of labor," "socialist planning," and "socialist trade."[17] Inside their covers, each of these books endeavored, and never failed, to establish the unique socialist characteristics of their subject, those that set it apart from similar policies and processes elsewhere. The way to prove the socialist pedigree of a current or proposed policy was to connect it to the writings of the "classics," that is, Marx, Engels, Lenin, and, for a part of the period, Stalin.

Gerschenkron (1953, 26; 1971, 287–88) argues forcefully that the only role of Marxist ideology in Soviet economic policy was post-factum justification of whatever the rulers decreed. One does not need to fully agree with him in order to see that this was indeed an important role. Connecting current practice to the writings of classics, whether done by mercenary propagandists or true believers, was a universal requirement for those wishing to write on economics subjects.

Soviet claims of Marxist origins and socialist specifics served, along with secrecy, as yet another veil covering the militarization of society and the economy. In the words of a German journalist, "The propagandist skill which consistently describes things military as socialist, and creates out of them an ostensibly new conception of the world, deserves admiration." (Just 1936, 19). A veteran Sovietologist with socialist leanings acknowledged it after the veil was off: "Marxist ideology and the class struggle were mobilized" to legitimize the creation and maintenance of "the material basis of a great power" in a relatively poor country (Nove 1994, 347).[18]

The mission of Sovietologists was to discern and evaluate the specifics of the first ever socialist economy. It presented far more than professional interest, as the question of the relative merits of socialism and capitalism was a live political issue in the West. For this task, researchers had to rely, to a large degree, on the Soviet books described in the previous paragraphs, and on other official materials, offering ready-made ideological explanations for various strange practices of the socialist economy. Sovietologists' acceptance of these explanations amounted to the civilianization of their subject.

Soviet characterizations and explanations of their economy are as indispensable for its study as the official statistics. The issue here, as in chapters 4 and 5 and in section 7.3.3, is not the resort to Soviet formulations per se, but their uncritical use.

The priority of heavy industry, the cornerstone of every military industrialization from Brazil to Japan in the late nineteenth and early twentieth centuries, acquired its socialist pedigree by being linked to Marx's schemes of reproduction. This was a clear case of post-factum legitimation, as it was never mentioned in Stalin's speeches or party documents prior to or during the First Five-Year Plan, yet it was accepted by most Sovietologists.[19] In an especially vivid formulation, the development strategy underlying industrialization is said to have "been conceived before the emergence of the first socialist country" (Ofer 1976, 219). This apparently meant in the 1860s, when Marx was writing the second volume of *Das Kapital*.

Implicit in some treatments is the notion that there exists a well-defined, stable idea of socialism from which specific policies derive. Thus, in making his case for the superior level of equality in the USSR, as described in 7.1.2, Hewett (1988, 2) refers to "the essence of socialism" and "a socialist state, which values equality more than capitalist states." This approach practically predetermines its own conclusion and leaves no space for such facts as the "extraordinarily great" inequality in wage and salary distribution of the 1940s and its decline to the level of the capitalist United Kingdom by the mid-1970s (Bergson 1984, 1063, 1076).

The "socialist essentialism" approach left little space to study the pursuit of military might. To quote a landmark review of Soviet growth, "While the defense effort cannot be considered an integral part of a 'socialist growth strategy' in an abstract sense, it clearly has a very strong impact on the realities of the Soviet growth pattern" (Ofer 1987, 1788). This assessment suggests the existence of such a thing as an abstract "socialist growth strategy," from which actual policies derive, and in which the overgrown military sector does not belong.

The historical record shows the futility of this approach. Socialism was a malleable concept that could be "built" by redefining its meaning, as argued in section 5.7. The new society established by the mid-1930s "was in many respects radically different from the vague and optimistic notions about the socialist future held by Marx and Engels and . . . Lenin" (Davies 1989a, 984). The actual policies of the rulers, adopted for a variety of reasons, to a large degree came to constitute socialism.

Reinforcing socialist essentialism was the positive disposition towards socialism on the part of many (though of course not all) Sovietologists. Some of them were members of the Communist Party, or associated with various socialist movements, and professed adherence to socialist ideas, such as Jasny, Erlich, and Nove. Most scholars, especially in the United States, did not belong to a movement or share the ideology, their sympathy towards socialism taking a more diffuse form. They would be inspired by the proclaimed aspirations of the Soviet system, seeing it as a "noble experiment," or hope to discern novel ways of solving social problems. The most technically adept would develop theoretical schemes to improve socialism, allowing planners to mimic the flexibility of the market along the lines of Lange (1938).[20]

Nothing prevented a scholar sympathetic to socialism from noticing the militarization of the Soviet economy. To the contrary, if addressing the Soviet military sector was politically incorrect, as I argue below, it may have taken a Communist to break the taboo, by a kind of "Nixon going to China" logic. Indeed, scholars associated with the University of Birmingham in England were found in chapter 3 to produce a disproportionately large share of publications on the military sector, while their "investigations were often motivated by a socialist political agenda" (Hessler 2004, 3). Generally, however, the military sector was of little interest, because the promise of socialism lay elsewhere, in the realm of efficiency and equality.

A study of American writing about the USSR in the 1930s documented a similar orientation on the part of the proto-Sovietologists. They too were not interested in understanding the country on its own terms. "American intellectuals looked to the Soviet Union for solutions to what they saw as the problems of modern America—or, more broadly, the problems of modernity itself" (Engerman 2003, 155). The creation of industrial capacity to support a prolonged war against the rest of the world was not seen as one of those problems.

## 7.3   *Politics*

Politics are beside the point in a scholarly debate, where arguments should be evaluated on their merit, without regard to the author's motives. But once the weakness of an argument has been demonstrated, it is legitimate to inquire into what caused it, and there is no reason to keep scholars' political beliefs out of consideration.

## 7.3.1 The politics and economics of science

Politics can be incorporated into the model of scientists' behavior outlined in section 7.1.1 in several ways:

  (i) A scholar may strive to "serve the cause," in which case advancing the favored view through one's work may be seen as an argument of his utility function, like satisfying curiosity in the standard model of research.

 (ii) One's political convictions may dictate a particular picture of the world or predispose a scholar to see things a certain way, playing the same role as a scientific paradigm.

(iii) Academics seek fame and fortune by earning the approval of their colleagues. If a scholarly community happens to share widely a particular political view relevant to its field, one would do well to orient one's work towards that view, or at least to avoid challenging it.

In cases (i) and (ii), it is the researcher's personal convictions that result in faulty research, while in case (iii), one yields to the prevailing climate of opinion, regardless of one's own views. Political and professional motives become interwoven in (ii) and (iii). As argued in the preceding sections, Sovietologists followed the professional standards of the larger discipline in choosing civilian topics. But the aversion to military issues in economics, which underlay these standards, was likely political in origin.[21] Socialist essentialism, which obscured the role of the military sector, could be just a methodological approach prompted by Soviet self-descriptions, or a reflection of a scholar's political predilections.

As usual when questions of motivation arise, proving political influence in scholarly work is difficult. Case (i) is impossible to demonstrate conclusively, unless a scholar proclaims his own political goals. For example, in response to my article documenting the persistent upward bias in Western forecasts of Soviet growth in the 1970s and early 1980s (Kontorovich 2001), Holland Hunter wrote, "we were fighting for peace" (personal communication). Such testimony is valuable, but in a discipline where the dispassionate analysis is the publicly endorsed norm, it is very rare.

If confessions of one's own political motivation are credible, allegations of other people's biases are less so. The chill cast over Sovietologists' efforts by criticism of "some émigrés, conservatives, and 'cold warriors'"

(Hunter 1998, 1029) would only matter if it were shown to be effective, that is, if there were evidence that it changed the behavior of its targets.

## 7.3.2 Can Sovietologists inform us of each other's bias?

In private conversation, Sovietologists were not above linking their colleagues' professional positions and political views. Yet such allegations very rarely appeared in print, not surprising for a field that largely eschewed even polite professional debate (section 1.3.1). I can hardly think of any published charges of political bias among Sovietologists in the 1970s and 1980s. Moskowitz's charges of bias (section 1.4.2) were made against the CIA analysts, not fellow academics.

Reviewing the history of the field after its demise, veterans would describe political passions animating outside critics of Sovietological research, while maintaining that insiders "struggled to bring detachment, balance and perspective to their assessments and to be cautious in addressing the future."[22]

It was a bit livelier earlier on. The members of the newly formed guild of Soviet economic studies stressed the inferiority of the earlier authors, "many of them rabidly partisan," though they avoided mentioning the names and the substance of partisanship.[23] Even then, little was being said about contemporaries. Wiles (1956b, 145) catalogued the biases of his colleagues, meaning to show that they were quite limited and few. Some "still trail clouds of the 'thirties behind them: they neglect . . . the role of forced labor, . . . mince their words about collectivization," and find it hard to see any enemies on the Left. Those of Russian origin "cannot forget their Russian patriotism. But all this comes out much more in their personal opinions and conversation than in their work." He also discounted Communists and fellow travelers. Elsewhere he called a book by Maurice Dobb *stalinisant* (Wiles 1964, 70). Naum Jasny is said to have, in private conversation and correspondence, called his opponents "friends of Moscow" and "fellow travelers." Dobb called Jasny a "propagandist" and his book a product of the "Cold War" in a published review (Laird and Laird 1976, 120, 123). Notice that these scrapes involved two British economists and an outsider, with American professors apparently observing proper academic etiquette.

In his encyclopedic history of Soviet studies, Engerman (2009, ch. 11) describes how the disciplines of history and political science split along political lines in the 1970s and 1980s. "Politics and profession had become so intertwined that it was difficult to understand historical arguments apart from political aims" (Engerman 2009, 307). This academic "trench warfare" (304) was highly visible, as its participants wore their political commitments on their sleeves. Nothing even remotely approaching this condition can be found in the publications on the Soviet economy. The particular subjects over which political scientists and historians fought were of little professional import for economists. However, the political passions underlying the fight over Soviet history and politics concerned American, not Soviet society, and it is implausible that they were not shared by broader social science academic circles, including the Sovietologists. Yet they left few traces in the literature.

In addition to being rare, published charges of political bias in economic Sovietology, like those cited earlier, are usually not specific enough to be informative, lack substantiation, and may well reflect the biases of the accuser as readily as those of the accused. A celebrated article, "Bias and Blunders in American Studies on the USSR," cites the suggestions that the USSR may one day collapse as one example of bias (or maybe blunder?) in the study of Soviet politics (Dallin 1973, 560, 564). Out of 16 reviews of the Sutton trilogy (described in section 6.2.3) written by economists, 14 are generally positive, with some serious substantive criticism of the books' methods. Yet two reviews accuse Sutton of being "very much in the cold-war tradition of the fifties."[24]

While charges of bias among one's colleagues are entertaining to read, they cannot be taken at face value. At the most, they may indicate how heated the political atmosphere in a field is. The absence of politicized controversy, as observed in Sovietology in the later decades, may just signify the uniformity of political outlook, rather than the detached professionalism of all the contributors. One needs a firmer basis for evaluating the role of politics.

## 7.3.3 Proliferation of digressions

When Sovietologists touched on military matters, they frequently made detours into areas far outside their professional competence. These excursions provide evidence of political influences on research into the military sector. An economist writing about an armaments industry buildup is interested in finding out where resources are coming from, how they are extracted and how they are directed to their new use, how much output is gained, and at what cost for the society. Harrison (1998b) is a good example of this approach. Professionally, an economist has nothing to say about, and is not obligated to pronounce on, the motives for the buildup and the likely uses of its products. These topics are beyond his area of expertise, in the realms of international relations, history, or military doctrine. If they need to be mentioned, the standard academic procedure is to cite the authorities in the corresponding disciplines.

Sovietologists regularly broke these norms, supplying unsourced, unsupported digressions on contemporary international relations and remote history meant to justify or explain the military matter in question. These detours did not accompany detailed discussions of the military sector, which were, as has been shown, rare. Mostly, they followed short references to the defense industry, and sometimes exceeded those in length (e.g., Hunter 1983b, 176). In addition to being tangential to the substance of the argument, and exceeding the author's competence, or perhaps because of this, the digressions were likely to be poorly thought out, inconsistent, or factually wrong.

One finds the largest number of unsourced geopolitical/historical digressions in the writings on industrialization, where references to the buildup of the defense sector tend to cluster. Attention to the defense industry in the First Five-Year Plan is explained as a response to the threat of an imminent war, at least as perceived by the Soviets. Nove (1969, 227–28) was perplexed that the immediate external threat could not quite explain the stress the Second Five-Year Plan (1933–37) put on heavy industry despite the stated intent to improve consumer welfare. "The basic reasons for this shift are not so easy to determine. They obviously include, as a major factor, the rise of Hitler." However, he noted, similar revisions of targets in favor of heavy industry at the expense of consumers also occurred in 1930, before Hitler, and again under Khrushchev many years later. This argument was also used in reverse, when Erlich (1960, 168) supported his denial of the military motivation of industrialization by arguing that the international situation in 1927–28 did not indicate an imminent war.[25] No war tomorrow, no reason to build up armaments production.

The standard formulations refer to unspecified Soviet "insecurities," "unfriendly neighbors," "fear of foreign intervention," "capitalist encirclement," or "external threat."[26] The defeat of the Chinese Communists, the breaking off of diplomatic relations by Britain, and the assassination of the Soviet ambassador to Warsaw are the specific events named, jointly or separately, as the signs of a war threat in 1927, on the eve of the First Five-Year

Plan.[27] Zaleski (1971, 106–7) also cites the conflict around the Soviet-run Chinese Eastern Railroad in 1929 as such a sign.

Trouble with these excursions begins even before our economists encroach on the other disciplines' turf. Investment projects of the kind undertaken in the First Five-Year Plan take years to complete, and would have been of no use in case of an immediate war threat. Interestingly, the most authoritative source on industrialization took a very long view when justifying it. He recounted alleged offenses against Russia from the Middle Ages on, and elsewhere stated that it would take the completion of three Five-Year Plans to protect the country against any eventuality (Stalin 1931, 38–39; 1946).

The list of events associated with the war threat is strictly one-sided. It portrays the USSR as an inert target of assaults with no initiative of its own. There is no hint of the Soviet policies that preceded and may have precipitated the hostile acts, which makes them look like manifestations of unreasoned enmity. There is no discussion of why these events could reasonably be considered signs of imminent war, and no surprise at the fact that the radical and permanent change in the structure of the economy came in response to a series of passing incidents on different continents.

The source for this characterization of the international situation usually is not given, but easy to establish. It is a conflation of two strands of Soviet propaganda, which explains its one-sidedness. A war scare whipped up by Soviet propaganda in 1927 did precede the adoption of the First Five-Year Plan, though there have long been doubts, later confirmed by archival research, that the official fears of the plots of Poincare and Chamberlain were real.[28] The list of incidents said to signal the danger of war in 1927 is borrowed, without attribution, from the celebrated official party history written with Stalin's participation (*Istoriia* [1938] 1997, 268). The latter, however, offers hostile incidents not as a motive for military-sector buildup, but as evidence of capitalist attempts to obstruct the progress of industrialization.

Digressions use the term "encirclement" without explanation, as if it were an ideologically neutral term. Thus, Holzman (1957, 401) ascribes planners' concern for defense considerations in industrial location to the "well-known Soviet fear of 'encirclement.'" This conjures an image of a blockade or "virtual siege conditions" (Munting 1982, 87). However, "encirclement" is not a description of a strategic situation, but rather a term of official ideology and propaganda denoting the mere existence of capitalist countries, which by itself, irrespective of actual behavior, presented a threat to the USSR. This threat could be eliminated only by getting rid of its source, the social system of the surrounding countries, through a series of revolutions (*Istoriia* [1938] 1997, 261–62). Like the encirclement of Germany by Jew-inspired enemies bent on its destruction, capitalist encirclement of the USSR was a "just-so story."[29] Scrupulous economists, appropriately skeptical of sources such as official Soviet statistics, channel raw propaganda when they touch on things military.

One long-term reason for the creation of the military sector in 1928–1932 advanced in the digressions is the preparation for war with Germany.[30] The line between a post-factum justification (Hitler's attack) and a discussion of the original motivations for the policy is blurred. The previous group of explanations was inspired by the Soviet propaganda of the time, and followed the common fallacy that if the war scare of 1927 preceded the adoption of defense-oriented policy, the former must have caused the latter. The "1941 justifies the economic strategy of 1927" reasoning comes close to explaining earlier events by later ones. In a more chronologically consistent fashion, Hunter (1998, 1027) names the publication of *Mein Kampf* in 1925–1926 as the reason for Soviet military buildup. Explaining the military side of the First Five-Year Plan by Nazi threat was also common among Soviet historians (Stone 2000, 114). But then again it was their job to justify government policies in whatever way possible.

There is no connection between Germany, let alone Hitler, and the First Five-Year Plan in contemporary sources. Two major speeches of the People's Commissar of Defense on the eve of the First Five-Year Plan, in their obligatory surveys of capitalist war preparations, mention a dozen countries, including Poland and Romania, but not Germany, and neither does a later military economy book.[31] And for a good reason: "Germany, despite the Russian aid to the Reichswehr, was still the military vacuum of Europe" (Gerschenkron 1962b, 147). Archival documents show "that the Soviet concern in the mid- to late 1920s was always with a war against Poland and Romania." An "enormous increase" in aircraft and tanks was planned by the USSR before Hitler came to power.[32]

Memory of the past invasions and defeats suffered by Russia is another long-term factor cited as the explanation of both industrialization and the level of the post-war defense burden.[33] Though usually unsourced, such digressions follow Stalin's famous justification of industrialization by presenting Russian history from the thirteenth century on as a continuous string of humiliations (Stalin 1931, 38–39). Singling out policies concerning the military sector as being driven by the traumas of the past, while policies in other sectors are analyzed in terms of rational decisionmaking based on the present conditions and the objectives for the future, is methodologically dubious.

The one-sided history of assaults on Russia cited in these excursions leaves the reader wondering how it had become one of the largest empires in the world.[34] Specific historical examples contain errors, exaggerations, and simplifications which could have easily been avoided by checking any standard reference, but then the list of alleged assaults on Russia would have been shorter, and the "historical trauma" origin of the military buildup less persuasive. Taking the list of offenses cited by Temin (1991, 588–89), the Russo-Japanese war was a colonial adventure on both sides, not an attack on Russia. "Invasion from the west in the early 1920s," which can only refer to the war with Poland in 1920, was not "barely repulsed," but saw Soviet forces almost reach Warsaw, while aspiring to go even further. And the Russian Civil War is, by definition, a bad example of external threat. Turning now to the list of Layard and Parker (1996, 47, 48), the situation in 1914 was too tangled for a one-sentence summary, but it was Russia who first breached German and Austro-Hungarian borders. Allied intervention in 1919 was limited to a few distant ports and involved minuscule military action, undermining the statement that "Russia was attacked in 1914, 1919, and 1941."[35]

A methodological note is in order. Since the opening of Soviet archives, the defensive nature of the Soviet military buildup was sometimes supported by the failure to locate the "grand Soviet plan of aggression."[36] For Sovietologists, well aware of the futility of long-term comprehensive planning, this is a strange argument to make. The largest empire in the world was once said to have been acquired in a fit of absentmindedness, that is, without a plan. Hitler had no plan for world conquest, or even much of a plan for what to do with Poland in 1939 (Overy 2010, 112–13). The "no plans for future conquests" argument would have been stronger if it could be shown that, say, the 1939–40 war with Finland or the 1979 invasion of Afghanistan had been planned far in advance.

In the Soviet political system, the intent that mattered in questions of war and peace was that of one man, or, in different periods, very few men, and it was not necessarily documented or shared with anyone. Consider Stalin's decision in 1935 to build an ocean-going navy—not an obvious use of resources for a poor, overstretched continental power facing threats on its land borders. What was the plan for the eventual use of these battleships and cruisers? The long-term minister of the navy, in charge of the buildup, did not know the answer. According to him, "The naval doctrine was only in Stalin's head" (Rohwer and Monakov 2001, 118). True, the Soviet war plans that have become known all started with the country being attacked, going on a counteroffensive, and waging war on the enemy territory. But "the goal of operations was to establish Soviet regimes in the defeated countries" (Samuelson 2000a, 53).

## 7.3.4 Interpretation: exculpatory incantations

A digression in the course of a scholarly presentation that serves no professional purpose may just reflect the author's lack of discipline. One would expect the content of such detours to vary across authors. If the geopolitical excursions were randomly selected from the record unfiltered by Soviet propaganda, then the list would have included some of the following: the invasions of Poland and Finland in 1939 and of the Baltic countries and Romania in 1940; the subjugation of Eastern Europe in 1945–48, of Hungary in 1956, and Czechoslovakia in 1968; shuttling Cuban troops to Angola; and supplying weapons to Somalis fighting Ethiopians and then to Ethiopians fighting Somalis. Such a list would have been on firmer factual ground than those cited in the previous section, though, in my opinion, equally out of place in an economics text. But it did not appear in Sovietological literature, to the best of my knowledge.

Connecting the buildup of the military industry to immediate external threats, or to Hitler's attack 14 years later, or to the memory of defeats in the distant past all convey the same message, that Soviet policy was purely, if not always rationally, defensive. There is no professional reason to do this, as armaments production capacity is equally compatible with either defensive or offensive intent. The two motives are in any case difficult to disentangle, as the saying about the best defense suggests. Even Hitler's military buildup was in part motivated by the need to defend against France and Poland (Tooze 2006, 57). It would seem prudent for an economist to withhold judgment on the subject, as Gregory and Stuart (1986, 363) do when describing the postwar Soviet military buildup.

Arming for defensive purposes is universally seen as justified. Painting the USSR's motives as exclusively defensive made its military might look less threatening, allayed suspicions of geopolitical rivals, and therefore, arguably, promoted the cause of peace.[37] Economists who followed references to the military sector by digressions into its defensive nature were producing excuses for it. I believe they did so to excuse themselves.

Researchers may be expected to conform to widely held political views to avoid sanctions, ranging from unfriendly questioning at an academic workshop to negative journal referee reports and worse. Touching on the topic of the military sector brought a Sovietologist uncomfortably close to one of the hottest issues of Western politics, that of Soviet military posture and intentions (Nove 1987, 175–79). There were two ways of dealing with this danger, avoidance and insurance. A risk-averse academic would keep clear of the sensitive subject and write about agriculture instead. In this way, political attitudes (not necessarily those of the author) change scholarly output without leaving any fingerprints, a gap in published research being difficult to interpret.

Alternatively, a researcher approaching a politically touchy subject may try to insure against possible sanctions by reciting an exculpatory incantation. A simple example is a digression on the author's political views in the course of a scholarly presentation. Thus, Jasny, while defending the reliability of his research findings that are unflattering to the Soviets, avers, "I certainly am not an enemy of socialism, state ownership of the means of production, planning, socialized medicine, and many other things" (Laird and Laird 1976, 127). I remember how Murray Feshbach started his talk about serious Soviet demographic problems at the University of Pennsylvania planning workshop in the early 1980s by assuring the audience of his liberal political views. These are but learned variants of the well known "some of my best friends are . . ." rhetorical strategy. Geopolitical digressions trailing the mention of the military sector were similar exculpating incantations designed to neutralize the politically hot issue.

The digressions referred to in the previous section have a standardized, perfunctory feel about them, and are carelessly put together. This, and the indirect way in which they excuse the military sector, suggests that the authors are buying insurance against disapproval of others, rather than voicing their own strong convictions. This is likely an example of case (iii) defined in section 7.3.1, rather than of case (i). Direct declarations that Soviet motives are purely peaceful are extremely rare in Sovietological literature, but consider the following one-word digression: "In 1940, the USSR . . . took the Baltic Republics as a (defensive) *place d'armes*" (Hunter and Szyrmer 1992, 140).

Exculpatory incantations result from the same causes as the avoidance of military sector. Unlike the latter, the incantations are visible and, if my reasoning here is correct, their content indicates the direction in which political opinion pushes the researchers. They offer evidence of a political climate that helps explain the relative neglect of the defense economy and its civilianization in the literature. In the minds of academics, dwelling on the dimensions of the Soviet military sector carried the risk of being considered a Cold Warrior, hostile to the first socialist country and not being able to impartially analyze its development. The reviewers' charges against A. Sutton, cited in section 7.3.2, illustrate this risk. Exculpatory incantations certified the author as a non–Cold Warrior.

## 7.4  Persistence of civilianization and Soviet economic history

While Sovietology's avoidance of the military sector is documented in chapter 3 only through 1991, the analysis of civilianization in chapters 4 and 5, and of exculpatory incantations in section 7.3.3 draws on both pre- and post-1991 texts. It shows that the standard, civilianized views of the objectives of planners and the nature of the First Five-Year Plan, as well as the war scare/historical trauma excuses for the powerful military industry remain accepted, if not dominant, well after the USSR's demise.

The civilian slant of Sovietology resulted from the need for a peripheral field to follow norms of the larger discipline, the attractions of socialism, and the pressure of prevailing political attitudes, in disregard of substantial contrary evidence. Weeding out false findings, the non-experimental field's equivalent of replication, was Sovietology's weak suit, as argued in section 1.3.2. The result was a fragmented literature containing both a civilianized picture of the Soviet economy, and on the other hand, a scattering of one-sentence remarks about the military sector's great importance, as well as a few more substantial investigations by the outsiders. Over time, the civilianized version acquired the authority and the inertia of the accepted interpretation, which insulate it from additional contradictory arguments and evidence.

A quarter of a century ago, Temin (1991, 573) noted that his military buildup explanation of industrialization, "although not a new view, . . . has dropped out of recent discussions of the Soviet economy and needs reemphasis." While historians of Germany reacted to the part of Temin's article dealing with that country, there was no response in print to the Soviet part, and thus no reemphasis. Massive new evidence became available after 1991, from intimations by the former Soviet officials and experts about the hypertrophied size of the military sector (sections 2.2.1 and 2.5) to archival materials on its genesis, development, and functioning. Yet this new information did not help the field overcome fragmentation, and in fact only deepened it.

The persistence of disproved or unproven claims in the literature is a common occurrence. In economics, there is a documented case of the long survival of the empirically unsupported and unused theory of the kinked oligopoly demand curve (Stigler 1978). In medicine, when the previously highly cited findings are overturned by subsequent experiments, researchers often continue relying on the contradicted results and do not even mention the contradicting evidence. "One wonders if any contradicted associations may ever be entirely abandoned" (Tatsioni et al. 2007, 2525). If this is the case in such a densely populated, experimental discipline as medicine, the long survival of contradicted claims should not be a surprise in the now practically deserted field of Soviet economic studies, where decisive refutation is harder to come by.

The persistence of civilianized Soviet economic history is not, however, solely a matter of intellectual inertia. The continued political touchiness of the subject of the defense industry is attested in an excellent study of its place in the First Five-Year Plan and the broader social processes of 1926–1933 (Stone 2000). The book bears the subtitle "The Militarization of the Soviet Union" and concludes, using abundant archival sources, that "No state in Europe would become as militarized in this sense [eliminating the distinction between civilian and military spheres] as Stalin's Soviet Union" (Stone 2000, 18). Yet the reader is forewarned: "Describing this process as militarization requires some caution. *Militarism* as a term can be as pejorative and vague as *imperialism*; additionally, it smacks of waging the cold war all over again" (Stone 2000, 7). Caution is needed in handling the evidence, but if it indicates militarism, what is the extra caution for? "Waging the cold war" is a political accusation, not a substantive criticism. The events described in the book occurred 20 years before the Cold War and 70 years before the time of publication, which itself happened 10 years after the end of the Cold War. The author in effect concedes that discussing the dimensions of the Soviet military may displease his readers, and asks to be heard out to the end. Apparently the impact of old political passions recedes slowly. According to Schama (1989, p. xv), historians have been underplaying the role of violence in the French Revolution two centuries after the event for fear of appearing counter-revolutionaries.

# *Notes*

1. Kitcher (1993, ch. 1) and Hands (1997, S107–S112) discuss changing views of science.
2. Stigler (1983, 530); Diamond (1996, 8); Stephan (1996, 1202–3).
3. Polanyi (1962); Goldman and Shaked (1991, 52–53); Brock and Durlauf (1999); Wade (2009).
4. Goldman and Shaked (1991); Kitcher (1993, ch. 8); Brock and Durlauf (1999).
5. See discussion in Stigler (1983, 532–35).
6. See the Brookings Institution celebration of the re-issue of the book on its 40th anniversary:     http://www.brookings.edu/events/2015/05/04-okun-equality-efficiency-tradeoff, visited March 18, 2016.
7. Broadberry and Harrison (2005, 1); Harrison (1998a, 2).
8. E.g., Grossman (1974); Köhler (1989).
9. Wolf (1996, 57); Leonard (1991).
10. The number of responses for each topic ranged from 22 to 47.
11. Arndt (1978, chs. 4 and 5); Abramowitz (1989, 3).
12. Wiles (1953); Congress for Cultural Freedom (1956); Hardt et al. (1961).
13. Also Crosland (1956); Kuznets (1963, 371).
14. Montias (1961); Dobb (1966, 2); World Bank (1991, 34).
15. Domar (1957); Bardhan (1993, 130).
16. Sah and Stiglitz (1984; 1987).
17. Notkin (1984), Kurskii (1945), and Sorokin (1946) can serve as examples.
18. But see his earlier reasoning quoted in section 5.7.
19. See references in sections 5.1 and 5.3.
20. This paragraph is based on my personal recollections and a personal communication from Richard Ericson.
21. Section 7.1.3. More on the reasons for social science aversion to things military in sections 8.2 and 8.3.
22. Schroeder (1995, 218). Also Hunter (1998).
23. Campbell (1961, 130). Also Gerschenkron (1968, 525).
24. Freeman (1972); also Sherman (1973).
25. Ulam (1974) made similar arguments, according to Stone (2000, 110), who shows them to be unconvincing.
26. Åslund (2002, 31); Boettke (1990, 168); Grossman (1974, 94); Offer (1987, 877); Hunter (1983b, 176); Harrison (1985, 46–47); Munting (1982, 74, 87); Temin (1991, 587–88); Davies (2010, 155).
27. Gerschenkron (1962b, 147); Gregory and Stuart (1986, 78); Hunter (1983b, 176); Munting (1982, 74); Davies (1989b, 462); Temin (1991, 588).
28. Doubters: Nove (1969, 121); Zaleski (1971, 106–7); and Davies (1989b, 462); and among historians, von Laue (1964, 209). Archival research: Samuelson (2000b, 35–36); Stone (2000, 44–49).

29. Hutton (1939, 533); Tooze (2006, 664).

30. Åslund (2002, 31); Nove (1969, 188); and Munting (1982, 87); with Erlich (1960, 168–69) disagreeing.

31. Voroshilov (1927a and 1927b); Ventsov (1931).

32. Stone (2000, 22); Samuelson (2000b, 162–63).

33. Temin (1991, 588); Barner-Barry and Hody (1995, 156–57); Layard and Parker (1996, 47–48).

34. See Odom (1998, 2) on the myth of Russia as a perennial victim of aggression.

35. On war with Poland and intervention, see Pipes (1995, 177–82, 8).

36. Hanson (2003, 31). Also a more cautious statement by Barber and Harrison (2000, 3–4).

37. As suggested by one of my former Soviet studies colleagues.

# 8

# *Civilianization Elsewhere*

TWO OF THE factors that led Sovietologists to avoid the military sector—the focus on socialism and the political climate of the field—were specific to the country being studied. The third, the aversion of the discipline of economics to things military, which Sovietology, its peripheral field, emulated, turns out to be a part of a more general pattern in the social sciences. Economists writing about the German economy in the 1930s largely ignored the military buildup, or civilianized it into an employment policy. Archeologists and anthropologists civilianized evidence of warfare in pre-literate societies, while academic historians marginalized their colleagues specializing in military history. Civilianizing tendencies in the study of other countries and in other disciplines support some of my arguments about Sovietology, and at the same time make its case all the more instructive.

## *8.1  Writings on the German economy in the 1930s*

My analysis of Sovietology invites comparison with economists' treatment of another great peacetime military buildup of the twentieth century, that of Hitler's Germany. There was no specialized field of Germanology comparable to Sovietology within the much smaller British and American academic economics of the 1930s. Still, Germany attracted significant attention by being the second largest economy in the world.[1] Unlike with Sovietology in the late 1940s, there was no need to teach economists the German language in order to create qualified researchers. Several hundred trained economists emigrated from

Germany and Austria in the 1930s, and 131 of them obtained university positions in their new countries of residence. Their professional caliber was high, with several dozen making lasting contributions to the discipline (Scherer 2000, 616, 618–22). These scholars possessed special interest and expertise in the economy of their country of origin, as well as the motivation to alert the world to the dangerous policies of the regime that made them flee their homes. The newcomers needed publications to establish themselves, and German economy was a natural topic for them to write about. Indeed, most articles on the German economy in 1934–43 appear to be written by authors of German origin (tables 8.1 and 8.2).

Table 8.1. Economics articles on German economy, 1934–1939.

| Year | All articles | Articles with war-related titles | Some discussion of rearmament | Rearmament mentioned in passing | No reference to rearmament |
| --- | --- | --- | --- | --- | --- |
| 1934 | 9 | o | o | Katona (1) | Baerwald; Bergstraesser; Drescher: Ham; Kessler; Nathan; O.L.L.; Wunderlich (8) |
| 1935 | 3 | o | o | Hegemann (1) | Brandt; Dessauer (2) |
| 1936 | 5 | o | o | Katona (1) | Selke; Ham; Kessler; Kraemer (4) |
| 1937 | 7 | o | Grebler a; Grebler b (2) | o | Solmssen; Brandt a; Brandt b; Schranz; Wehner (5) |
| 1938 | 8 | Wunderlich (1) | Balogh (1) | Bresciani; Feiler; Mittelman; Vollweiler (4) | Kessler; Egle (2) |
| 1939 | 6 | o | Hutton; Balogh; Cole (3) | Sweezy (1) | Galbraith; Spiegel (2) |
| Total | 38 | 1 | 6 | 8 | 23 |

*Sources*: See appendix 8.1.

**Table 8.2. Economics articles on German economy, 1940–1943.**

| Year | All articles | Articles with war-related titles | Some discussion of rearmament | Rearmament mentioned in passing | No reference to rearmament |
|---|---|---|---|---|---|
| 1940 | 7 | Spiegel; Singer; Hillmann (3) | Sweezy (1) | Guillebaud; Humber (2) | Ellis (1) |
| 1941 | 7 | Singer a, b, c, d; Strauss (5) | Domeratzky (1) | Einzig (1) | 0 |
| 1942 | 8 | Block; Singer a, b, c; Nathan (5) | Grunfeld (1) | Brady (1) | Doblin (1) |
| 1943 | 11 | Schweitzer; Singer a, b, c, d (5) | Block; Livchen; Ludmer; Merlin (4) | Brady; Rostas (2) | 0 |
| Total | 33 | 18 | 7 | 6 | 2 |

*Sources*: See appendix 8.1.

## 8.1.1 Hitler's military economy

Economists' relative neglect of the 1930s militarization would only matter if the overlooked phenomenon was worth noticing. Yet the extent of the Nazi military-economic buildup has been a subject of controversy after the war.[2] One school of thought, originating with the US Strategic Bombing Survey in 1945, held pre-war economic mobilization to be incomplete and half-hearted. The adherents of this school, dubbed "revisionists" by Lorell (1976, 12), maintained that in 1933–34, the main economic goal of the dictatorship was to reduce unemployment and spur economic recovery. Rearmament became the priority only afterwards.[3] In the years leading up to the war, the mobilization of resources for the military was moderated by a concern for domestic consumers and other non-military considerations. The rearmament program was "shallow," stressing the current production of weapons, but not the creation of capacities for a "total war."[4] The strategy of *Blitzkrieg* was developed specifically to accommodate the under-mobilized economy unable to support protracted fighting.

With much archival research, new data sources put into use, and more rigorous reasoning, the revisionist views have now been superseded.

Historians see no sharp distinction between the early employment-oriented policy and the later rearmament phase (Scherner 2013, 497). Rearmament was Hitler's top priority from the first days of his rule, initially fueled by syphoning off a third of the funds the previous government budgeted for work creation. In mid-1933, a 35-billion-Reichsmark (RM), eight-year program of rearmament was approved. This compares to the total national income that year of 43 billion RM, and implies annual spending an order of magnitude higher than that of the Weimar Republic. While the civilian work creation measures of 1933 were the subject of a noisy propaganda campaign, and rearmament decisions were kept secret, the military spending package greatly exceeded anything intended for the jobs program. Military spending growth outpaced economic recovery, with the defense burden in current prices doubling or quadrupling in the second year of Nazi rule, and reaching 8%–10% in the third (table 2.3).[5] This is an unusually, perhaps unprecedentedly rapid increase for a country at peace.[6]

As in the USSR, military-economic efforts far exceeded the scope of military expenditures conventionally defined. Massive investment went into the development of domestic substitutes for imported raw materials: synthetic oil, synthetic rubber, and steel made out of low-grade domestic iron ore. Similarly to Stalin's canals, construction of the highway system was justified in terms of its purported strategic value, whether the military asked for it or not.[7]

No evidence has been found to support the hypothesis that *Blitzkrieg* was a deliberate strategy to compensate for the economy being less than fully committed to war. New data on investment suggest that, in addition to equipping their armed forces, the Nazis pursued rearmament "in depth," creating production capacities necessary for waging a prolonged war.[8] In sum, "the Third Reich shifted more resources in peacetime into military uses than any other capitalist regime in history" (Tooze 2006, 660). It is this latest view of the German economy of the 1930s that serves here as a baseline for evaluating the economists' handling of the rearmament.

## 8.1.2  Rearmament in the economics journals of the time

In 1934–43, 71 articles on the German economy appeared in English-language economics journals.[9] In tables 8.1 and 8.2, they are classified into four groups: those with military terms in the title; those with a civilian title but a discussion of the rearmament of some length; those mentioning rearmament in passing; and those without any mention of rearmament.

Economists' interest in a particular topic may be measured by the number of articles devoted to it. Of the 38 articles on German economy from 1934 to 1939, only one, Wunderlich (1938), had the cautious term "defense economy" in its title (table 8.1). Assuming that the main subject of an article is indicated in its title, the greatest peacetime rearmament effort received as much attention as did the German tourism industry (Selke 1936).

The distribution of titles shows that, in the 1930s, economists were primarily interested in labor and unemployment, which accounted for nine articles. Five more pieces dealt with the closely related subject of recovery from the Great Depression. The second largest group of articles, eight, was about agriculture.[10] Out of six articles on the German economy published as late as 1939, two concerned hereditary land (Galbraith 1939) and tenancy problems and policies (Spiegel 1939). This curiously parallels the situation in Sovietology, which devoted more articles and book chapters to agriculture than to any other sector. Other titles included general surveys and studies of banking, cartels, and international trade.

Two-thirds of the articles published in 1934–39 lacked any mention of the military buildup, arguably the main economic phenomenon of the time. In 1934–36, only three out of 17 articles on the German economy mentioned rearmament, and that in passing (table 8.1). A passing reference, as used here, consists of a few sentences scattered through the article, unconnected to one another and lacking background and elaboration. Thus, an investigation of the causes of economic recovery since 1932 mentioned that the world press attributed it to rearmament efforts but that the evidence for this was insufficient (Katona 1934, 32). An article on regional planning mentioned the preference given to the import of war material over that of foodstuffs, and the military purpose of the highway construction program (Hegemann 1935). Another investigation of the recovery stated several times that it was propelled by both public works projects and rearmament (Katona 1935).

The six articles with more than just a passing mention of rearmament all appeared in 1937–39. They addressed military issues in the context of a more conventional economic topic, such as a survey of the job creation policy (Grebler 1939 a and b), an analysis of the sources of Hitler's success in reducing unemployment (Cole 1939; Balogh 1938), or an inquiry into stability of German economy (Balogh 1939; Hutton 1939).

An earlier study addressing a somewhat different question also found economists of the 1930s interested in recovery and unemployment, but not in the military buildup. Lorell (1976) investigated the claim that pre-war writers allegedly exaggerated the extent of militarization.[11] While my goal is to see how many of those writing about the German economy said anything about rearmament, Lorell looked into what the authors who did write about the rearmament had to say. His sample of the literature is broader than mine, including business, foreign policy, and general interest publications.

Taking the revisionist, minimalist view of rearmament as his baseline, Lorell (1976, viii) found no exaggeration of the extent of military buildup by the pre-war writers. He noted that the economists' interests lay elsewhere, in recovery from the Great Depression and reduction of unemployment. "Many experts were understandably more impressed with the positive achievements of National Socialism, particularly with the rapid recovery of German industrial output and the liquidation of unemployment, than with the signals that economic war preparations were being undertaken." "Pre-war experts were primarily concerned with two issues: the nature of the German economic recovery and the economic stability of the Nazi regime." "Calculating the actual level of German Government expenditures on rearmament was obviously a problem of considerable import for pre-war economists. This problem, however, was most often dealt with in the context of the nature of the overall German economic recovery" (Lorell 1976, vii, 67).

## 8.1.3 Why economists neglected rearmament

As in the Soviet case, the neglect of the German military buildup cannot be attributed to a lack of information. While the first steps of rearmament were kept secret, already in 1934 the published state budget revealed an extraordinary increase in military expenditures, and foreign observers were becoming aware of what was afoot (Tooze 2006, 59, 79–80). Hitler publicly declared Germany's rearmament on March 16, 1935, with the abrogation of the Versailles Treaty. Since that moment, concealment gave way to official bluffing, with foreign politicians and journalists shown staged, exaggerated displays of new weapons (Whaley 1984, 50, 56). Germans publicly discussed the economics of the military buildup. "The intensive occupation with the economic aspects of war preparation and warfare which started in Germany with the advent of the Hitler regime resulted in a stupendous volume of literary output." Research institutes and university chairs for war economics were established and treatises on the subject were published (Spiegel 1940, 713).

References to rearmament in the articles on civilian topics show that economists were aware of the phenomenon and its economic consequences. Thus, a survey of job creation policies noted that rearmament aborted the market-driven economic recovery, distorted foreign trade by favoring the importation of specific commodities, and changed the structure of employment by sector. The article also supplied quantitative estimates of the impact of rearmament on the credit market, all the while declining to discuss "the general importance of armaments."[12] Several civilian-titled articles each contained enough material for an article on military buildup, though this is not how the authors chose to frame their work.[13] There were significantly more military references in the articles in table 8.1 than one could find in a comparable sample of Sovietological writings.

The distribution of article titles changed after 1939. Out of 33 articles on the German economy published in 1940–43, 18 bore titles with the words "war," "war economy," and similar terms (table 8.2). These numbers overstate the economics profession's turn towards the problems of war economy, as 11 of the war-titled articles were penned by just one author, H. W. Singer. The number of articles that did not mention military matters at all dwindled. No new data sources appeared after 1939 to support all this writing on war economy. Rather, international developments made economists look differently on the information already available.

The German peacetime military buildup was a new and relatively short-lived phenomenon that started from a low level, with a burden of defense of just 1% in 1932 (table 2.3). This may explain why many economists writing about Germany in the 1930s continued to pursue their established, specialized interests, such as the organization of farm laborers and the use of unemployment insurance funds for works purpose.[14] Rearmament was too remote from these topics to justify even a passing reference.

Those writing on the current state of the economy, its recovery, and the reduction of unemployment were in a different situation, for rearmament was at the center of their subject matter. After 1933, rearmament projects drove the reduction of unemployment. "The military spending package [of June 1933] vastly exceeded anything ever contemplated for work creation . . . Not a single Reichsmark of new money was allocated to national work creation projects in 1934 or at any point thereafter."[15]

Rearmament gave the recovery its peculiar shape, with suppressed consumption and hypertrophied heavy-industry growth. By 1935, while GDP recovered to its pre-slump level, private consumption remained at 7%, and private investment at 22% below that of 1928, while government spending grew by 70% (Tooze 2006, 65). As if Preobrazhenskii and Feldman were inspiring not only Stalin but also Hitler, investment in consumer goods industries failed to reach the level of 1929 [apparently, by 1938—VK], while investment in heavy industry exceeded it by 170% (Overy 1995, 192). In 1935, the production of textiles stood at less than 90% of the 1929 level, while that of investment goods at more than 150%. The per capita meat consumption in 1938 was still below the 1929 level.[16]

Just as Sovietologists presented the military industrialization of the First Five-Year Plan as a peculiar growth strategy, writers on German economy analyzed rearmament-driven recovery in terms of countercyclical and job-creation policies. As noticed by a contemporary observer, "The great depression was only an occasion for this policy of centralized planning which itself was motivated by the desire for war preparation. This point is missed by such writers who interpret the slump as the cause of Nazi economic policy, and economic recovery as its goal. . . . see C. W. Guillebaud, *The Economic Recovery of Germany* (London, 1939). To him, Hitler is a Keynesianized promoter of recovery. War as a goal of Nazi economic policy is hardly mentioned in the lengthy monograph" (Spiegel 1940, 714). Even when the role of the military buildup was acknowledged, it was discussed as a complement to public works or a component of the "German experiment in recovery."[17]

As in the Soviet case, economists on the periphery of the discipline sought mainstream relevance by squeezing their subject into a topic of general interest. Massive peacetime military buildup was a specifically German phenomenon, of little professional interest to economists elsewhere. American and British economists were primarily concerned with the pressing problems of their own economies, unemployment and recovery. "The most timely problem confronting economists in the 1930's was the urgent necessity to understand and to find means to overcome the unprecedented crisis" (Lorell 1976, 68). Authors of articles on unemployment reduction and recovery emphasized the importance of their subject beyond Germany. Thus, a survey of German work creation policy was justified by the interest it presented for other countries (Grebler 1937a, 330). Other authors noted Hitler's greater success in reducing unemployment compared to Western democracies, discussed the applicability of the

German experience to other countries and the utility of the German experience as an empirical test of the universal multiplier effect.[18] The military buildup was ignored or deemphasized in these accounts.

## 8.2 (No) violence in primitive societies

Among primitive societies, war was extremely frequent and much deadlier than the wars among nation-states in the period of 1800–1945. Yet anthropology and archeology in the second half of the twentieth century largely ignored warfare in pre-literate societies. The most popular archeological textbooks had no references to warfare until the discussion of urban civilization came up. While tens of thousands of books were published on warfare in civilized societies, only three complete books on war before civilization were published in the twentieth century.[19]

The two authors charging anthropology and archeology with the neglect of war before civilization, Keeley (1996) and LeBlanc (2003), do not provide a comprehensive survey of professional publications, in the manner of my chapter 3. To support their claim, they rely on their own experience as researchers and their career's worth of exposure to the literature. Both books received generally positive reviews and drew no overall rebuttals.

As with Sovietology, there was a degree of fragmentation in the literature, as prehistoric violence was not completely absent from research publications. "Information on the topic is . . . tucked away in technical journals or scattered as brief passages in ethnographic and archeological reports" (Keeley 1996, 4). Also as with Sovietology, the silence on prehistoric warfare could not be blamed on lack of information. Evidence included arrowheads or spear points embedded in bones; skulls with fractures from a blunt instrument, scalping marks, and specific types of bone fractures; walls, moats, and settlements located on hilltops; burned-down settlements with possessions still intact; caches of weapons and stocks of projectiles; piles of unburied or improperly buried human remains; artistic depictions of warfare; oral traditions written down by outside observers or by subject groups themselves upon the acquisition of literacy; and accounts from anthropologists, missionaries, and government agents (LeBlanc 2003, 59–66). To sum up, the concept of prehistoric peace, common in the literature, was "extremely contrary to ethnographic and archeological fact" (Keeley 1996, 163).

These facts were dealt with by means of "studied silence or fashionable reinterpretation" (Keeley 1996, 4). Log palisades encircled by ditches were explained as symbols of exclusion, and armor and weapons as status symbols, or as a form of money. Such "interpretive pacification" advanced hypotheses that were rarely implausible or manifestly wrong, just tenuous and "ignoring more violent interpretations directly supported by evidence." Similarly to the civilizing interpretations in chapters 4 and 5, "they ignore the bellicosely obvious for the peaceably arcane" (Keeley 1996, 18–20).

If scholarly silence about primitive warfare was not imposed by lack of information, neither was it the matter of explicit individual decisions. The autobiographical passages in Keeley (1996) and LeBlanc (2003) describe the workings of professional norms, something we could only hypothesize about in the case of Sovietology (section 7.1). The authors recount the ease with which they ignored the evidence of violence they themselves unearthed throughout their careers. The standard assumption of archeology that "warfare and prehistory did not mix" was inculcated strongly enough in the process of professional training to make scholars overlook unambiguous physical evidence to the contrary. Most archeologists are said to be pacifying the past "almost unconsciously."[20] Internalized beliefs were reinforced by the threat of ostracism. Heretics could face ruinous professional sanctions, exemplified by the case of Napoleon Chagnon, who studied Yanomamo people of the Amazon and wrote about their violent ways (Dreger, 2011).

Keeley hypothesizes that the causes of the "prevailing studied silence about prestate warfare" lie outside academic anthropology, in the spirit of the times. This he describes as an aversion for anything connected with warfare, bred by the experience of the two world wars and the Cold War, as well as "anxiety, malaise, and dissatisfaction with Western civilization." The myth-making about primitive warfare resulted "from the current Western attitude of self-reproach."[21] Such broad statements, unsupported by textual evidence, may easily be reversed, as Guilaine and Zammit (2005, 8) do, when ascribing the pacification of the past to the peaceful post–World War II environment, rather than the shock of that war.

Explanations that may plausibly be based on scholars' introspection are more credible. "Archeologists and ethnologists have an audience. The audience wants to hear about peace." Also, archeologists become attached to and identify with the ancient people they study, and are reluctant to see them as aggressors, though may more readily acknowledge defensive warfare (LeBlanc 2003, 4).

## 8.3 The marginalization of military history

Academic military historians have been bemoaning their field's status for many decades. They are, of course, an interested party, but I found nothing to contradict their testimony. The general complaints include difficulty finding academic positions and publishing in respectable outlets, graduate students avoiding military topics, and the non-replacement of retiring professors at the leading institutions.[22] Some authors imply a downward trend in the status and size of the military history field: "its academic footprint continues to shrink" (Citino 2007, 1070). Others report a series of ups and downs.[23]

Fragmentary quantitative evidence supports the assertion that military history occupies a marginal place in academia. In 2007, Harvard University had no military historians among the 58 members of its history department. Neither did Johns Hopkins University. Among the 91 history departments rated by the *US News and World Report*, only four had more than one military history specialist. Altogether, military historians made up less than two percent of the faculty of the top 25 history departments, as well as of the membership of the American History Association. A survey of the main professional journal, *American Historical Review*, from 1976 to 2006 found only a handful of articles even tangentially dealing with military issues. Only two out of 85 history courses offered at Harvard in the spring of 2007, and two out of 61 offered at Johns Hopkins, were principally concerned with war.[24] A celebrated historian saw it necessary to justify "the space given to military campaigns" in his prize-winning book on the American Civil War (McPherson 1988, x).[25]

The field's position in academia does not reflect the public appeal of its subject. Military history books, some of them written by esteemed historians, have been in high demand among readers, and military topics have been attracting TV viewers.[26] Undergraduates flock to military history courses, which should earn the field the favor of university administrators.[27] It is the fellow academic historians who hold military history in low regard and diminish its role in the discipline.

Explanations of the low status of military history refer to broad political attitudes similar to those cited by the archaeologists in the preceding section. Withdrawal of interest from military history was intensified by "the emotional and ideological perspectives of the years between 1960 and 1979" (Kaegi, 300). Different authors name "the fallout of the Vietnam era" with its antiwar movement, "the nuclear pessimism" and "unthinking militaristic mind-set" of the Cold War, the effects of the two world wars, or McCarthyism as ruining the reputation of military history with academics.[28] The field is viewed as "politically and morally questionable." Many historians empathize with their subjects—women, racial groups, workers—and see their job as involving the promotion of a political cause. The military historian's lack of obvious social cause becomes evidence of perverted values.[29]

The authors do not provide any evidence for these explanations, which presumably reflect the insiders' informal reading of the academic atmosphere. The fact that different historical events are used to explain the same phenomenon, aversion to military history, also suggests that the issue is the general attitude, the *zeitgeist*, as with archeology's civilizing bias.

The same authors also identify factors working against their field that are internal to the discipline of history, such as the change of academic fashions in favor of social history, and more recently, the even narrower categories of race, class, gender, and labor.[30] The continued success of popular military history made its academic cousin appear suspect in the eyes of other academics (Morillo and Pavkovic 2012, 39). There is even a one-page survey of the history of social thought in support of the thesis that history and other social sciences "have mostly avoided giving war the attention it deserves" because of how they developed in the last couple of centuries (Bell, 2007).

## Notes

1. See Maddison (2006, 428, 429, 463) for historical GDP data.
2. The first 30 years of this controversy are reviewed in Lorell (1976, 1–28).
3. Overy (1995, 182); Abelshauser (1998, 126–27, 132).
4. Milward (1965, 6).
5. A range of estimates is cited here in view of the the uncertainties in the measurement of German military spending mentioned in section 2.2.1.
6. This paragraph follows Tooze (2006, 38–65, 659).
7. Abelshauser (1998, 145), Tooze (2006, 46).
8. Scherner (2013), Tooze (2006, 334–5).
9. The search criteria by which the articles were selected are described in appendix 8.1.
10. One article in my sample deals with labor in agriculture and is included in both groups.
11. Klein (1959, 3–4); Milward (1965, 1–2).
12. Grebler (1937a, 350–51 and 1937b, 506, 510).

13. Balogh (1939); Hutton (1939).
14. Ham (1936); Mittelman (1938).
15. Tooze (2006, 55, 61). Also Tooze (2006, ch. 2).
16. Tooze (2005, 95); Abelshauser (1998, 147).
17. Katona (1935, 350); Grebler (1937a, 349); Balogh (1938, 462).
18. Cole (1939, 55); Balogh (1939, 462, 496); Bresciani-Turroni (1938).
19. Keeley (1996, 4, 18, 28; 32–33; 88–91).
20. Keeley (1996, viii–ix, 20); LeBlanc (2003, xii–xiii, 2–3).
21. Keeley (1996, 163, 164, 169, 179).
22. Kaegi (1981, 301); Coffman (2013, 119), Lynn (2008, 33–34).
23. Kennedy (1991, 10); Lynn (1997, 777–78); Morillo and Pavkovic (2012, 38).
24. Bell (2007); Lynn (2008, 31, 35); Hanson (2011, 9).
25. As noticed by Keeley (1996, 165).
26. Bell (2007); Kaegi (1981, 310); Bunting (2008, 13); Lynn (2008, 20); Hanson (2013, 11).
27. Kaegi (1981, 301), Coffman (2013, 124); Bell (2007); Bunting (2008, 13); Lynn (2008, 34); Hanson (2013, 11).
28. Coffman (2013, 119); Hanson (2013, 6–7); Morillo and Pavkovic (2017, 38).
29. Lynn (1997, 782; 2008, 32–33).
30. Kaegi (1981, 299); Lynn (1997, 780); Hanson (2013, 8).

# Conclusion

THE ACADEMIC STUDY of the Soviet economy in the United States was founded to help fight the Cold War, a conflict that would have been impossible without the ability of the Soviet economy to turn out large numbers of technologically sophisticated weapons. For Sovietology to fulfill the purpose for which it was created, it would have to study the workings of the military sector and its relation to the rest of the economy. The leading scholars of the field promised just that when arguing for continued public support. And in this case, there was no contradiction between the demands of the national interest and those of scholarship, as the military sector was the most successful, top-priority part of the economy deserving attention on its own merits.

Yet Sovietological literature paid little attention to the military sector, compared to other, less important ones. Most of the books on topics for which the military sector is relevant either did not mention it, referred to it in a perfunctory way, or acknowledged its importance in a few sentences without explanation or follow-up. Journal articles also scarcely addressed the subject. Several important aspects of the economy that had military significance according to the Soviets were civilianized in Sovietological literature.

The militarization of the Soviet economy belongs with the other momentous events in the Communist world that were overlooked or glossed over in the West, such as the Soviet famine of 1932–33 and Chinese famine of 1959–61.[1] The major difference is that the blame for ignoring the famines is broadly shared by scholars and journalists, while only one scholarly guild, American academic economists, neglected the militarized nature of the Soviet economy.

The Sovietologists did not overlook the military sector because it was shrouded in secrecy. If nothing else, they could read about it in the *New York Times*, or in the work of their colleagues at the RAND Corporation. Sovietologists paid scant attention to the sector in their work because professional norms in economics directed their attention towards other topics. Also, the military sector was unrelated to the main object of interest, the socialist nature of the Soviet economy. And by stressing the militarized nature of the economy, one risked being viewed as a Cold War monger.

The tendency to adhere to the norms of the larger discipline, even if they do not fit one's subject, is not specific to the Soviet case. The 1930s writings on the German economy interpreted Hitler's rearmament as a jobs policy that could provide an answer to the main problem facing Western economists at the time. A critical look at Middle Eastern studies ascribes its failures in part to the scholars in this marginal field trying to win legitimacy within the discipline of political science by adopting the current general theories, however inappropriate for their subject.[2]

The conflict identified in this book between academic incentives and the needs of national security has broad relevance. The fields of social science that are important for national security are those that study other societies. These fields are also likely to be peripheral in their academic disciplines, where the mainstream deals with American, or at any rate Western, problematics, and sets the research agenda accordingly. Practitioners in peripheral fields may be expected to seek professional respectability and acceptance by adopting topics and approaches from the mainstream of their discipline, even if ill-fitting to the task at hand.

The case of Sovietology shows the professional and political incentives operating in academia to be stronger than the government's power of the purse in determining the direction of research. Admittedly, this is a local result, and at some higher level of government funding, the outcome may have been different. Still, a tiny academic field created specifically for national security purposes got away with ignoring the priorities of its sponsors. This casts a doubt on the strain of "Cold War science" writing that argues that government funding of university research deformed, and perhaps corrupted, academic disciplines (Kontorovich 2014).

Despite Sovietology's consistent unresponsiveness to the government's priorities, public funding of the field continued. Perhaps the reason is that the amounts involved were a pittance on the scale of the federal budget, as Kramer (2001, 126) noted with respect to a similar situation in Middle Eastern studies. Interestingly, proposals by academics to boost support for research on the Soviet economy in the late 1970s, when Sovietology was threatened with extinction, involved the formation of an extra-academic research institute, a structure more responsive to the sponsors' needs.

Sovietologists' preference for civilian topics was bad for scholarship, for keeping policymakers informed, and for educating the public. Any analysis of the Soviet economy that glossed over its dominant sector was at best incomplete, quite apart from the interests of the United States and its allies. The advice that academics offered to the policy makers was based on this incomplete analysis. Scholars who ignored the military sector in their publications are very unlikely to have given full weight to its role in the Soviet economy when advising the government, testifying, or writing consulting reports.

Academics' lack of interest in the military economy did not leave the government completely in the dark. Work on the sector was done in-house and by the outside contractors such as RAND. This division of labor was unusual if not unique. Thus, the CIA produced Soviet national income accounts and published estimates of total factor productivity, but most research on growth and related topics was done in academia. The US Department of Agriculture conducted research on the Soviet farm economy, but this sector also attracted much Sovietological attention. Turning to the American domestic economy, fine work done by the Departments of Commerce and Labor was but a small part of research into the subject.

Governments have well-known disabilities as providers of research, which is why most research is done elsewhere. New ideas and techniques for the study of the Soviet economy, and for economics generally, originated in academia. Much in-house government research was, of necessity, technical and short-term. Government researchers, good as they were, would have done a better job of understanding the Soviet economy and its military sector if academics also had played their part.

The prospect of the demise of Soviet studies in the late 1970s and 1980s elicited expressions of alarm at the coming government monopoly on research. "If the Federal government acquires a near-monopoly [on Soviet economic expertise] then the universities, and also the society they serve, stand mute and disarmed" (Field 1984, vii). "Foreign affairs analysis of a higher order is of course carried out in Washington, and again it might be assumed that national needs could be met this way. The record demonstrates, however, that independent scholarly research, conducted outside the government, can provide extremely valuable historical perspective, alternative judgments, diversity, and creative initiative."[3] But as far as the military sector goes, this near-monopoly was a reality.

In a democracy, public opinion is crucial for the conduct of conflicts, especially protracted ones, like the Cold War. The CIA was not structured to and lacked the credibility for educating the public on the nature of the Soviet economy. It was academics who channeled their knowledge of the Soviet society and economy to their students, the media, and the general public. College textbooks that barely mention the militarization of the Soviet economy serve as a sign that society was not properly informed.

A wide-ranging history of Soviet studies in the United States concluded that their downfall was due to the attempt to serve scholarship and national security, or Minerva and Mars, at the same time (Engerman 2009, 10, 339). My inquiry into how one field of Soviet studies dealt with one (albeit very important) task finds no contradiction between acquiring new knowledge and telling the government and the public what they needed to know. Both Mars and Minerva are best served by an accurate representation of the rival society. By failing to notice the military sector, Sovietology failed both deities.

There will never again be so many economists studying the Soviet economy as there were in the West between 1948 and 1991. The writings from this period will long dominate the extant literature on the subject and impact the way Soviet history—both economic and general—will be written. Yet Sovietological inheritance suffers from a civilizing bias, which is perpetuated over time through the chain of citing established authorities. Works based on the post-1991 archival findings did much to elucidate the importance of the military considerations for the functioning of the Soviet economy. They now exist side by side with the old civilized interpretations that they failed to supersede.

A reexamination of the Soviet economy with the primacy of the military sector in mind may help resolve its many puzzles and find explanations for the features currently attributed to the rulers' obsessions, planners' miscalculations, and ideological imperatives. An economic history of the USSR built around changes in military doctrine and the life cycle of specific weapons acquisition programs, as attempted by Belousov (2000a and b), waits to be written.

# *Notes*

1. Engerman (2000); Mosher (1990, 110–18); Waldron (2002).
2. Kramer (2001, 16, 108, 109, 122). See also Anderson (1999, 2).
3. U.S. House (1971, 1133–34). Also Atkinson (1988, 192).

# Appendices

The estimate of the number of PhD Sovietologists cited in section 1.3.1 is well documented in Millar (1980 and 1995). Other sources cite somewhat different, but equally minuscule estimates. Thus, US Senate (1982, 64, 69) puts the number of full-time equivalents of researchers on the Soviet economy in academia, government, and business at 135, and those working on Eastern European economies at 90.

There is a case for including specialists on East European economies in the number of Sovietologists. The former published in the same journals, spoke at the same workshops, and belonged to the same professional society (Association for Comparative Economic Studies) as the latter. Both groups drew support from the NCSEER. Their subjects represented variants of the same economic system that operated in the USSR, or, in case of Yugoslavia, possibilities for its modification. Some scholars worked on specific problems of both the Soviet and East European economies (David Granick, Ed Hewett). The study of the Chinese economy appears to have been somewhat further removed from Sovietology.

The American Association for the Advancement of Slavic Studies (AAASS) compiled the AAASS *Directory of Programs*, covering Soviet and East European area-studies programs in about 250 higher education institutions. According to this directory, there were 139 faculty members teaching Soviet and East European economics, at an unspecified date in the 1980s. The AAASS membership directory listed 197 members as economists, reflecting both academics and non-academics (Atkinson 1988, 398, 404).

I surveyed the English language literature, both original and translations of works of Western authors in other languages. Western translations of authors living in

Communist countries and Soviet publications of Western authors (e.g., Victor Perlo) in English were excluded. The survey covered the years 1948–1991 for articles and 1948–1992 for books, adding one year to compensate for publication lag. Books were located by searching the Harvard and Princeton library catalogs for the keywords "Soviet economy," "command economy," and "planned economy." I considered multiple editions of a title to be separate books.

For each category of literature (textbooks, books on growth, management, etc.) I considered all volumes dealing with the Soviet economy, as well as with socialist or centrally planned economies, based on the title. Books dealing only with particular socialist economies other than the Soviet one (e.g., Polish or Chinese) were excluded. For most of the categories, the authors of the books were economists, though a few were affiliated with other social-science disciplines and writing about the economy. For R&D and technology, agriculture, foreign trade, and the military sector, a large proportion of the authors were non-economists, a vexatious issue discussed in the main text.

Material on the World War II military economy was not counted here, because the distinctive feature of the Soviet economy was the size and the role of military industry in peacetime.

The subject of the book is the performance of the academics studying the Soviet economy, and so it is based on the survey of books and journal articles, the usual outlets for academic research. The exclusion of think tank publications, unpublished research reports, and oral briefings may misrepresent the true picture of Sovietological effort. In particular, academic researchers could have done the government's bidding to study the military sector, but expressed their results in these "non-academic" forms. Yet this is highly unlikely. Normally, contract research by academics filters into their publications. Thus, according to Mirowski (2002), economists, having worked on projects sponsored by the military, at RAND and elsewhere, carried the methods developed there into their academic research.

Besides, the core activities of academics are teaching and publishing books and articles. The absence of the military sector from the textbooks and from the primary scholarly media means that it was not taught to students, played no role in the academic analysis of the Soviet economy, and was not presented to the public.

Books on the military sector (table 3.12, appendix 3.3) were located by searching the Harvard University Library Hollis catalog and the Haverford College Catalog for the keywords "Soviet military economy," "Soviet military industry," "Soviet arms industry," "Soviet arms," "Soviet armaments," "Soviet defense industries," "Soviet defense," "defense conversion," and "defense industry conversion."

### APPENDIX 3.2 COUNTING INDEX ENTRIES IN BOOKS

For each book, I calculated the number of pages on which, according to the index, the words "defense," "military," "arms," "weapons," and their derivatives (e.g., "armaments," but not "arms control") are mentioned. "Army" was counted in contexts concerning costs and provisions, but not those concerning political force, as much as one can judge by the index. For most books, these four words exhausted the references to military matters in the index. If one of these index entries referred to another entry (e.g., "munitions industry" or "tanks"), the pages under the latter were counted, as well. However, second-order references were not followed.

As with book chapters and articles, references to the wartime economy were not counted. As far as the index makes it clear, references to non-Soviet subjects under these entries (e.g., US Defense Department) and metaphorical uses (e.g., militarization of labor under War Communism) were not counted. If the index had references to specific weapons (e.g., tanks, missiles) or other clearly domestic military-economic matters in addition to the aforementioned terms, I counted the corresponding pages. Thus, references to weapons systems exported by the USSR in pursuit of its foreign policy goals in Bornstein (1981) were not counted, while references to weapons systems designed and produced in the USSR in Amann and Cooper (1982) were. References to the aviation or shipbuilding industries or to electronics may mean either military or civilian output, and were not counted. References to defense policy vis-à-vis foreign countries (e.g., Hewett 1988, 382–86) were not counted. Military superiority or parity was counted, because it was crucially dependent on the output of military industry. I occasionally checked the text to see the exact meaning of the reference.

Each page number was counted only once, no matter how many times it was listed under the appropriate index entries. Thus, if a book's index showed "tanks," "defense," and "munitions" mentioned on page 101, this counted as one page. The last column in tables 3.1–3.7 gives the absolute number of pages with military references and their percentage in the total number of pages of a book. This is the number of the last page of the text, before the bibliography and index. This measure tends to overstate the space given to the subject, because even a passing reference is counted as if it occupies the whole page. No perfect justice is done to individual authors, since a book with five passing references to the military sector on different pages will get a higher indicator than a book with three pages of solid discussion of the same matter.

On the other hand, some relevant references may not be indexed. Thus, Grossman (1974) mentions the rapid increase of military production on two pages, only one of which is indexed. There are several references to the Soviet military sector in Schnitzer and Nordyke textbooks, none of which are indexed (both in table 3.14).

APPENDIX 3.3 BOOKS ON THE SOVIET MILITARY SECTOR

Holzman, Franklyn D. 1975. *Financial Checks on Soviet Defense Expenditures.* Lexington, MA: DC Heath and Company,

Lee, William Thomas. 1977. *The Estimation of Soviet Defense Expenditures, 1955–75: An Unconventional Approach.* New York: Praeger.

Becker, Abraham S. 1977. *Military Expenditure Limitation for Arms Control: Problems and Prospects.* Cambridge, MA: Ballinger.

Rosefielde, Steven, ed. 1980. *World Communism at the Crossroads: Military Ascendancy, Political Economy, and Human Welfare.* Boston: Martinus Nijhoff.

Rosefielde, Steven. 1982. *False Science: Underestimating the Soviet Arms Buildup: An Appraisal of the CIA's Direct Costing Effort, 1960–80.* New Brunswick, NJ: Transaction Books.

Holloway, David. 1983. *The Soviet Union and the Arms Race.* New Haven, CT: Yale University Press.

Holloway, David. 1984. *The Soviet Union and the Arms Race.* 2nd ed. New Haven, CT: Yale University Press.

Harrison, Mark. 1985. *Soviet Planning in Peace and War, 1938–1945.* Cambridge, UK: Cambridge University Press.

Rosefielde, Steven. 1987. *False Science: Underestimating the Soviet Arms buildup: An Appraisal of the CIA's Direct Costing Effort, 1960–1985.* Rev. 2nd ed. New Brunswick, NJ: Transaction Books.

Jacobsen, Carl G., ed. 1987. *The Soviet Defence Enigma: Estimating Costs and Burden.* New York: Oxford University Press.

Maddock, Rowland T. 1988. *The Political Economy of Soviet Defence Spending.* Basingstoke: Macmillan.

Efrat, Moshe. 1988. *The Political Economy of Soviet Arms Transfers to the Third World.* New York: Simon and Schuster.

Evangelista, Matthew. 1988. *Innovation and the Arms Race: How the United States and the Soviet Union Develop New Military Technologies.* Ithaca, NY: Cornell University Press.

Cooper, Leo. 1989. *Political Economy of Soviet Military Power.* Basingstoke: Macmillan.

Rowen, Henry S., and Charles Wolf Jr., eds. 1990. *The Impoverished Superpower: Perestroika and the Burden of Soviet Military Spending.* San Francisco: Institute for Contemporary Studies Press.

Almquist, Peter, *Red Forge: Soviet Military Industry Since 1965.* 1990. New York: Columbia University Press.

Sapir, Jacques. 1991. *The Soviet Military System.* Cambridge: Polity Press.

Allison, Roy, ed. 1991. *Radical Reform in Soviet Defence Policy.* London: Macmillan.

Cooper, Julian. 1991. *The Soviet Defence Industry: Conversion and Economic Reform.* New York: Council on Foreign Relations.

Malleret, Thierry. 1992. *Conversion of the Defense Industry in the Former Soviet Union.* Boulder, CO: Westview Press.

APPENDIX 3.4 BOOKS ON PARTICULAR SECTORS OF
THE SOVIET ECONOMY OTHER THAN EXTERNAL
AND AGRICULTURE PUBLISHED BEFORE 1975

Arnold, Arthur Z. 1937. *Banks, Credit, and Money in Soviet Russia*. New York: Columbia University Press.

Clark, Mills Gardner. 1956. *The Economics of Soviet Steel*. Cambridge, MA: Harvard University Press.

Hunter, Holland. 1957. *Soviet Transportation Policy*. Cambridge, MA: Harvard University Press.

Williams, Ernest W. Jr. 1962. *Freight Transportation in the Soviet Union, Including Comparisons with the United States*. Princeton, NJ: Princeton University Press.

Goldman, Marshall I. 1963. *Soviet Marketing: Distribution in a Controlled Economy*. New York: Free Press.

Westwood, J. N. 1964. *Soviet Railways Today*. New York: Citadel Press.

Campbell, Robert W. 1968. *The Economics of Soviet Oil and Gas*. Baltimore, Johns Hopkins Press.

Abouchar, Alan. 1971. *Soviet Planning and Spatial Efficiency: The Prewar Cement Industry*. Bloomington, Indiana University Press.

Hemy, Geoffrey W. 1971. *The Soviet Chemical Industry*. New York: Barnes and Noble.

Greer, Thomas V. 1973. *Marketing in the Soviet Union*. New York: Praeger.

Podolski, T. M. 1973. *Socialist Banking and Monetary Control: The Experience of Poland*. Cambridge University Press.

Ofer, Gur. 1973. *The Service Sector in Soviet Economic Growth: A Comparative Study*. Cambridge, MA: Harvard University Press.

Hanson, Philip. 1974. *Advertising and Socialism: The Nature and Extent of Consumer Advertising in the Soviet Union, Poland, Hungary, and Yugoslavia*. White Plains, NY: International Arts and Sciences Press.


APPENDIX 3.5 BOOKS ON SOVIET AGRICULTURE

The following list was compiled by searching Princeton University Library's main catalog and Harvard University Library's Hollis catalog for "Soviet agriculture" and "Russian agriculture."

Research Staff of Free Europe Press. 1954. *Satellite Agriculture in Crisis: A Study of Land Policy in the Soviet Sphere*. New York: Praeger.

Bass, Robert H. 1957. *Force Versus Food: A Short History of Agriculture in the Soviet Sphere*. New York: Free Europe Press.

Walston, Henry David. 1962. *Agriculture Under Communism*. London: Bodley Head.

Wesson, Robert G. 1963. *Soviet Communes*. New Brunswick, NJ: Rutgers University Press.

Laird, Roy D., ed. 1963. *Soviet Agricultural and Peasant Affairs.* Lawrence: University of Kansas Press.

Jasny, Naum. 1965. *Khrushchev's Crop Policy.* Glasgow: G. Outram.

Laird, Roy D., ed. 1965. *Soviet Agriculture: The Permanent Crisis.* New York: Praeger.

Ploss, Sidney I. 1965. *Conflict and Decision-Making in Soviet Russia: A Case Study of Agricultural Policy, 1953–1963.* Princeton, NJ: Princeton University Press.

Karcz, Jerzy F., ed. 1967. *Soviet and East European Agriculture.* Berkeley: University of California Press.

Conquest, Robert, ed. 1968. *Agricultural Workers in the U. S. S. R.* New York: Praeger.

Strauss, Erich. 1969. *Soviet Agriculture in Perspective: A Study of its Successes and Failures.* New York: Praeger.

Miller, Robert F. 1970. *One Hundred Thousand Tractors: The MTS and the Development of Controls in Soviet Agriculture.* Cambridge, MA: Harvard University Press.

Volin, Lazar. 1970. *A Century of Russian Agriculture: From Alexander II to Khrushchev.* Cambridge, MA: Harvard University Press.

Laird, Roy D., and Betty A. Laird. 1970. *Soviet Communism and Agrarian Revolution.* Harmondsworth, UK: Penguin.

Conklin, David W. 1970. *An Evaluation of the Soviet Profit Reforms, with Special Reference to Agriculture.* New York: Praeger Publishers.

Millar, James R., ed. 1971. *The Soviet Rural Community: A Symposium.* Urbana: University of Illinois Press.

Jackson, Douglas W. A., ed. 1971. *Agrarian Policies and Problems in Communist and Non-Communist Countries.* Seattle: University of Washington Press.

Adams, Arthur E., and Jan S. Adams. 1971. *Men Versus Systems: Agriculture in the USSR, Poland, and Czechoslovakia.* New York: Free Press.

Symons, Leslie. 1972. *Russian Agriculture: A Geographic Survey.* London: Bell.

Hahn, Werner G. 1972. *The Politics of Soviet Agriculture, 1960–1970.* Baltimore: Johns Hopkins University Press.

Stuart, Robert C. 1972. *The Collective Farm in Soviet Agriculture.* Lexington, MA: Lexington Books.

Wadekin, Karl Eugen. 1973. *The Private Sector in Soviet Agriculture.* Berkeley: University of California Press.

Osofsky, Stephen. 1974. *Soviet Agricultural Policy: Toward the Abolition of Collective Farms.* New York: Praeger.

Lewin, Moshe. 1975. *Russian Peasants and Soviet Power: A Study of Collectivization.* New York: Norton.

McCauley, Martin. 1976. *Khrushchev and the Development of Soviet Agriculture: The Virgin Land Programme, 1953–1964.* New York: Holmes and Meier Publishers.

Solomon, Susan Gross. 1977. *The Soviet Agrarian Debate: A Controversy in Social Science, 1923–1929.* Boulder, CO: Westview Press.

Shaffer, Harry G., ed. 1977. *Soviet Agriculture: An Assessment of its Contributions to Economic Development.* New York: Praeger.

Laird, Roy D., Joseph Hajda, and Betty A. Laird, ed. 1977. *The Future of Agriculture in the Soviet Union and Eastern Europe: The 1976–80 Five Year Plans*. Boulder, CO: Westview Press.

Nell Cowden. 1980. *Soviet Agricultural Policy: Stalin-Malenkov-Krushchev-Kosygin-Breznev*. Maryville: Northwest Missouri State University.

Davies, R. W. 1980. *The Socialist Offensive: The Collectivisation of Soviet Agriculture, 1929–1930*. Cambridge, MA: Harvard University Press

Francisco, Ronald A., Betty A. Laird, and Roy D. Laird, eds. 1980. *Agricultural Policies in the USSR and Eastern Europe*. Boulder, CO: Westview Press.

Khan, Azizur Rahman, and Dharam Ghai. 1980. *Collective Agriculture and Rural Development in Soviet Central Asia*. New York: St. Martin's.

Gustafson, Thane. 1981. *Reform in Soviet Politics: The Lessons of Recent Policies on Land and Water*. New York: Cambridge University Press.

Wädekin, Karl-Eugen. 1982. *Agrarian Policies in Communist Europe: A Critical Introduction*. Totowa, NJ: Rowman and Allanheld.

Stuart, Robert C., ed. 1983. *The Soviet Rural Economy*. Totowa, NJ: Rowman and Allanheld.

Johnson, D. Gale, and Karen McConnell Brooks. 1983. *Prospects for Soviet Agriculture in the 1980s*. Bloomington: Indiana University Press.

Hedlund, Stefan. 1984. *Crisis in Soviet Agriculture*. New York: St. Martin's.

Wädekin, Karl-Eugen, ed. 1985. *Agriculture in Inter-System Comparison: Communist and Non-Communist Cases*. Berlin: Duncker and Humbolt.

Conquest, Robert. 1986. *The Harvest of Sorrow: Soviet Collectivization and the Terror-Famine*. New York: Oxford University Press.

Deutsch, Robert. 1986. *The Food Revolution in the Soviet Union and Eastern Europe*. Boulder, CO: Westview Press.

Kaplan, Cynthia S. 1987. *The Party and Agricultural Crisis Management in the USSR*. Ithaca, NY: Cornell University Press.

Litvin, Valentin. 1987. *The Soviet Agro-Industrial Complex: Structure and Performance*. Boulder, CO: Westview Press.

Brada, Josef C., and Karl-Eugen Wädekin. 1988. *Socialist Agriculture in Transition: Organizational Response to Failing Performance*. Boulder, CO: Westview Press.

Wädekin, Karl-Eugen, ed. 1989. Communist Agriculture: Farming in the Soviet Union and Eastern Europe. New York: Routledge.

Hedlund, Stefan. 1989. *Private Agriculture in the Soviet Union*. New York: Routledge.

Gray, Kenneth R., ed. 1990. *Soviet Agriculture: Comparative Perspectives*. Ames: Iowa State University Press.

Moskoff, William, ed. 1990. *Perestroika in the Countryside: Agricultural Reform in the Gorbachev Era*. Armonk, NY: M. E. Sharpe.

Yin, John. 1991. *Infrastructure of the Soviet Agriculture*. Sudbury, ON: Northernmost View Press.

APPENDIX 3.6 BOOKS ON SOVIET FOREIGN ECONOMIC RELATIONS

Strange, Susan. 1959. *The Soviet Trade Weapon*. London: Phoenix House.

Wiles, P. J. D. 1969. *Communist International Economics*. New York: Praeger.

Wilczynski, J. 1969. *The Economics and Politics of East-West Trade*. New York: Praeger.

Boltho, Andrea. 1971. *Foreign Trade Criteria in Socialist Economies*. Cambridge University Press.

Marer, Paul. 1972. *Soviet and East European Foreign Trade, 1946–1969: Statistical Compendium and Guide*. Bloomington, Indiana University Press.

Smith, Glen Alden. 1973. *Soviet Foreign Trade: Organization, Operations, and Policy, 1918–1971*. New York: Praeger.

Grzybowski, Kazimierz, comp. 1973. *East-West Trade*. Dobbs Ferry, NY: Oceana Publications.

Wolf, Thomas A. 1973. *U. S. East-West Trade Policy: Economic Warfare Versus Economic Welfare*. Lexington, MA: Lexington Books.

Holzman, Franklyn D. 1974. *Foreign Trade Under Central Planning*. Cambridge: Harvard University Press.

Hewett, Edward A. 1974. *Foreign Trade Prices in the Council for Mutual Economic Assistance*. Cambridge University Press.

Quigley, John. 1974. *The Soviet Foreign Trade Monopoly: Institutions and Laws*. Columbus: Ohio State University Press.

Stowell, Christopher E. 1975. *Soviet Industrial Import Priorities: With Marketing Considerations for Exporting to the USSR*. New York: Praeger.

Holzman, Franklyn D. 1976. *International Trade Under Communism: Politics and Economics*. New York: Basic Books.

Friesen, Connie M. 1976. *The Political Economy of East-West Trade*. New York: Praeger.

Turpin, William Nelson. 1977. *Soviet Foreign Trade: Purpose and Performance*. Lexington, MA: Lexington Books.

Levcik, Friedrich, and Jan Stankovsky. 1979. *Industrial Cooperation Between East and West*. London: Macmillan.

Marer, Paul, and John Michael Montias, eds. 1980. *East European Integration and East-West Trade*. Bloomington: Indiana University Press.

Hanson, Philip. 1981. *Trade and Technology in Soviet-Western Relations*. New York: Columbia University Press.

Gardner, Stephen H. 1983. *Soviet Foreign Trade: The Decision Process*. Boston: Kluwer-Nijhoff.

Paarlberg, Robert L. *Food Trade and Foreign Policy: India, the Soviet Union, and the United States*. Ithaca: Cornell University Press, 1985.

Jentleson, Bruce W. 1986. *Pipeline Politics: The Complex Political Economy of East-West Energy Trade*. Ithaca, NY: Cornell University Press.

Sokoloff, Georges. 1987. *The Economy of Détente: The Soviet Union and Western Capital*. New York: St. Martin's.

Perry, Charles M., and Robert L. Pfaltzgraff, Jr., eds. 1987. *Selling the Rope to Hang Capitalism: The Debate on West-East Trade & Technology Transfer.* Washington: Pergamon-Brassey's.

McMillan, Carl H. 1987. *Multinationals from the Second World: Growth of Foreign Investment by Soviet and East European Enterprises.* New York: St. Martin's.

Holzman, Franklyn D. 1987. *The Economics of Soviet Bloc Trade and Finance.* Boulder, CO: Westview Press.

Wolf, Thomas A. 1988. *Foreign Trade in the Centrally Planned Economy.* New York: Harwood Academic Publishers.

Funigiello, Philip J. 1988. *American-Soviet Trade in the Cold War.* Chapel Hill: University of North Carolina Press.

Liebowitz, Ronald D., ed. 1988. *Gorbachev's New Thinking: Prospects For Joint Ventures.* Cambridge, MA: Ballinger.

Hansen, Carol Rae. 1988. *U.S.-Soviet Trade Policy.* Lanham, MD: Foreign Policy Institute, School of Advanced International Studies, Johns Hopkins University. Distributed by University Press of America.

Shelton, Judy. 1989. *The Coming Soviet Crash.* New York: Free Press.

Michael Kraus, and Ronald D. Liebowitz, eds. 1990. *Perestroika and East-West Economic Relations: Prospects for the 1990s.* New York: New York University Press.

Friedländer, Michael, ed. 1990. *Foreign Trade in Eastern Europe and the Soviet Union.* Boulder, CO: Westview Press.

Murrell, Peter. 1990. *The Nature of Socialist Economies: Lessons from Eastern European Foreign Trade.* Princeton, NJ: Princeton University Press.

Razvigorova, Evka, and Gottfried Wolf-Laudon, eds. 1991. *East-West Joint Ventures: The New Business Environment.* Cambridge, MA: Blackwell.

Zloch-Christy, Iliana. 1991. *East-West Financial Relations: Current Problems and Future Prospects.* New York: Cambridge University Press.

Marer, Paul, and András Köves, eds. 1991. Foreign Economic Liberalization: Transformations in Market and Socialist Economies. Boulder, CO: Westview Press.

Haus, Leah A. 1992. *Globalizing the GATT: The Soviet Union's Successor States, Eastern Europe, and the International Trading System.* Washington, DC: Brookings Institution.

APPENDIX 4.1 HOW THE LITERATURE WAS SURVEYED
FOR CHAPTER 4

Chapter 4 is based on a subset of the books surveyed in chapter 3. This covers 24 out of 47 separate editions of textbooks, excluding, for the most part, multiple editions of the same title. The planning and growth titles are almost the same as in chapter 3. For each book, the table of contents was checked for a section on goals and the index for the words "goals" and "objectives." The introduction and sometimes the foreword or preface, as well as sections offering historical background that discussed the revolution and/or industrialization, were also searched for statements on planners' objectives. Priorities mentioned in sections on planning or investment were taken to be closely associated with objectives. Sometimes consumption or welfare sections contained statements relevant to the objectives of the rulers. The search did not cover every page of every book surveyed, and some statements on objectives were doubtless missed.

### APPENDIX 8.1 HOW LITERATURE WAS SURVEYED FOR SECTION 8.1

JSTOR and Google Scholar were searched for articles on "German/Nazi/Hitler's economy/ industry/recovery/employment/banking/production/consumption/economic policy/economic planning/economic conditions/finance/trade/agriculture/manufacture/transportation" for the period of 1934–43. A separate search, limited to economics journals, was conducted for the terms "German/Nazi/Hitler's/Reich rearmament/war economy/war industry/military preparations."

The findings were pruned to exclude articles that did not belong to the discipline of economics. This involved a degree of discretion, since at the time, the line between economics and other social sciences was less well defined than it is now (Scherer 2000, 617). Of the 71 articles selected, 40 appeared in what are now premier economics journals. The rest were published in the journals of allied disciplines (farm economics, economic geography, accounting, and regional planning), *International Labor Review, Social Research,* and foreign affairs periodicals. Articles in non-economics periodicals were selected only if the title suggested economics content (e.g., Cole [1939], published in *Political Quarterly* with the title "Nazi Economics").

When classifying articles as mentioning rearmament in passing or containing a discussion of rearmament, references to ostensibly civilian but strategically significant autarchic policies, such as securing self-sufficiency in farm products (Brandt 1937a) or developing synthetic substitutes for imported rubber and petroleum (Solmssen 1937, 233) were not counted.

# Bibliography

Abelshauser, Werner. 1998. "Germany: guns, butter, and economic miracles." In Harrison 1998, 122–76.

Abouchar, Alan. 1979. *Economic Evaluation of Soviet Socialism*. New York: Pergamon.

Abramowitz, Moses. 1989. *Thinking about Growth and Other Essays on Economic Growth and Welfare*. Cambridge, UK: Cambridge University Press.

ACDA (United States Arms Control and Disarmament Agency). 1995. *World Military Expenditures and Arms Transfers, 1993–1994*. Washington, DC: GPO. https://www.state.gov/t/avc/rls /rpt/wmeat/c50834.html.

ACDA (US Arms Control and Disarmament Agency). 1997. *World Military Expenditures and Arms Transfers, 1996*. Washington DC: GPO. http://www.state.gov/www/global/arms /wmeat96/wmeat96.html.

Agarwal, B. L. 1989. *Alternative Economic Structures*. Shimla: Indian Institute of Advanced Study.

Agursky, Mikhail. 1983. *Sovetskii Golem*. London: Overseas Publications Interchange.

Alexeev, Michael, and Clifford G. Gaddy. 1993. "Income Distribution in the USSR in the 1980s." *Review of Income and Wealth* 39 (1): 23–36.

Alexeev, Michael, and Lee Walker, eds. 1991. *Estimating the Size of the Soviet Economy: Summary of a Meeting*. Washington, DC: National Academy Press.

Allen, Robert C. 2003. *Farm to Factory: A Reinterpretation of the Soviet Industrial Revolution*. Princeton, NJ: Princeton University Press.

Amann, Ronald, and Julian Cooper, eds. 1982. *Industrial Innovation in the Soviet Union*. New Haven, CT: Yale University Press.

Amann, Ronald, and Julian Cooper, eds. 1986. *Technical Progress and Soviet Economic Development*. New York: Basil Blackwell.

Amann, Ronald, Julian Cooper, and R. W. Davies, eds. 1977. *The Technological Level of Soviet Industry*. London: Yale University Press.

Ames, Edward. 1965. *Soviet Economic Processes*. Homewood, IL: Richard D. Irwin.

Amuzegar, Jahangir. 1981. *Comparative Economics: National Priorities, Policies, and Performance*. Cambridge, MA: Winthrop Publishers.

Anderson, Lisa. 1999. "Politics in the Middle East." In *Area Studies and Social Science: Strategies for Understanding Middle East Politics*, edited by Mark Tessler, 1–11. Bloomington: Indiana University Press.

Angresano, James. 1992. *Comparative Economics*. Englewood Cliffs, NJ: Prentice Hall.

Arndt, Heinz W. 1978. *The Rise and Fall of Economic Growth: A Study in Contemporary Thought*. Chicago: University of Chicago Press.

Arndt, Heinz W. 1987. *Economic Development: The History of an Idea*. Chicago: University of Chicago Press.

Assistant to the National Intelligence Officer for Political Economy. 1978. Memorandum. January 4, 1978. CIA-RDP81B00401R002400200071-9. CREST System, National Archives at College Park.

Åslund, Anders. 1989. *Gorbachev's Struggle for Economic Reform*. Ithaca, NY: Cornell University Press, 1989.

Åslund, Anders. 1991. *Gorbachev's Struggle for Economic Reform*. Updated and expanded edition. Ithaca, NY: Cornell University Press.

Åslund, Anders, ed. 1992. *Market Socialism or the Restoration of Capitalism?* Cambridge, UK: Cambridge University Press.

Åslund, Anders. 2002. *Building Capitalism: The Transformation of the Former Soviet Bloc*. New York: Cambridge University Press.

Asselain, Jean-Charles. 1984. *Planning and Profits in Socialist Economies*. Translated by Jill Rubery and Andrew Wilson. London: Routledge.

Atkinson, Dorothy. 1987. "Understanding the Soviets: The Development of U.S. Expertise on the USSR." *The Washington Quarterly* 10 (3): 183–201.

Atkinson, Dorothy. 1988. "Soviet and East European Studies in the United States." *Slavic Review* 47 (3): 397–413.

Babakov, A. A. 1987. *Vooruzhennye sily SSSR posle voiny (1945–1986): istoria stroitel'stva*. Moscow: Voenizdat.

Backhouse, Roger E. 2002. *The Ordinary Business of Life: A History of Economics from the Ancient World to the Twenty-First Century*. Princeton, NJ: Princeton University Press.

Backhouse, Roger E., and Philippe Fontaine. 2010. Introduction to *The History of the Social Sciences since 1945*, edited by Roger E. Backhouse and Philippe Fontaine, 1–16. Cambridge, UK: Cambridge University Press.

Baerwald, Friedrich. 1934. "How Germany Reduced Unemployment." *American Economic Review* 24 (4): 617–30.

Bahry, Donna, and James R. Millar. 1975. "An Evaluation of Research Opportunities and Allocations in Studies of the Soviet and East European Economies." *ACES Bulletin* 17 (1): 90–96.

Baibakov, N. K. 1998. *Ot Stalina do Iel'tsina*. Moscow: GazOil Press.

Bailes, K. E. 1979. Review of *The Technological Level of Soviet Industry*, edited by Robert Amann, Julian Cooper, and R. W. Davies. *Isis* 70 (1): 158–59.

Bairam, Erkin. 1988. *Technical Progress and Industrial Growth in the USSR and Eastern Europe: An Empirical Study, 1961–75*. Aldershot, UK: Avebury.

Baldwin, Hanson W. 1967. "Soviet Military Advances Pose a Challenge for U.S." *New York Times*, October 30.

Balinky, Alexander, Abram Bergson, John N. Hazard, and Peter Wiles. 1967. *Planning and the Market in the U.S.S.R.: The 1960's*. New Brunswick, NJ: Rutgers University Press.

Balogh, T. 1938. "The National Economy of Germany." *The Economic Journal 48* (191): 461–97.

Balogh, T. 1939. "The Economic Background in Germany." *International Affairs (Royal Institute of International Affairs 1931–1939)* 18 (2): 227–48.

Balzer, Harley D. 1989. *Soviet Science on the Edge of Reform*. Boulder, CO: Westview Press.

Barber, Elinor G., and Warren Ilchman. 1980. "The Preservation of the Cosmopolitan Research University in the United States: The Prospect for the 1980s." *The ANNALS of the American Academy of Political and Social Science* 449 (1): 59–79.

Barber, John, and Mark Harrison, eds. 2000. *The Soviet Defense-Industry Complex from Stalin to Khrushchev*. New York: St. Martin's Press.

Barber, John, Mark Harrison, Nikolai Simonov, and Boris Starkov. 2000. "The Structure and Development of the Soviet Defense-Industry Complex." In Barber and Harrison 2000, 3–32.

Bardhan, Pranab. 1993. "Economics of Development and the Development of Economics." *The Journal of Economic Perspectives* 7 (2): 129–42.

Barner-Barry, Carol, and Cynthia A. Hody. 1995. *The Politics of Change: The Transformation of the Former Soviet Union*. New York: St. Martin's.

Barro, Robert J., and Xavier Sala-i-Martin. 2004. *Economic Growth*. 2nd ed. Cambridge, MA: MIT Press.

Baumol, William J. 1988. *Economics: Principles and Policy*. 4th ed. San Diego: Harcourt Brace Jovanovich.

Baumol, William J., and Alan S. Blinder. 1982. *Economics: Principles and Policy*. 2nd ed. New York: Harcourt Brace Jovanovich.

Baumol, William J., and Alan S. Blinder. 1985. *Economics: Principles and Policy*. 3rd ed. San Diego: Harcourt Brace Jovanovich.

Baumol, William J., and Alan S. Blinder. 1991. *Economics: Principles and Policy*. 5th ed. San Diego: Harcourt Brace Jovanovich.

Becker, Abraham S. 1969. *Soviet National Income 1958–1964: National Accounts of the USSR in the Seven Year Plan Period*. Berkeley: University of California Press.

Becker, Abraham S. 1994. "Intelligence Fiasco or Reasoned Accounting?: CIA Estimates of Soviet GNP." *Post-Soviet Affairs* 10 (4): 291–329.

Becker, Gary. 1988. "The Economic Approach to Human Behavior." In *Rational Choice*, edited by Jon Elster, 108–22. Oxford: Basil Blackwell.

Beissinger, Mark R. 1984. Review of *Industrial Innovation in the Soviet Union*, by Ronald Amann and Julian Cooper. *Bulletin of the Atomic Scientists* 40 (5): 42–44.

Beissinger, Mark R. 1988. *Scientific Management, Socialist Discipline, and Soviet Power.* Cambridge, MA: Harvard University Press.

Belanovsky, Sergei. 1998. "The Arms Race and the Burden of Military Expenditures." In Ellman and Kontorovich 1998, 40–70.

Bell, David A. 2007. "Military History Bites the Dust." *New Republic Online*, May 7. https://newrepublic.com/article/64680/casualty-war-military-history-bites-the-dust.

Belousov, Andrei. 2000a. "Stanovlenie sovetskoi industrial'noi sistemy." *Rossiia XXI*, no. 3, 28–78.

Belousov, Andrei. 2000b. "Stanovlenie sovetskoi industrial'noi sistemy." *Rossiia XXI*, no. 3, 20–70.

Bennett, John. 1989. *The Economic Theory of Central Planning.* New York: Basil Blackwell.

Berend, Ivan T. 2006. *An Economic History of Twentieth-Century Europe: Economic Regimes from Laissez-Faire to Globalization.* New York: Cambridge University Press.

Bergson, Abram. 1948. "Russian Defense Expenditures." *Foreign Affairs* 26 (2): 373–76.

Bergson, Abram, ed. 1953a. *Soviet Economic Growth: Conditions and Perspectives.* Evanston, IL: Row, Peterson.

Bergson, Abram. 1953b. *Soviet National Income and Product in 1937.* New York: Colombia University Press.

Bergson, Abram. 1953c. "Comments." In Bergson 1953a, 33–36.

Bergson, Abram. 1961. *The Real National Income of Soviet Russia since 1928.* Cambridge, MA: Harvard University Press.

Bergson, Abram. 1964. *The Economics of Soviet Planning.* New Haven, CT: Yale University Press.

Bergson, Abram. 1973. "Toward a New Growth Model." *Problems of Communism* 22 (2): 1–9.

Bergson, Abram. 1978. *Productivity and the Social System: The USSR and the West.* Cambridge, MA: Harvard University Press.

Bergson, Abram. 1984. "Income Inequality under Soviet Socialism." *Journal of Economic Literature* 22 (3): 1052–1099.

Bergson, Abram. 1989. *Planning and Performance in Socialist Economies: The USSR and Eastern Europe.* Boston: Unwin Hyman.

Bergson, Abram. 1991. "The USSR before the Fall: How Poor and Why." *Journal of Economic Perspectives* 5 (4): 29–44.

Bergson, Abram, and Hans Heymann, Jr. 1954. *Soviet National Income and Product, 1940–48.* New York: Columbia University Press.

Bergson, Abram, and Simon Kuznets, eds. 1963. *Economic Trends in the Soviet Union.* Cambridge, MA: Harvard University Press.

Bergson, Abram, and Herbert Levine, eds. 1983. *The Soviet Economy: Toward the Year 2000*. London: Allen & Unwin.

Bergsträsser, Arnold. 1934. "The Economic Policy of the German Government." *International Affairs (Royal Institute of International Affairs 1931–1939)* 13 (1): 26–46.

Berkowitz, Bruce, and Jeffrey Richelson. 1995. "The CIA Vindicated: The Soviet Collapse *Was* Predicted." *National Interest*, no. 41, 36–47.

Berkowitz, Daniel M., Joseph S. Berliner, Paul R. Gregory, Susan J. Linz, and James R. Millar. 1993. "Survey Article: An Evaluation of the CIA's Analysis of Soviet Economic Performance, 1970–1990." *Comparative Economic Studies* 35 (2): 33–57.

Berliner, Joseph S. 1957. *Factory and Manager in the USSR*. Cambridge, MA: Harvard University Press.

Berliner, Joseph S. 1966. "The Economics of Overtaking and Surpassing." In Rosovsky 1996, 159–85.

Berliner, Joseph S. 1976. *The Innovation Decision in Soviet Industry*. Cambridge, MA: MIT Press.

Berliner, Joseph S. 1988. *Soviet Industry from Stalin to Gorbachev: Essays on Management and Innovation*. Ithaca, NY: Cornell University Press.

Bernard, Philippe J. 1966. *Planning in the Soviet Union*. Translated by I. Nove. Oxford: Pergamon.

Bernstein, Michael A. 2001. *A Perilous Progress: Economics and Public Purpose in Twentieth-Century America*. Princeton, NJ: Princeton University Press.

Berri, L. Ia., ed. 1973. *Planirovanie narodnogo khoziaistva SSSR*. 2nd ed. Moscow: Ekonomika.

Berry, Michael J., ed. 1988. *Science and Technology in the USSR*. Harlow: Longman.

Birman, Igor. 1980a. "The Financial Crisis in the USSR." *Soviet Studies* 32 (1): 84–105.

Birman, Igor. 1980b. Review of *The Soviet Economy: How It Really Works*, by Konstantin A. Krylov. *Soviet Studies* 32 (4): 603–6.

Birman, Igor. 1983a. *Ekonomika nedostach*. New York: Chalidze.

Birman, Igor. 1983b. "Pochemu oni nas ne slushaiut. . . ." *Kontinent*, no. 35, 207–30.

Blanchard, Olivier, and Stanley Fischer. 1989. *Lectures on Macroeconomics*. Cambridge, MA: The MIT Press.

Blank, Stephen J. 1995. "Reform and Revolution in Russian Defense Economics." *Journal of Slavic Military Studies* 8 (4): 691–717.

Bleaney, Michael. 1988. *Do Socialist Economies Work?: The Soviet and East European Experience*. Oxford: Basil Blackwell.

Block, Herbert. 1942. "Subcontracting in German Defense Industries." *Social Research* 9 (1): 4–21.

Block, Herbert. 1943. "Industrial Concentration versus Small Business: The Trend of Nazi Policy." *Social Research* 10 (2): 175–99.

Boettke, Peter J. 1990. *The Political Economy of Soviet Socialism: The Formative Years, 1918–1928*. Boston: Kluwer Academic Publishers.

Boeva, Irina, Vyacheslav Shironin, and Tat'yana Dolgopyatova. 1992. "Soviet Arms Manufacturers in the Summer of 1991." *Communist Economies and Economic Transformation* 4 (2): 269–78.

Bonstingl, John J. 1991. *Scholastic Economics*. New York: Scholastic.

Bornstein, Morris. 1974. *Comparative Economic Systems: Models and Cases*. 3rd ed. Homewood, IL: Richard. D. Irwin.

Bornstein, Morris. 1979. *Comparative Economic Systems: Models and Cases*. 4th ed. Homewood, IL: Richard. D. Irwin.

Bornstein, Morris, ed. 1981. *The Soviet Economy: Continuity and Change*. Boulder, CO: Westview Press.

Bornstein, Morris. 1985. *Comparative Economic Systems: Models and Cases*. 5th ed. Homewood, IL: Richard D. Irwin.

Bornstein, Morris. 1989. *Comparative Economic Systems: Models and Cases*. 6th ed. Homewood, IL: Richard D. Irwin.

Bornstein, Morris, and Daniel R. Fusfeld, eds. 1962. *The Soviet Economy: A Book of Readings*. Homewood, IL: Richard. D. Irwin.

Bornstein, Morris, and Daniel R. Fusfeld, eds. 1966. *The Soviet Economy: A Book of Readings*. Rev. ed. Homewood, IL: Richard D. Irwin.

Bornstein, Morris, and Daniel R. Fusfeld, eds. 1970. *The Soviet Economy: A Book of Readings*. 3rd ed. Homewood, IL: Richard D. Irwin.

Bornstein, Morris, and Daniel R. Fusfeld, eds. 1974. *The Soviet Economy: A Book of Readings*. 4th ed. Homewood, IL: Richard. D. Irwin.

Boulier, Bryan, and Robert Goldfarb. 1998. "On the Use and Nonuse of Surveys in Economics." *Journal of Economic Methodology* 5 (1): 1–21.

Bowen, H. R. 1953. "Graduate Education in Economics." *American Economic Review* 43 (4): 341–52.

Brada, Joseph C. "Editor's Note." 1985. *Comparative Economic Studies* 27 (1): iii.

Brady, Robert A. 1942. "Modernized Cameralism in the Third Reich: The Case of the National Industry Group." *Journal of Political Economy* 50 (1): 65–97.

Brady, Robert. A. 1943. "Industrial Policy." *Journal of Economic History*, 3 (1): 108–23.

Brandt, Karl. 1935. "The German Back-to-the-Land Movement." *Journal of Land & Public Utility Economics* 11 (2): 123–32.

Brandt, Karl. 1937. "German Agricultural Policy: Some Selected Lessons." *Journal of Farm Economics* 19 (1): 287–99.

Bresciani-Turroni, C. 1938. "The 'Multiplier' in Practice: Some Results of Recent German Experience." *The Review of Economics and Statistics* 20 (2): 76–88.

Brezhnev, L. I. 1981. *Otchetnyi doklad Tsentral'nogo Komiteta KPSS XXVI siezdu Kommunisticheskoi Partii Sovetskogo Soiuza i ocherednye zadachi partii v oblasti vnutrennei i vneshnei politiki*. Moscow: Politizdat.

Broad, William J. 1993. "Russian Says Soviet Atom Arsenal Was Larger Than West Estimated." *New York Times*, September 26.

Broadberry, Stephen, and Peter Howlett. 1998. "The United Kingdom: 'Victory at all Costs.'" In Harrison 1998, 43–80.

Broadberry, Stephen, and Mark Harrison, eds. 2005. *The Economics of World War I*. Cambridge, UK: Cambridge University Press.

Brock, Gregory. 1998. "Public Finance in the ZATO Archipelago." *Europe-Asia Studies* 50 (6): 1065–81.

Brock, William A., and Steven N. Durlauf. 1999. "A Formal Model of Theory Choice in Science." *Economic Theory* 14 (1): 113–30.

Brutzkus, Boris. 1935. *Economic Planning in Soviet Russia*. London: Routledge.

Buck, Trevor, and John Cole. 1987. *Modern Soviet Economic Performance*. Oxford: Basil Blackwell.

Bunting, Josiah III. 2008. "Why Military History?" *Academic Questions* 21 (1): 12–17.

Burenok, V. M. 2011. "O podkhodakh k mobilizatsionnoi podgotovke promyshlennosti v sovremennykh usloviiakh." *Vooruzhenie i ekonomika* 2 (14): 5–8.

Byrnes, Robert F. 1962. "Academic Exchange with the Soviet Union." *The Russian Review* 21 (3): 213–25.

Byrnes, Robert. F. 1964. "USA: Work at the Universities." *Survey: A Journal of Soviet and East European Studies* 50, 24–30.

Cairncross, Alec and Peter Sinclair. 1982. Introduction to economics. London: Butterworths.

Cameron, Norman, E. 1975. Review of *Western Technology and Soviet Economic Development, 1945–1965*, by Antony C. Sutton. *Canadian Slavonic Papers* 17 (2/3): 536–37.

Campbell, Robert W. 1960. *Soviet Economic Power: Its Organization, Growth, and Challenge*. Cambridge, MA: Houghton Mifflin.

Campbell, Robert W. 1961. "Research on the Soviet Economy: Achievements and Prospects." In Spulber, 1961, 129–43.

Campbell, Robert. W. 1966. *Soviet Economic Power: Its Organization, Growth, and Challenge*. 2nd ed. Cambridge, MA: Houghton Mifflin.

Campbell, Robert W. 1974. *The Soviet-Type Economies*. Boston: Houghton Mifflin.

Campbell, Robert W. 1979. Review of *The Technological Level of Soviet Industry*, edited by Amann et al. *Slavic Review* 38 (3): 504–6.

Campbell, Robert W. 1991. *The Socialist Economies in Transition. A Primer on Semi-Reformed Systems*. Bloomington: Indiana University Press.

Campbell, Robert W. 1992. *The Failure of Soviet Economic Planning. System, Performance, Reform*. Bloomington: Indiana University Press.

Carr, Edward Hallett, and R. W. Davies. 1969. *Foundations of a Planned Economy, 1926–1929*. London: Palgrave Macmillan.

Carr, William. 1973. *Arms, Autarky and Aggression. A Study in German Foreign Policy, 1933–1939*. New York: W. W. Norton & Company, Inc.

Carroll, Berenice. 1968. *Design for Total War: Arms and Economics in the Third Reich*. The Hague, Netherlands: Mouton.

Carson, Richard L. 1973. *Comparative Economic Systems*. New York: Macmillan.

Carson, Richard L. 1990. *Comparative Economic Systems*. Vol 2, *Socialist Alternatives*. Armonk, NY: M. E. Sharpe.

Case, Karl E., and Ray C. Fair. 1989. *Principles of Economics*. Englewood Cliffs, NJ: Prentice Hall.

Cave, Martin. 1980. *Computers and Economic Planning: The Soviet Experience*. Cambridge, UK: Cambridge University Press.

Chamberlin, Wiliam H. 1935. *Russia's Iron Age*. Boston: Little, Brown, and Company.

Checinski, Michael. 1985. "The Economics of Defense in the USSR." *Survey* 29(1): 59–79.

Cherniaev, A. 2003. *Byl li u Rossii shans? On-poslednii*. Moscow: Sobranie.

CIA. 1979. "Sovsim: A Model of the Soviet Economy." Washington, DC: CIA.

CIA. 1982. *Soviet Statistics on Capital Formation: A Reference Aid*. Washington, DC: CIA.

Citino, Robert M. 2007. "Military Histories Old and New: A Reintroduction." *American Historical Review* 112 (4): 1070–90.

Clark, Colin. 1956. "The Soviet Crisis." In Congress for Cultural Freedom 1956.

Clarke, Roger A. 1983. "The Study of Soviet-Type Economies: Some Trends and Conclusions." *Soviet Studies* 35 (4): 525–32.

Clayton, Gary E., and James E. Brown. 1988. *Economics: Principles and Practices*. Columbus, OH: Merrill.

Cocks, Paul M. 1980. *Science Policy: USA/USSR*. Vol. 2, *Science Policy in the Soviet Union*. Washington, DC: GPO.

Coffman, Edward M. 2013. *The Embattled Past*. Lexington: University of Kentucky Press.

Cohn, Stanley H. 1970. *Economic Development in the Soviet Union*. Lexington, MA: D. C. Heath.

Cohn, Stanley H. 1972. "National Income Growth Statistics." In Treml and Hardt 1972, 120–47.

Cohn, Stanley H. 1981. "A Comment on Alec Nove, 'A Note on Growth, Investment and Price Indexes.'" *Soviet Studies* 33 (2): 296–99.

Colander, David. 1989. "Research on the Economics Profession." *Journal of Economic Perspectives* 3 (4): 137–48.

Cole, G. D. H. 1939. "Nazi Economics: How Do They Manage It?" *Political Quarterly* 10 (1): 55–68.

Coleman, John R., Ted C. Soens, and Edwin Fenton. 1968. *Comparative Economic Systems: An Inquiry Approach*. New York: Holt, Rinehart and Winston.

Congress for Cultural Freedom. 1956. *The Soviet Economy: A Discussion*. London: Martin Secker and Warburg.

Conyngham, William J. 1982. *The Modernization of Soviet Industrial Management*. Cambridge, UK: Cambridge University Press.

Cooper, Julian. 1976. *Defence Production and the Soviet Economy, 1929–1941.* Birmingham, UK: University of Birmingham.

Cooper, Julian. 1982. "Innovation for Innovation in Soviet Industry." In Amann and Cooper 1982, 453–512.

Cooper, Julian. 1991. *The Former Soviet Defence Industry: Conversion and Reform.* London: Royal Institute of International Affairs.

Cooper, Julian. 1993. *The Conversion of the Former Soviet Defence Industry.* London: Royal Institute of International Affairs.

Cooper, Julian. 1998. "The Military Expenditure of the USSR and the Russian Federation, 1987–97." In *SIPRI Yearbook 1998: Armaments, Disarmament and International Security.* New York: Oxford University Press.

Cooper, Julian. 2013. "The Fate of the Military Economy." In *Handbook of the Economics and Political Economy of Transition*, edited by Paul Hare and Gerard Turley. London: Routledge.

Cooper, Leo. 1989. *Political Economy of Soviet Military Power.* Basingstoke: Palgrave Macmillan.

Cooper, Leo. 1991. *Soviet Reforms and Beyond.* Basingstoke: Macmillan.

Cowles, Gardner. 1958. Foreword to *Soviet Progress vs. American Enterprise*, Committee for Economic Development, 7–9. Garden City, NY: Doubleday.

Crane, Keith. 1988. "Military Spending in Czechoslovakia, Hungary, and Poland." *Journal of Comparative Economics* 12 (4): 1–35.

Craven, John. 1984. *Introduction to Economics: An Integrated Approach to Fundamental Principles.* New York: Blackwell.

Crosland, C. A. R. 1956. "Discussion." In Congress for Cultural Freedom 1956, 87–91.

Crowther-Heyck, Hunter. 2006. "Patrons of the Revolution: Ideas and Institutions in Postwar Behavioral Sciences." *Isis* 97 (3): 420–26.

Dallin, Alexander. 1973. "Bias and Blunders in American Studies on the USSR." *Slavic Review* 32 (3): 560–76.

Dallin, Alexander. 1982. "Soviet and East European Studies in the United States." In *Soviet and East European Studies in the International Framework*, edited by Arnold Buchholz. New York: Transnational Publishers.

Dalton, George. 1974. *Economic Systems and Society: Capitalism, Communism, and the Third World.* Baltimore: Penguin.

Davies, R. W. 1974. "A Note on Defence Aspects of the Urals-Kuznetsk Combine." *Soviet Studies* 26 (2): 272–74.

Davies, R. W. 1981. "Economic Planning in the USSR." In Borstein 1981, 7–38.

Davies, R. W. 1989a. "Economic and Social Policy in the USSR, 1917–1941." In *The Cambridge Economic History of Europe*, edited by Peter Mathias and Sidney Pollard, 984–1087. Vol. 8. Cambridge, UK: Cambridge University Press.

Davies, R. W. 1989b. *The Soviet Economy in Turmoil, 1929–1930.* Cambridge, MA: Harvard University Press.

Davies, R. W. 1993. "Soviet Military Expenditure and the Armaments Industry, 1929–1933: A Reconsideration." *Europe-Asia Studies* 45 (4): 577–86.

Davies, R. W. 1994. "Industry." In *The Economic Transformation of the Soviet Union, 1913–1945*, edited by R. W. Davies, Mark Harrison, and S. G. Wheatcroft, 131–58. Cambridge, UK: Cambridge University Press.

Davies, R. W. 2010. "The Economic History of the Soviet Union Reconsidered." *Kritika: Explorations in Russian and Eurasian History* 11 (1): 145–59.

Davis, Christopher. 2002. "Country Survey XVI: The Defence Sector in the Economy of a Declining Superpower: Soviet Union and Russia, 1965–2001." *Defence and Peace Economics* 13 (3): 145–77.

Degras, Jane, and Alec Nove, eds. 1964. *Soviet Planning: Essays in Honour of Naum Jasny*. Oxford: Basil Blackwell.

Desai, Padma. 1987. *The Soviet Economy: Problems and Prospects*. New York: Basil Blackwell.

Desai, Padma. 1989. *Perestroika in Perspective: The Design and Dilemmas of Soviet Reform*. Princeton, NJ: Princeton University Press.

De Schweinitz, Karl, Jr. 1964. Review of *Soviet Strategy for Economic Growth*, by Nicolas Spulber. Bloomington: Indiana University Press. *American Economic Review* 54 (6): 1135–37.

Despres, Laure, and Ksenya Khinchuk. 1990. "The Hidden Sector in Soviet Agriculture: A Study of the Military Sovkhozy and Auxiliary Farms." *Soviet Studies* 42 (2): 269–93.

Dessauer, Marie. 1935. "The German Bank Act of 1934." *Review of Economic Studies* 2 (3): 214–24.

Diamond, Arthur. M., Jr. 1996. "The Economics of Science." *Knowledge and Policy: The International Journal of Knowledge Transfer and Utilization* 9 (2–3): 6–49.

Diamond, Arthur M., Jr., and Donald R. Haurin. 1995. "Changing Patterns of Subfield Specialization among Cohorts of Economists from 1927–1988." *Research in the History of Economic Thought and Methodology* 13, 103–23.

Dienes, Leslie. 1991. "Siberia: *Perestroika* and Economic Development." *Soviet Geography* 32 (7): 445–57.

Dienes, Leslie. 2002. "Reflections on a Geographic Dichotomy: Archipelago Russia." *Eurasian Geography and Economics* 43 (6): 443–58.

Djilas, Milovan. 1962. *Conversations with Stalin*. New York: Harcourt Brace.

Dobb, Maurice. 1928. *Russian Economic Development since the Revolution*. New York: E. P. Dutton.

Dobb, Maurice. 1933. "Economic Theory and the Problems of a Socialist Economy." *The Economic Journal* 43 (172): 588–98.

Dobb, Maurice. 1955. "Comparative Rates of Growth in Industry: A Comment on Strumilin's Article on 'Expanded Reproduction.'" *Soviet Studies* 7 (1): 52–58.

Dobb, Maurice. 1966. *Soviet Economic Development since 1917*. New York: International Publishers.

Dobb, Maurice. 1967. *Papers on Capitalism, Development, and Planning.* London: Routledge and Kegan Paul.

Doblin, Ernest. 1942. "The German 'Profit Stop' of 1941." *Social Research* 9 (3): 371–78.

Dobrynin, Anatolii. 1996. *Sugubo doveritel'no.* Moscow: Avtor.

Dodge, Norton T., and Dana G. Dalrymple. 1966. "The Stalingrad Tractor Plant in Early Soviet Planning." *Soviet Studies* 18 (2): 164–68.

Dodge, Norton T., and Charles K. Wilber. 1970. "The Relevance of Soviet Industrial Experience for Less Developed Countries." *Soviet Studies* 21 (3): 330–49.

Domar, E. D. 1957. *Essays in the Theory of Economic Growth.* New York: Oxford University Press.

Domeratzky, Louis. 1941. "The Industrial Power of the Nazis." *Foreign Affairs* 19 (3): 641–54.

DOS (US Department of State) and AVC (Bureau of Arms Control, Verification and Compliance). 2002. *World Military Expenditures and Arms Transfers, 1999–2000.* Washington, DC: GPO.

Douglass, Joseph D., Jr. 1995. "Chemical and Biological Warfare Unmasked." *Wall Street Journal,* November 2.

Dowlah, Abu F. 1992. *Soviet Political Economy in Transition: From Lenin to Gorbachev.* New York: Greenwood Press.

Dreger, Alice. 2011. "Darkness's Descent on the American Anthropological Association." *Human Nature* 22 (3): 225–46. doi: 10.1007/s12110-011-9103-y.

Drescher, Leo. 1934. "The New German Inheritance Law for Agriculture (Erbhofgesetz)." *Journal of Farm Economics* 16 (1): 149–51.

Dulleck, Uwe, and Rudolf Kerschbamer. 2006. "On Doctors, Mechanics, and Computer Specialists: The Economics of Credence Goods." *Journal of Economic Literature* 44 (1): 5–42.

Dunmore, Timothy. 1980. *The Stalinist Command Economy: The Soviet State Apparatus and Economic Policy 1945–1953.* New York: St. Martin's.

Dyker, David A. 1976. *The Soviet Economy.* New York: St. Martin's Press.

Dyker, David A. 1983. *The Process of Investment in the Soviet Union.* Cambridge, UK: Cambridge University Press.

Dyker, David A. 1985. *The Future of the Soviet Economic Planning System.* Armonk, NY: M. E. Sharpe.

Dyker, David A., ed. 1987. *The Soviet Union under Gorbachev: Prospects for Reform.* London: Croom Helm.

Dyker, David A. 1992. *Restructuring the Soviet Economy.* London: Routledge.

Earle, John S., and Ivan Komarov. 1998. "Measuring Defense Conversion in Russian Industry." SITE Working Paper no. 134, Stockholm Institute of Economics, Stockholm, Sweden.

Easterly, William. 2001. *The Elusive Quest for Growth.* Cambridge, MA: MIT Press.

Easterly, William, and Stanley Fischer. 1995. "The Soviet Economic Decline." *World Bank Economic Review* 9 (3): 341–71.

Eatwell, John, Murray Milgate, and Peter Newman, eds. 1990. *Problems of the Planned Economy.* New York: W. W. Norton.

Eckstein, Alexander, ed. 1971. *Comparison of Economic Systems: Theoretical and Methodological Approaches.* Berkeley: University of California Press.

"Editorial." 1949. *Soviet Studies* 1 (1): 1–2.

Editors of *Survey*, eds. *The State of Soviet Science.* 1965. Cambridge, MA: MIT Press.

Edmondson, Linda, and Peter Waldron, eds. 1992. *Economy and Society in Russia and the Soviet Union, 1860–1930: Essays for Olga Crisp.* New York: St. Martin's.

Egle, Walter. 1938. "The Progress of Mass Production and the German Small-Scale Industries." *Journal of Political Economy* 46 (3): 376–95.

Einzig, Paul. 1941. "Hitler's 'New Order' in Theory and Practice." *Economic Journal* 51 (201): 1–18.

Ekspertnyi Institut. 1996. *Oboronnnaia promyshlennost' Rossii: konversiia ili rekonstruktsiia?* Moscow: Agentstvo Informart.

Elliott, John E. 1973. *Comparative Economic Systems.* Englewood Cliffs, NJ: Prentice Hall.

Elliott, John E., and Robert W. Campbell. 1985. *Comparative Economic Systems.* Belmont, CA: Wadsworth.

Ellis, Howard S. 1940. "German Exchange Control, 1931–1939: From an Emergency Measure to a Totalitarian Institution." *Quarterly Journal of Economics* 54 (4): 1–158.

Ellman, Michael. 1971. *Soviet Planning Today: Proposals for an Optimally Functioning Economic System.* Cambridge, UK: Cambridge University Press.

Ellman, Michael. 1973. *Planning Problems in the USSR: The Contribution of Mathematical Economics to Their Solution 1960–1971.* Cambridge, UK: Cambridge University Press.

Ellman, Michael. 1989. *Socialist Planning.* New York: Cambridge University Press.

Ellman, Michael. 1990a. "Evgenii Alexeyevich Preobrazhensky." In Eatwell et al. 1990, 214–17.

Ellman, Michael. 1990b. "Grigorii Alexandrovich Fel'dman." In Eatwell et al. 1990, 109–12.

Ellman, Michael. 2004. "Soviet Industrialization: A Remarkable Success?" *Slavic Review* 4 (63): 841–59.

Ellman, Michael. 2006. "Churchill on Stalin: A Note." *Europe-Asia Studies* 58 (6): 965–71.

Ellman, Michael. 2008a. "Abram Bergson (1914–2003)." In *The New Palgrave Dictionary of Economics*, edited by Steven N. Durlauf and Lawrence E. Blume. 2nd ed. Vol. 7. New York: Palgrave Macmillan.

Ellman, Michael. 2008b. "The Political Economy of Stalinism in the Light of the Archival Revolution." *Journal of Institutional Economics* 4 (1): 99–125.

Ellman, Michael. 2009. "What Did the Study of the Soviet Economy Contribute to Mainstream Economics?" *Comparative Economic Studies* 51 (1): 1–19.

Ellman, Michael. 2014. *Socialist Planning.* 3rd ed. Cambridge, UK: Cambridge University Press.

Ellman, Michael, and Vladimir Kontorovich, eds. 1992. *The Disintegration of the Soviet Economic System.* London: Routledge.

Ellman, Michael, and Vladimir Kontorovich. 1997. "The Collapse of the Soviet System and the Memoir Literature." *Europe-Asia Studies,* 49 (2): 259–79.

Ellman, Michael, and Vladimir Kontorovich, eds. 1998. *The Destruction of the Soviet Economic System: An Insider's History.* Armonk, NY: M. E. Sharpe.

Engerman, David C. 1999. "New Society, New Scholarship: Soviet Studies Programmes in Interwar America." *Minerva* 37 (1): 25–43.

Engerman, David C. 2000. "Modernization from the Other Shore: American Observers and the Costs of Soviet Economic Development." *American Historical Review* 105 (2): 383–416.

Engerman, David C. 2003. *Modernization from the Other Shore: American Intellectuals and the Romance of Russian Economic Development.* Cambridge, MA: Harvard University Press.

Engerman, David C. 2004. "The Ironies of the Iron Curtain." *Cahiers du Monde Russe* 45 (3–4): 465–96.

Engerman, David C. 2009. *Know Your Enemy: The Rise and Fall of America's Soviet Experts.* New York: Oxford University Press.

Epstein, David F. 1990. "The Economic Cost of Soviet Security and Empire." In Rowen and Wolf Jr. 1990, 127–54.

Erickson, John. 1962. *The Soviet High Command: A Military-Political History, 1918–1941.* London: Macmillan.

Erickson, John. 1983. "Over to you, Mr. Andropov." *Nature* 301 (3): 443–44.

Ericson, Paul. 1976. "Soviet Efforts to Increase Exports of Manufactured Products to the West." In Congress 1976.

Ericson, Richard E. 1979. "A Theoretical and Institutional Analysis of Industrial Supply in the USSR: A Study of Resource Allocation under Uncertainty." CRMS Working Paper IP-276. University of California, Berkeley.

Ericson, Richard E. 2008. "Command Economy." In *The New Palgrave Dictionary of Economics,* edited by Steven N. Durlauf and Lawrence E. Blume. 2nd ed. Vol. 7. New York: Palgrave Macmillan.

Erlich, Alexander. 1950. "Preobrazhenskii and the Economics of Soviet Industrialization." *Quarterly Journal of Economics* 64 (1): 57–88.

Erlich, Alexander. 1960. *The Soviet Industrialization Debate, 1924–1928.* Cambridge, MA: Harvard University Press.

Erlich, Alexander. 1967. *The Soviet Industrialization Debate, 1924–1928.* Reprint, Cambridge, MA: Harvard University Press.

Erlich, Alexander. 1978. "Dobb and the Marx-Feldman model: A Problem in Soviet Economic Strategy." *Cambridge Journal of Economics* 2 (2): 203–14.

Evangelista, Matthew. 1988. *Innovation and the Arms Race: How the United States and the Soviet Union Develop New Military Technologies.* Ithaca, NY: Cornell University Press.

Eydelman, Moisei. 1998. "Monopolized Statistics under a Totalitarian Regime." In Ellman and Kontorovich 1998, 70–76.

Fallenbuchl, Zbigniew M. 1970. "The Communist Pattern of Industrialization." *Soviet Studies* 21 (4): 458–84.

Fallenbuchl, Zbigniew M., ed. 1975. *Economic Development in the Soviet Union and Eastern Europe.* Vol. 1, *Research, Technology, and Income Distribution.* New York: Praeger.

Fallenbuchl, Zbigniew M., ed. 1976. *Economic Development in the Soviet Union and Eastern Europe.* Vol. 2, *Sectoral Analysis.* New York: Praeger.

Feiler, Arthur. 1938. "International Trade under Totalitarian Governments." *Social Research* 5 (4): 424–41.

Feldman, Grigorii A. (1928) 1964. "K teorii tempob rosta narodnogo dokhoda." *Planovoe Khoziaistvo* 11, 146–70. Translated as "On the Theory of Growth Rates of National Income I," in Spulber 1964, 174–202.

Ferrero, Mario. 1993. "Why Were Investment Ratios So High in Soviet-Type Economies?: A Public Choice Approach." *Eastern Economic Journal* 19 (1): 1–14.

Field, Daniel. "From the Editor: Economists." 1984. *The Russian Review* 43 (4): v–vii.

Filtzer, Donald. 1979. "Portrait: Evgeny Preobrazhensky." *Challenge* 22 (1): 64–66.

Firth, Noel, and James Noren. 1998. *Soviet Defense Spending: A History of CIA Estimates, 1950–1990.* College Station: Texas A&M University Press.

Fishlow, Albert. 1991. Review of *Handbook of Development Economics*, by Hollis Chenery and T. N. Srinivasan. *Journal of Economic Literature* 29 (4): 1728–37.

Fomin, D. A. 2006. "Politicheskaia ekonomiia: panegirik vmesto epitafii?" *EKO* 7, 166–90.

Fortescue, Stephen. 1986. *The Communist Party and Soviet Science.* Baltimore: Johns Hopkins University Press.

Fortescue, Stephen. 1990. *Science Policy in the Soviet Union.* London: Routledge.

Fourcade-Gourinchas, Marion. 2001. "Politics, Institutional Structures, and the Rise of Economics: A Comparative Study." *Theory and Society* 30, 397–447.

Frank, 1973. Victor S. 1964. "Soviet Studies in Western Europe: Britain." *Survey* 50, 90–96.

Freeman, Christopher. 1972. Review of *Western Technology and Soviet Economic Development, 1930–1945*, by Antony C. Sutton. *The Journal of Political Economy* 81 (2): 511–12.

Freeman, Derek. 1999. *The Fateful Hoaxing of Margaret Mead: A Historical Analysis of Her Samoan Research.* Boulder, CO: Westview Press.

Freris, Andrew. 1984. *The Soviet Industrial Enterprise: Theory and Practice.* New York: St. Martin's Press.

Friedberg, Aaron L. 2000. *In the Shadow of the Garrison State*. Princeton, NJ: Princeton University Press.

Friedman, Milton. 1953a. "The Methodology of Positive Economics." In Friedman 1953b, 3–43.

Friedman, Milton. 1953b. *Essays in Positive Economics*. Chicago: University of Chicago Press.

Friedman, Norman. 2000. *The Fifty-Year War: Conflict and Strategy in the Cold War*. Annapolis: Naval Institute Press.

Fusfeld, Daniel R. 1982. *Economics: Principles of Political Economy*. Glenview, IL: Scott Foresman.

Gaddy, Clifford G. 1996. *The Price of the Past: Russia's Struggle with the Legacy of a Militarized Economy*. Washington, DC: Brookings Institution Press.

Gaidar, Yegor. 2003. "The Inevitability of Collapse of the Socialist Economy." *The Economics of Transition*, edited by Yegor Gaidar, 19–30. Cambridge, MA: MIT Press.

Galbraith, J. K. 1939. "Hereditary Land in the Third Reich." *Quarterly Journal of Economics* 53 (3): 465–76.

Gansler, Jacques S. 1982. *The Defense Industry*. Cambridge, MA: MIT Press.

Garbuzov, V. F., ed. 1984. *Finansovo-kreditnyi slovar'*. Vol. 1. Moscow: Finansy i statistika.

Gardner, Harold S. 1988. *Comparative Economic Systems*. Chicago, IL: Dryden Press.

Gatrell, Peter. 1994. *Government, Industry and Rearmament in Russia, 1900–1914: The Last Argument of Tsarism*. Cambridge, UK: Cambridge University Press.

Gatrell, Peter. 2005. *Russia's First World War: A Social and Economic Study*. Harlow, UK: Pearson Education.

Gay, David E. R. 1980. *The Soviet Economy. How It Really Works*, by Constantin A. Krylov. *Slavic Review* 39 (3): 750–76.

Gelman, Harry. 1992. *The Rise and Fall of National Security Decisionmaking in the Former USSR*. Santa Monica, CA: RAND Corporation.

Gerschenkron, Alexander. 1953. "Comment." In Bergson 1953a, 23–32.

Gerschenkron, Alexander. 1962a. "The Changeability of a Dictatorship." *World Politics* 14 (4): 576–604.

Gerschenkron, Alexander. 1962b. *Economic Backwardness in Historical Perspective*. Cambridge, MA: Belknap Press.

Gerschenkron, Alexander. 1968. "American Research on the Soviet Economy." In *Continuity in History and Other Essays*. Cambridge, MA: Belknap Press.

Gerschenkron, Alexander. 1970. *Europe in the Russian Mirror: Four Lectures in Economic History*. Cambridge, UK: Cambridge University Press.

Gerschenkron, Alexander. 1971. "Ideology as a System Determinant." In Eckstein 1971, 269–89.

Goldman, Alvin I., and Moshe Shaked. 1991. "An Economic Model of Scientific Activity and Truth Acquisition." *Philosophical Studies* 63 (1): 31–55.

Goldman, Marshall, I. 1964. *Comparative Economic Systems: A Reader.* 1st ed. New York: Random House.

Goldman, Marshall I. 1968. *The Soviet Economy: Myth and Reality.* Englewood Cliffs, NJ: Prentice Hall.

Goldman, Marshall, I. 1971. *Comparative Economic Systems: A Reader* 2nd ed. New York: Random House.

Goldman, Marshall I. 1983. *USSR in Crisis: The Failure of an Economic System.* New York: W. W. Norton.

Goldman, Marshall I. 1987. *Gorbachev's Challenge: Economic Reform in the Age of High Technology.* New York: W. W. Norton.

Goldman, Marshall I. 1991. *What Went Wrong with Perestroika.* New York: W. W. Norton.

Goldstein, Edward R. 1971. *Military Aspects of Russian Industrialization: The Defense Industries, 1890–1917.* Unpublished PhD diss., Case Western Reserve University.

Goodwin, Craufurd D., ed. 1991. *Economics and National Security: A History of Their Interaction.* Durham, NC: Duke University Press.

Gorbachev, Mikhail. 1995. *Zhizn' i reformy.* Vol. 1. Moscow: Novosti.

Gorshkov, S. G. 1979. *Morskaia moshch' gosudarstva.* 2nd ed. Moscow: Voenizdat.

Goskomstat SSSR. 1988. *Narodnoe khoziaistvo SSSR v 1987 g.* Moscow: Finansy i statistika.

Goskomstat SSSR. 1991. *Narodnoe khoziaistvo SSSR v 1990 g.* Moscow: Finansy i statistika.

Gosplan SSSR. 1969. *Metodicheskie ukazaniia k razrabotke gosudarstvennykh planov razvitiia narodnogo khoziaistva SSSR.* Moscow: Ekonomika.

Gosplan SSSR. 1974. *Metodicheskie ukazaniia k razrabotke gosudarstvennykh planov razvitiia narodnogo khoziaistva SSSR.* Moscow: Ekonomika.

Gottlieb, Manuel. 1984. *A Theory of Economic Systems.* Orlando, FL: Academic Press.

Graham, Thomas, Jr. 2002. *Disarmament Sketches: Three Decades of Arms Control and International Law.* Seattle: University of Washington Press.

Granick, David. 1954. *Management of the Industrial Firm in the USSR: A Study in Soviet Planning.* New York: Columbia University Press.

Granick, David. 1960. *The Red Executive: A Study of the Organization in Russian Industry.* Garden City, NY: Doubleday.

Granick, David. 1962. "An Organizational Model of Soviet Industrial Planning." In Holzman 1962.

Grayson, T. J. 1975. Review of *Western Technology and Soviet Economic Development, 1945 to 1965,* by Antony C. Sutton. *Soviet Studies* 27 (1): 301–4.

Grebler, Leo. 1937a. "Work Creation Policy in Germany, 1932–1935: I." *International Labor Review* 35 (3): 329–51.

Grebler, Leo. 1937b. "Work Creation Policy in Germany, 1932–1935: II." *International Labor Review* 35 (4): 505–27.

Green, Donald W., and Christopher I. Higgins. 1977. *SOVMOD I: A Macroeconometric Model of the Soviet Economy.* New York: Academic Press.

Gregory, Paul R. 1970. *Socialist and Nonsocialist Industrialization Patterns: A Comparative Appraisal.* New York: Praeger.

Gregory, Paul R. 1974. "Economic Growth, US Defense Expenditures and the Soviet Defence Budget: A Suggested Model." *Soviet Studies* 26 (1): 71.

Gregory, Paul R. 1990. *Essentials of Economics.* 2nd ed. Glenview, IL: Scott Foresman.

Gregory, Paul R. 2004. *The Political Economy of Stalinism: Evidence from the Soviet Secret Archives.* Cambridge, UK: Cambridge University Press.

Gregory, Paul R., and Mark Harrison. 2005. "Allocation under Dictatorship: Research in Stalin's Archives." *Journal of Economic Literature,* 43 (3): 721–61.

Gregory, Paul R., and Robert C. Stuart. 1980. *Comparative Economic Systems.* Boston, MA: Houghton Mifflin.

Gregory, Paul R., and Robert C. Stuart. 1981. *Soviet Economic Structure and Performance.* 2nd ed. New York: Harper and Row.

Gregory, Paul R., and Robert C. Stuart. 1985. *Comparative Economic Systems.* 2nd ed. Boston, MA: Houghton Mifflin.

Gregory, Paul R., and Robert C. Stuart. 1986. *Soviet Economic Structure and Performance.* 3rd ed. New York: Harper and Row.

Gregory, Paul R., and Robert C. Stuart. 1989. *Comparative Economic Systems.* 3rd ed. Boston, MA: Houghton Mifflin.

Gregory, Paul R., and Robert C. Stuart. 1990. *Soviet Economic Structure and Performance.* 4th ed. New York: Harper and Row.

Gregory, Paul R., and Robert C. Stuart. 1992. *Comparative Economic Systems.* 4th ed. Boston, MA: Houghton Mifflin.

Gregory, Paul R., and Robert C. Stuart. 2001. *Russian and Soviet Economic Performance and Structure.* 7th ed. Boston: Addison-Wesley.

Gregory, Paul R., and Roy J. Ruffin. 1989. *Basic Economics.* Glenview, IL: Scott Foresman.

Grossman, Gregory. 1953. "National Income." In Bergson, 1953, 1–37.

Grossman, Gregory. 1958. "Thirty Years of Soviet Industrialization." *Survey* 26, 15–21.

Grossman, Gregory. 1959. "Economics." In *American Research on Russia,* edited by Harold H. Fisher, 34–50. Bloomington: Indiana University Press.

Grossman, Gregory, ed. 1960. *Value and Plan: Economic Calculation and Organization in Eastern Europe.* Berkeley: University of California Press.

Grossman, Gregory. 1963. "Notes for a Theory of the Command Economy." *Soviet Studies* 15, 101–23.

Grossman, Gregory. 1974. *Economic Systems.* 2nd ed. Englewood Cliffs, NJ: Prentice Hall.

Grossman, Gregory. 1983. "Economics of Virtuous Haste: A View of Soviet Industrialization and Institutions." In *Marxism, Central Planning, and the Soviet*

*Economy: Economic Essays in Honor of Alexander Erlich*, edited by Padma Desai, 198–206. Cambridge, MA: MIT Press.

Gruchy, Allan G. 1977. *Comparative Economic Systems: Competing Ways to Stability, Growth, and Welfare*. 2nd ed. Boston, MA: Houghton Mifflin.

Grunfeld, Judith. 1942. "Mobilization of Women in Germany." *Social Research*, 9 (4): 476–94.

Guilaine, Jean, and Jean Zammit. 2005. *The Origins of War: Violence in Prehistory*. Malden, MA: Blackwell.

Guillebaud, C. W. 1940. "Hitler's New Economic Order for Europe." *Economic Journal* 50 (200): 449–60.

Guroff, Gregory, and Fred V. Carstensen. 1983. *Entrepreneurship in Imperial Russia and the Soviet Union*. Princeton, NJ: Princeton University Press.

Habeck, Mary. 2002. "Dress Rehearsals, 1937–1941." In *The Military History of the Soviet Union*, edited by Robin Higham and Frederick W. Kagan, 93–109. New York: Palgrave.

Hacker, Barton C. 1977. "The Weapons of the West: Military Technology and Modernization in 19th-Century China and Japan." *Technology and Culture* 18 (1): 16–58.

Haitani, Kanji. 1986. Comparative Economic Systems: Organizational and Managerial Perspectives. Englewood Cliffs, NJ: Prentice Hall.

Ham, William T. 1934. "Labor under the German Republic." *Quarterly Journal of Economics* 48 (2): 203–28.

Ham, William T. 1936. "The Organization of Farm Laborers in Germany." *Journal of Political Economy* 44 (3): 374–97.

Hamermesh, Daniel S. 2007. "Replication in Economics." NBER Working Paper 13026, National Bureau of Economic Research, Cambridge MA.

Hands, D. Wade. 1997. "Caveat Emptor: Economics and Contemporary Philosophy of Science." In "Proceedings of the 1996 Biennial Meetings of the Philosophy of Science Association. Part II: Symposia Papers," supplement, *Philosophy of Science* 64, S107–S116.

Hanson, Philip. 1981. *Trade and Technology in Soviet-Western Relations*. New York: Columbia University Press.

Hanson, Philip. 2003. *The Rise and Fall of the Soviet Economy*. London: Pearson Education.

Hanson, Victor Davis. 2011. *The Father of Us All: War and History, Ancient and Modern*. New York: Bloomsbury Press.

Hara, Akira. 1998. "Japan: Guns before Rice." In Harrison 1998, 224–64.

Hardt, John P. 2004. "Abram Bergson and the Development of Soviet Economic Studies." *Problems of Post-Communism* 51 (4): 34–39.

Hardt, John P., Marvin Hoffenberg, Norman Kaplan, and Herbert S. Levine, eds. 1967. *Mathematics and Computers in Soviet Economic Planning*. New Haven, CT: Yale University Press.

Hardt, John P., and Carl H. McMillan, eds. *Planned Economies: Confronting the Challenges of the 1980s*. New York: Cambridge University Press, 1988.

Hardt, John P., with C. Darwin Stolzenbach and Martin J. Kohn. 1961. *The Cold War Economic Gap: The Increasing Threat to American Supremacy*. New York: Praeger.

Hare, P. *Central Planning*. 1991. Chur, Switzerland: Harwood Academic Publishers.

Harris, Chauncy D. 1997. "Russian, Slavic, and Soviet Studies in the United States: Some Memories and Notes." *Russian History/Histoire Russe* 24 (4): 441–56.

Harrison, Mark. 1985. *Soviet Planning in Peace and War 1938–1945*. Cambridge, UK: Cambridge University Press.

Harrison, Mark. 1998a. "The Economics of World War II: An Overview." In Harrison 1998b, 1–42.

Harrison, Mark. 1998b. *The Economics of World War II: Six Great Powers in International Comparison*. Cambridge, UK: Cambridge University Press.

Harrison, Mark. 2003. "How Much Did the Soviets Really Spend on Defence?: New Evidence from the Close of the Brezhnev Era." PERSA Working Paper no. 24, Department of Economics, University of Warwick.

Harrison, Mark. 2006. "Five-Year plan." In *Europe since 1914: Encyclopedia of the Age of War and Reconstruction*, edited by John Merriman and Jay Winter, 1097–1101. Detroit, MI: Scribner's.

Harrison, Mark, ed. 2008. *The Defense Industry in the Stalinist State*. New Haven, CT: Guns and Rubles.

Harrison, Mark, and R. W. Davies. 1997. "The Soviet Military-Economic Effort during the Second Five-Year Plan (1933–1937)." *Europe-Asia Studies* 49 (3): 369–406.

Harrison, Mark, and Nikolai Simonov. 2000. "Voenpriemka: Prices, Costs, and Quality Assurance in Interwar Defence Industry." In Barber and Harrison 2000, 223–45.

Harvey, Mose L., Leon Goure, and Vladimir Prokofieff. 1972. *Science and Technology as an Instrument of Soviet Policy*. Miami: Center for Advanced International Studies, University of Miami.

Haynes, Michael, and Rumy Husan. 2003. *A Century of State Murder? Death and Policy in Twentieth-Century Russia*. London: Pluto Press.

Heckscher, Eli F. 1935. *Mercantilism*. London: Allen and Unwin.

Hegemann, Werner. 1935. "Recent Trends in German Regional Planning." *Journal of the American Institute of Planners* 1 (4): 85–86.

Helpman, Elhanan. 2004. *The Mystery of Economic Growth*. Cambridge, MA: Belknap Press.

Herman, Leon. 1963. *Varieties of Economic Secrecy in the Soviet Union*. Santa Monica, CA: RAND Corporation.

Hessler, Julie. 2004. *A Social History of Soviet Trade*. Princeton, NJ: Princeton University Press.

Hewett, Ed A. 1988. *Reforming the Soviet Economy: Equality versus Efficiency*. Washington, DC: Brookings Institution.

Heyck, Hunter, and Kaser, David. 2010. "Introduction." *Isis* 101 (2): 362–66.

Higgs, Robert. 1994. "The Cold War Economy: Opportunity Costs, Ideology, and the Politics of Crisis." *Explorations in Economic History* 31 (3): 283–312.

Hill, Fiona, and Clifford Gaddy. 2003. *The Siberian Curse: How Communist Planners Left Russia Out in the Cold.* Washington, DC: Brookings Institution Press.

Hillmann, H. C. 1940. "Analysis of Germany's Foreign Trade and the War." *Economica*, n.s, 7 (25): 66–88.

Hirsch, Hans. 1961. *Quantity Planning and Price Planning in the Soviet Union.* Philadelphia: University of Pennsylvania Press.

Hirschman, Albert O. 1981. *Essays in Trespassing: Economics to Politics and Beyond.* Cambridge, UK: Cambridge University Press.

Hodgman, Donald R. 1954. *Soviet Industrial Production 1928–1951.* Cambridge, MA: Harvard University Press.

Hoeffding, Oleg. 1954. *Soviet National Income and Product in 1928.* New York: Columbia University Press.

Holden, Constance. 1984. "A Comeback for Soviet Studies: After a 15-Year Decline, Scholarship on the U.S.S.R. and East Europe Is Being Bolstered by New Programs and Money." *Science*, n.s., 223 (4638): 795–96.

Holesovsky, Vaclav. 1977. *Economic Systems: Analysis and Comparison.* New York: McGraw-Hill.

Holliday, George D. 1979. *Technology Transfer in the USSR, 1928–1937 and 1966–1975: The Role of Western Technology in Soviet Economic Development.* Boulder, CO: Westview Press.

Holloway, David. 1982. "Innovation in the Defence Sector." In Amann and Cooper 1982, 276–367.

Holloway, David. 1983. *The Soviet Union and the Arms Race.* New Haven, CT: Yale University Press.

Holzman, Franklyn D. 1957. "The Soviet Ural-Kuznetsk Combine: A Study in Investment Criteria and Industrialization Policies." *The Quarterly Journal of Economics* 71 (3): 368–405.

Holzman, Franklyn D., ed. 1962. *Readings on the Soviet Economy.* Chicago: Rand McNally.

Holzman, Franklyn D. 1982. *The Soviet Economy: Past, Present, and Future.* Headline Series 260. New York: Foreign Policy Association.

Holzman, Franklyn D. 1994. "Politics, Military Spending and the National Welfare." *Comparative Economic Studies* 36 (3): 1–14.

Hubbard, Raymond, and Daniel E. Vetter. 1992. "The Publication Incidence of Replication and Critical Commentary in Economics." *The American Economist* 36 (1): 29–34.

Humber, John Richard. 1940. "The Effects of German Clearing Agreements and Import Restrictions on Cotton, 1934–1939." *Southern Economic Journal* 6 (4): 419–39.

Humphreys, David. 1994. *Mining and Metals in the CIS: Between Autarky and Integration*. London: Royal Institute for International Affairs.

Hunter, Holland. 1957. *Soviet Transportation Policy*. Cambridge, MA: Harvard University Press.

Hunter, Holland. 1964. "Priorities and Shortfalls in Prewar Soviet Planning." In Degras and Nove 1964, 3–31.

Hunter, Holland. 1972. "Soviet Economic Statistics: An Introduction." In Treml and Hardt 1972, 3–20.

Hunter, Holland. 1974. Review of *Western Technology and Soviet Economic Development, 1945–1965*, by Antony C. Sutton. *Russian Review* 33 (4): 435–36.

Hunter, Holland. 1983a. Review of *Industrial Innovation in the Soviet Union*, by Ronald Amann and Julian Cooper. *Journal of Economic History* 43 (4): 1026–27.

Hunter, Holland. 1983b. "The New Tasks of Soviet Planning in the Thirties." In *Marxism, Central Planning, and the Soviet Economy: Economic Essays in Honor of Alexander Erlich*, edited by Padman Desai, 173–97. Cambridge, MA: MIT Press.

Hunter, Holland. 1998. "Tracking Economic Change with Ambiguous Tools: Soviet Planning, 1928–1991." *Journal of Economic History* 58 (4): 1027–31.

Hunter, Holland, and Janusz M. Szyrmer. 1992. *Faulty Foundations: Soviet Economic Policies, 1928–1940*. Princeton, NJ: Princeton University Press.

Hutching, Raymond. 1971. *Soviet Economic Development*. Oxford: Blackwell.

Hutchings, Raymond. 1976. *Soviet Science, Technology, Design: Interaction and Convergence*. London: Oxford University Press.

Hutchings, Raymond. 1977. *Soviet Economic Development*. New York: New York University Press.

Hutchings, Raymond. 1982. *Soviet Economic Development*. 2nd ed. New York: New York University Press.

Hutchings, Raymond. 1984. Review of *Industrial Innovation in the Soviet Union*, by Ronald Amann and Julian Cooper. *Soviet Studies* 36 (1): 149–51.

Hutchings, Raymond. 1987. *Soviet Secrecy and Non-Secrecy*. London: Macmillan.

Hutton, Graham. 1939. "German Economic Tension: Causes and Results." *Foreign Affairs* 17 (3): 524–37.

Iaremenko, Iu. 1990. "Ekonomika khanzhestva." *Pravda*, September 1.

Iaremenko, Iu. 1997. *Prognozirovanie razvitiia narodnogo khoziaistva i varianty ekonomicheskoi politiki*. Izbrannye trudy v trekh knigakh, vol 2. Moscow: Nauka.

IMELS (Institut Marksa-Engelsa-Lenina-Stalina) pri TsK KPSS. 1953. *Kommunisticheskaia partiia Sovetskogo Soiuza v rezoliutsiiakh i resheniiakh siezdov, konferentsii i plenumov TsK, 1898–1953*. Part 2. Moscow: Gospolitizdat.

IMELS (Institut Marksa-Engelsa-Lenina-Stalina) pri TsK KPSS. 1954. *Kommunisticheskaia partiia Sovetskogo Soiuza v rezoliutsiiakh i resheniiakh siezdov, konferentsii i plenumov TsK, 1898–1954*. Moscow: Gospolitizdat.

Ioannidis, John P. A. 2012a. "Why Science Is Not Necessarily Self-Correcting." *Perspectives of Psychological Science* 7 (6): 645–54.

Ioannidis, John P. A. 2012b. "Scientific Inbreeding and Same-Team Replication: Type D Personality as an Example." *Journal of Psychosomatic Research* 73 (6): 408–10.

Ioannidis, John P. A., and Chris Doucouliagos. 2013. "What's to Know about the Credibility of Empirical Economics?" *Journal of Economic Surveys* 27 (5): 997–1004.

Ioffe, Ia. 1948. *Planirovanie promyshlennogo proizvodstva.* Moscow: Gosplanizdat.

*Istoriia vsesoiuznoi kommunisticheskoi partii (bol'shevikov). Kratkii kurs.* (1938) 1997. Moscow: Pisatel'.

Isaev, A. 1989. "Reforma i oboronnye otrasli." *Kommunist*, no. 5, 24–31.

Jacobsen, Carl G., ed. 1987. *The Soviet Defence Enigma: Estimating Costs and Burdens.* New York: Oxford University Press.

Jasny, Naum. 1951. *The Soviet Economy during the Plan Era.* Stanford, CA: Stanford University Press.

Jasny, Naum. 1956. "On the Wrong Track." *Soviet Studies* 8 (1): 50–76.

Jasny, Naum. 1961. *Soviet Industrialization: 1928–1952.* Chicago: University of Chicago Press.

Jasny, Naum. 1962. *Essays on the Soviet Economy.* Chicago: University of Chicago Press.

Jasny, Naum. 1964. Review of *Soviet Strategy for Economic Growth*, by Nicolas Spulber. *Annals of the American Academy of Political and Social Science* 356, 213–14.

Jasny, Naum. 1976. *To Live Long Enough.* Edited, with biographical comments by Betty A. Laird and Roy D. Laird. Lawrence: University of Kansas Press.

Jeffries, Ian. 1990. *A Guide to the Socialist Economies.* London: Routledge.

Just, Artur W. 1936. *The Red Army.* London: Figurehead.

Kaegi, Walter Emil, Jr. 1981. "The Crisis in Military Historiography." *Armed Forces and Society* 7 (2): 299–316.

Kagel, John, Raymond Battalio, Howard Rachlin, and Leonard Green. 1981. "Demand Curves for Animal Consumers." *The Quarterly Journal of Economics* 96 (1): 1–15.

Karagedov, R. G. 1970. "Reforma glazami direktora." *Ekonomika i organizatsiia promyshlennogo proizvodstva*, no. 1.

Kaser, Michael. 1970. *Soviet Economics.* New York: McGraw-Hill.

Kaser, Michael. 1972. "The Publication of Soviet Statistics." In Treml and Hardt, 1972, 45–69.

Katona, George M. 1934. "How Real Is the German Recovery." *Foreign Affairs* 13 (1): 26–44.

Katona, George M. 1935. "The 'Miracle' of German Recovery." *Foreign Affairs* 14 (2): 348–50.

Katsenelinboigen, Aron. 1978. "Interaction of Foreign and Economic Policy in the Soviet Union." *The Papers of the Peace Science Society (International)* 28: 26–36.

Kaufman, Richard F. 1978. *Western Perceptions of Soviet Economic Trends.* A staff study prepared for the use of the Subcommittee on Priorities and Economy in Government of the Joint Economic Committee. 95th Cong. 2nd sess.

Keeley, Lawrence H. 1996. *War before Civilization: The Myth of the Peaceful Savage.* New York: Oxford University Press.

Keizer, Willem. 1971. *The Soviet Quest for Economic Rationality: The Conflict of Economic and Political Aims in the Soviet Economy 1953–1968*. Economic Series, vol. 9. Rotterdam: Rotterdam University Press.

Keller, Bill. 2002. "The Fighting Next Time." *New York Times Magazine*, March 10.

Kennedy, Paul. 1991. "The Fall and Rise of Military History." *MHQ: The Quarterly Journal of Military History* 3 (2): 9–12.

Kershaw, Joseph A. 1951. "The Economic War Potential of the USSR." *American Economic Review* 41 (2): 475–82.

Kershaw, Joseph. A. 1961. "Directions for Future Growth of the Soviet Economy." In Spulber 1961, 3–16.

Kessler, William C. 1938. "The German Corporation Law of 1937." *American Economic Review* 28 (4): 653–62.

Kessler, W. C. 1934. "The New German Cartel Legislation." *American Economic Review* 24 (3): 477–82.

Kessler, William C. 1939. "German Cartel Regulation under the Decree of 1923." *Quarterly Journal of Economics* 50 (4): 680–93.

Khanin, Grigorii. 1998. "An Uninvited Advisor." In Ellman and Kontorovich 1998, 76–85.

Khlevniuk, O. V. 1996. *Politburo. Mekhanizmy politicheskoi vlasti v 1930-e gody*. Moscow: Rosspen.

Khlusov, M. I. 1971. *Industrializatsiia SSSR 1933–1937 gg. Dokumenty i materialy*. Moscow: Nauka.

Khrushchev, Sergei. 2000a. *Rozhdenie sverkhderzhavy. Kniga ob otse*. Moscow: Vremia.

Khrushchev, Sergei. 2000b. "The Military-Industrial Complex, 1953–1964." In *Nikita Khrushchev*, edited by William Taubman, Sergei Khrushchev, and Abbott Gleason, 242–74. New Haven, CT: Yale University Press.

Kitcher, Philip. 1993. *The Advancement of Science: Science without Legend, Objectivity without Illusions*. New York: Oxford University Press.

Klein, Burton. 1959. *Germany's Economic Preparations for War*. Cambridge, MA: Harvard University Press.

Köhler, Heinz. 1966. *Welfare and Planning: An Analysis of Capitalism versus Socialism*. New York: Wiley.

Köhler, Heinz. 1989. *Comparative Economic Systems*. Glenview, IL: Scott Foresman.

Kokoshin, A. A. 1995. *Armiia i politika: Sovetskaia voenno-politicheskaia i voenno-strategicheskaia mysl, 1918–1991 gody*. Moscow: Mezhdunarodnye otnosheniia.

Kolkowicz, Roman. 1962. *The Use of Soviet Military Labor in the Civilian Economy: A Study of Military "Shefstvo."* Santa Monica, CA: RAND Corporation.

Kolodnyi, M. G., and A. P. Stepanov. 1975. *Planirovanie narodnogo khoziaistva SSSR*. Kiev: Vyshcha shkola.

*Konstitutsiia (osnovnoi zakon) SSSR*. 1960. Moscow: Iuridicheskaia literatura.

*Konstitutsiia SSSR i razvitie sovetskogo zakonodatel'stva*. 1983. Moscow: Iuridicheskaia literatura.

Kontorovich, Vladimir. 1986. "What Do Bosses in Command Economies Do?" Working Paper, Princeton Junction, NJ: Command Economies Research. https://www.haverford.edu/sites/default/files/Department/Economics/WhatDoBosses.pdf.

Kontorovich, Vladimir. 1988. "Prototype Statistics as Indicators of Soviet R&D Priorities in Civilian and Military Machinebuilding." *Comparative Economic Studies* 30 (3): 1–16.

Kontorovich, Vladimir. 1989. "Inflation in the Soviet Investment and Capital Stock Data." *Soviet Studies* 41 (2): 318–29.

Kontorovich, Vladimir. 1996. "Economists and the Collapse." https://www.haverford.edu/sites/default/files/Department/Economics/FAIR2.pdf.

Kontorovich, Vladimir. 1998. "Economic System and the Valuation of National Income." https://www.haverford.edu/sites/default/files/Department/Economics/COSTMAX2.pdf.

Kontorovich, Vladimir. 2001. "Economists, Soviet Growth Slowdown, and the Collapse." *Europe-Asia Studies* 53 (5): 675–95.

Kontorovich, Vladimir. 2011. "A Child, Not a Tool of the Cold War." Review of Engerman 2009. *Kritika* 12 (3): 691–703.

Kontorovich, Vladimir. 2014. "A Cold War Creature Which Sat Out the War." *Europe-Asia Studies* 66 (5): 811–29.

Kornai, János. 1986. "The Soft Budget Constraint." *Kyklos* 39, fasc. 1.

Kornai, János. 1992. *The Socialist System: The Political Economy of Communism.* Princeton, NJ: Princeton University Press.

Korol, Alexander G. 1965. *Soviet Research and Development: Its Organization, Personnel, and Funds.* Cambridge, MA: MIT Press.

Koropeckyj, Iwan S. 1967. "The Development of Soviet Location Theory before the World War II." *Soviet Studies* 19 (2): 232–44.

Kotkin, Stephen. 2001. *Armageddon Averted: The Soviet Collapse, 1970–2000.* New York: Oxford University Press.

Koval', N. S., ed. 1973. *Planirovanie narodnogo khoziaistva SSSR.* Moscow: Vysshaia shkola.

Kraemer, Erich. 1936. "Supplementary Farming Homesteads in Recent German Land Settlement." *Journal of Land & Public Utility Economics* 12 (2): 177–90.

Kramer, Martin. 2001. *Ivory Towers on Sand: The Failure of Middle Eastern Studies in America.* Washington, DC: The Washington Institute for Near East Policy.

Krause, Keith. 1992. *Arms and the State: Patterns of Military Production and Trade.* Cambridge, UK: Cambridge University Press.

Kreps, David M. 1990. *A Course in Microeconomic Theory.* Princeton, NJ: Princeton University Press.

Kreps, David M. 1997. "Economics: The Current Position." *Daedalus* 126 (1): 59–85.

Krugman, Paul. 1998. "The Rise and Fall of Development Economics." In *Development, Geography, and Economic Theory,* 1–30. Cambridge, MA: MIT Press.

Krylov, Constantin. A. 1979. *The Soviet Economy: How It Really Works*. Lexington, MA: D. C. Heath.

Kuhn, Thomas. S. 1962. *The Structure of Scientific Revolutions*. Chicago: University of Chicago Press.

Kuhn, Thomas S. 2000. *The Road since Structure*. Chicago: University of Chicago Press.

Kuratov, Oleg. 2004. *Khroniki russkogo byta 1950–1990*. Moscow: DeLi Print.

Kurnysheva, I., and K. Petrov. 1998. "Itogi demilitarizatsii ekonomiki." *Voprosy ekonomiki*, no. 9, 21–34.

Kurskii, A. D. 1945. *Sotsialisticheskoe planirovanie narodnogo khoziaistva SSSR*. Moscow: Gosplanizdat.

Kurskii, A. D. 1955. *Planirovanie narodnogo khoziaistva SSSR*. Moscow: Gosudarstvennoe izdatel'stvo politicheskoi literatury.

Kushnirsky, Fyodor. I. 1982. *Soviet Economic Planning, 1965–1980*. Boulder, CO: Westview Press.

Kushnirsky, Fyodor I. 1991. "Conversion, Civilian Production, and Goods Quality in the Soviet Economy." *Comparative Economic Studies* 33 (1): 23–56.

Kushnirsky, Fyodor I. 1993. "Lessons from Estimating Military Production of the Former Soviet Union." *Europe-Asia Studies* 45 (3): 483–503.

Kuznets, Simon. 1963. "A Comparative Appraisal." In Bergson and Kuznets 1963, 333–82.

Kuzyk, Boris. 1999. *Oboronno-promyshlennyi kompleks Rossii: proryv v XXI vek*. Moscow: Russkii biograficheskii institut.

Laband, David N., and Michael J. Piette. 1994. "The Relative Impact of Economics Journals: 1970–1990." *Journal of Economic Literature* 32 (2): 640–66.

Laird, Betty A., and Roy D. Laird. 1976. *To Live Long Enough: The Memoirs of Naum Jasny, Scientific Analyst*. Lawrence, KS: University Press of Kansas.

Lange, Oskar. 1938. "On the Economic Theory of Socialism." In *On the Economic Theory of Socialism*, edited by Benjamin E. Lippincott, 55–142. Minneapolis: University of Minnesota Press.

Lappo, G., and P. Polian. 1998. "Zakrytye goroda." *Sotsiologicheskie issledovaniia*, no. 2, 43–48.

Layard, Richard, and John Parker. 1996. *The Coming Russian Boom: A Guide to New Markets and Politics*. New York: Free Press.

LeBlanc, Steven A., with Katherine E. Register. 2003. *Constant Battles. The Myth of the Peaceful, Noble Savage*. New York: St. Martin's.

Lee, William Thomas. 1977. *The Estimation of Soviet Defense Expenditures, 1955–75: An Unconventional Approach*. New York: Praeger.

Leeman, Wayne A. 1963. *Capitalism, Market Socialism, and Central Planning: Readings in Comparative Economic Systems*. Boston: Houghton Mifflin.

Leeman, Wayne A. 1977. *Centralized and Decentralized Economic Systems: The Soviet-Type Economy, Market Socialism, and Capitalism*. Chicago, IL: Rand McNally.

Leijonhufvud, Axel. 1973. "Life among the Econ." *Western Economic Journal* 11 (3): 327–37.

Leonard, Robert. J. 1991. "War as a 'Simple Economic Problem': The Rise of an Economics of Defense." In Goodwin 1991, 261–83.

Leontiev, A. 1946. *Sovetskii metod industrializatsii*. Moscow: Pravda.

Leontief, Wassily. 1960. "The Decline and Rise of Soviet Economic Science." *Foreign Affairs* 38 (2): 223–36.

Lewis, Robert. 1979. *Science and Industrialization in the USSR*. New York: Holmes and Meier.

Liebowitz, Stan. J., and John P. Palmer. 1984. "Assessing the Relative Impacts of Economic Journals." *Journal of Economic Literature* 22 (1): 77–88.

Lieven, Dominic. 2000. *Empire: The Russian Empire and Its Rivals*. New Haven, CT: Yale University Press.

Lindblom, Charles E. 1975. "The Sociology of Planning: Thought and Social Interaction." In *Economic Planning: East and West*, edited by Morris Bornstein, 23–60. Cambridge, MA: Ballinger.

Linz, Susan J., and William Moskoff, eds. 1988. *Reorganization and Reform in the Soviet Economy*. Armonk, NY: M. E. Sharpe.

Lipsits, I. 1995. "Problemy Rossiiskoi konversii." *Ekonomist*, no. 1, 14–21.

Livchen, René. 1943. "Wage Trends in Germany from 1929 to 1942." *International Labor Review* 48, 714–32.

Lockwood, William W. 1954. *The Economic Development of Japan: Growth and Structural Change 1968–1938*. Princeton, NJ: Princeton University Press.

Lokshin, E. I. 1947. *Promyshlennost' SSSR*. Moscow: Gosplanizdat.

Lorell, Mark Allen. 1976. *The Politics of Economic Debate: Anglo-American Perceptions of Germany's Economic Preparations for War 1937–1939*. Unpublished Ph.D. diss., University of Washington.

Loucks, William N., and William G. Whitney. 1973. *Comparative Economic Systems*. 9th ed. New York: Harper and Row.

Liuboshits, Efim, and Vitalii Tsymbal. 1992. "Kak sformirovat' oboronnyi biudzhet Rossii." *Nezavisimaia gazeta*, July 9.

Lubrano, Linda L., and Susan Gross Solomon, eds. 1980. *The Social Context of Soviet Science*. Boulder, CO: Westview Press.

Lucas, Robert E. 1988. "On the Mechanics of Economic Development." *Journal of Monetary Economics* 22, 3–42.

Ludmer, A. Henry. 1943. "German Financial Mobilization." *Accounting Review* 18 (1): 34–39.

Lynn, John A., II. 1997. "The Embattled Future of Academic Military History." *The Journal of Military History* 61 (4): 777–89.

Lynn, John A., II. 2008. "Breaching the Walls of Academe: The Purposes, Problems, and Prospects of Military History." *Academic Questions* 21 (1): 18–36.

MacEachin, Douglas J. 1996. *CIA Assessments of the Soviet Union: The Record versus the Charges.* Washington, DC: Center for the Study of Intelligence, CIA.

Maddison, Angus. 1969. *Economic Growth in Japan and the USSR.* New York: W. W. Norton.

Maddison, Angus. 1998. "Measuring the Performance of a Communist Command Economy: An Assessment of the CIA Estimates for the USSR." *Review of Income and Wealth* 44 (3): 307–23.

Maddison, Angus. 2006. *The World Economy.* Paris: Development Centre of the OECD.

Maddock, Rowland T. 1988. *The Political Economy of Soviet Defence Spending.* Basingstoke, UK: Macmillan.

Malei, Mikhail. 1993. "Reforma voenno-promyshlennogo kompleksa." *Nezavisimaia gazeta,* August, 27.

Malia, Martin. 1994. *The Soviet Tragedy: A History of Socialism in Russia, 1917–1991.* New York: Free Press.

Mansfield, Edwin W. 1986. *Economics.* 5th ed. New York: Norton.

Mansfield, Edwin W. 1989. *Economics: Principles, Problems, Decisions* 6th ed. New York: Norton.

Mansfield, Edwin W. 1992. *Economics: Principles, Problems, Decisions* 7th ed. New York: Norton.

Marczewski, Jean. 1974. *Crisis in Socialist Planning: Eastern Europe and the USSR.* New York: Praeger.

Mas-Colell, Andreu, Michael Whinston, and Jerry Green. 1995. *Microeconomic Theory.* Oxford: Oxford University Press.

Masliukov, Iu. D., and E. S. Glubokov. 1999. "Planirovanie i finansirovanie voennoi promyshlennosti v SSSR." In *Sovetskaia voennaia moshch' ot Stalina do Gorbacheva,* edited by A. V. Minaev, 82–129. Moscow: Voennyi parad.

*Materialy XXIV s'ezda KPSS.* 1972. Moscow: Politizdat.

McCann, Frank D. 1984. "The Formative Period of Twentieth-Century Brazilian Army Thought, 1900–1922." *Hispanic American Historical Review* 64 (4): 737–65.

McCarty, Marilu H. 1982. *Dollars and Sense: An Introduction to Economics.* 3rd ed. Glenview, IL: Scott Foresman.

McCarty, Marilu H. 1988. *Dollars and Sense: An Introduction to Economics.* 5th ed. Glenview, IL: Scott Foresman.

McConnell, Campbell R. 1981. *Economics: Principles, Problems, and Policies.* 8th ed. New York: McGraw-Hill.

McConnell, Campbell R. 1984. *Economics: Principles, Problems, and Policies.* 9th. ed. New York: McGraw-Hill.

McConnell, Campbell R. 1987. *Economics: Principles, Problems, and Policies.* 10th ed. New York: McGraw-Hill.

Mcfadden, Robert D. 2004. "Harry Schwartz, 85, Times Editorial Writer, Dies." *New York Times*, November 12. http://www.nytimes.com/2004/11/12/obituaries/harry-schwartz-85-times-editorial-writer-dies.html.

McKay, John P. 1979. Review of *The Technological Level of Soviet Industry*, edited by Robert Amann, Julian Cooper, and R. W. Davies. *The Business History Review* 53, (3): 436–38.

McPherson, James M. (1988) 2003. *Battle Cry of Freedom: The Civil War Era*. Oxford: Oxford University Press.

Medvedev, Vadim. 1998. "Under Andropov and Gorbachev." In Ellman and Kontorovich 1998, 94–97.

Meier, Gerald M. 2005. *Biography of a Subject: Evolution of Development Economics*. Oxford: Oxford University Press.

Melnikova-Raich, Sonia. 2010. "The Soviet Problem with Two 'Unknowns': How an American Architect and a Soviet Negotiator Jump-Started the Industrialization of Russia, Part I: Albert Kahn." *Journal of the Society for Industrial Archeology* 36 (2): 57–80.

Mendershausen, Horst. 1943. *The Economics of War*. New York: Prentice Hall.

Merlin, Sidney. 1943. "Trends in German Economic Control since 1933." *Quarterly Journal of Economics* 57 (2): 169–207.

Middleton, Drew. 1980. "Soviet Arms Technology Has Shown Steady Gains." *New York Times*, December 8.

Millar, James R. 1976. "What's Wrong with the 'Standard Story.'" *Problems of Communism* 25 (4): 50–55.

Millar, James R. 1980. "Where Are the Young Specialists on the Soviet Economy and What Are They Doing?" *Journal of Comparative Economics* 4 (4): 317–29.

Millar, James R. 1981. *The ABCs of Soviet Socialism*. Urbana: University of Illinois Press.

Millar, James R. 1990. *The Soviet Economic Experiment*. Urbana: University of Illinois Press.

Millar, James R. 1994. "A Comment on 'Politics, Military Spending and the National Welfare.'" *Comparative Economic Studies* 36 (3): 15–18.

Millar, James R. 1995. "Rethinking Soviet Economic Studies." In *Beyond Soviet Studies*, edited by Daniel Orlovsky, 225–59. Washington, DC: Woodrow Wilson Center.

Miller, Jack. 1965. Review of *Soviet Strategy for Economic Growth*, by Nicolas Spulber. *Economic Journal* 75 (300): 834–35.

Miller, Jack. 1973. "The Origins of Soviet Studies: A Personal Note." *Soviet Studies* 25 (2): 167–69.

Miller, Roger L. 1984. *Economics: Today and Tomorrow*. Mission Hills, CA: McGraw-Hill.

Milward, Alan S. 1965. *The German Economy at War*. London: Athlone Press.

Minaev, A. V. 1999. "Istoki sovetskoi voennoi moshchi." In *Sovetskaia voennaia moshch' ot Stalina do Gorbacheva*, edited by A.V. Minaev, 18–35. Moscow: Voennyi parad.

Mirowski, Philip. 2002. *Machine Dreams: Economics Becomes a Cyborg Science.* New York: Cambridge University Press.

Mittelman, E. B. 1938. "The German Use of Unemployment-Insurance Funds for Works Purposes." *Journal of Political Economy* 46 (4): 515–36.

Monakov, M. 1998. "Zachem Stalin stroil okeansii flot?" *Morskoi sbornik*, no. 12, 74–9.

Montias, John M. 1957. "Rational Prices and Marginal Costs in Soviet-Type Economies." *Soviet Studies* 8 (4): 369–79.

Montias, John M. 1961. "The Soviet Model and the Underdeveloped Areas." In Spulber 1961, 57–80.

Montias, John M. 1962. *Central Planning in Poland.* New Haven, CT: Yale University Press.

Moore, Harriet L. 1939. "The National Defense Program of the Soviet Union." *American Quarterly on the Soviet Union*, 3–18.

Moorsteen, Richard, and Raymond P. Powell. 1966. *The Soviet Capital Stock, 1928–1962.* Homewood, IL: Richard D. Irwin.

Moravcik, I. 1965. "The Priority of Heavy Industry as an Objective of Soviet Economic Policy." *Soviet Studies* 17, (2): 245–51.

Morgan, Mary S., and Malcolm Rutherford. 1998. "American Economics: The Character of Transformation." In *From Interwar Pluralism to Postwar Neoclassicism*, edited by Mary S. Morgan and Malcolm Rutherford, 1–26. Durham, NC: Duke University Press.

Morillo, Stephen, and Michael F. Pavkovic. 2012. *What Is Military History?* 2nd ed. Cambridge, UK: Polity.

Morukov, Mikhail. 2003. "The White Sea-Baltic Canal." In *The Economics of Forced Labor: The Soviet Gulag*, edited by Paul R. Gregory and Valery Lazarev, 151–62. Stanford, CA: Hoover Institution Press.

Mosely, Philip E. 1959. "The Growth of Russian Studies." In *American Research on Russia*, edited by Harold H. Fisher, 1–22. Bloomington: Indiana University Press.

Mosher, Steven W. 1990. *China Misperceived. American Illusions and Chinese Realities.* New York: Basic Books.

Moskoff, William. 1981. "CIA Publications of the Soviet Economy." *Slavic Review* 40 (2): 269–72.

Mozhin, Vladimir. 1998. "Rulers Did Not Know What to Do." In Ellman and Kontorovich 1998, 120–22.

Mueller, Dennis. 1989. *Public Choice II.* Cambridge, UK: Cambridge University Press.

Munting, Roger. 1982. *The Economic Development of the USSR.* New York: St. Martin's.

Naimark, Norman. 1998. "On the 50th Anniversary: The Origins of the AAASS." *AAASS NewsNet* 38 (3): 1–5.

Nathan, Otto. 1934. "Some Considerations on Unemployment Insurance in the Light of German Experience." *Journal of Political Economy* 42 (3): 289–327.

Nathan, Otto. 1942. "Consumption in Germany during the Period of Rearmament." *Quarterly Journal of Economics* 56 (3): 349–84.

National Security Council. (1950) 1975. *NSC-68: United States Objectives and Programs for National Security.* Reprinted in *Naval War College Review* 27, 51–108. Citations refer to reprint.

Neuberger, E., and William J. Duffy. 1976. *Comparative Economic Systems: A Decision-Making Approach.* Boston, MA: Allyn and Bacon.

Noren, James H. 1995. "The Controversy over Western Measures of Soviet Defense Expenditures." *Post-Soviet Affairs* 11 (3): 238–76.

North, Douglass. C. 2005. *Understanding the Process of Economic Change.* Princeton, NJ: Princeton University Press.

Notkin, A. I. 1984. *Problemy sotsialisticheskogo vosproizvodstva.* Moscow: Nauka.

Nove, Alec. 1961. *The Soviet Economy: An Introduction.* New York: Frederick A. Praeger.

Nove, Alec. 1962. "Social Welfare in the USSR." In Holzman 1962, 661–70.

Nove, Alec. 1964. "Towards a Theory of Planning." In Degras and Nove 1964, 193–204.

Nove, Alec. 1964. *Economic Rationality and Soviet Politics or Was Stalin Really Necessary?* New York: Frederick A. Praeger.

Nove, Alec. 1966. "Planners' Preferences, Priorities and Reform." *Economic Journal* 76 (302): 267–77.

Nove, Alec. 1969. *An Economic History of the U.S.S.R.* Baltimore: Penguin.

Nove, Alec. 1977. *Soviet Economic System.* London: Allen and Unwin.

Nove, Alec. 1979. *Political Economy and Soviet Socialism.* London: George Allen and Unwin.

Nove, Alec. 1980. *Soviet Economic System.* London: Allen and Unwin.

Nove, Alec. 1982. *An Economic History of the USSR.* New York: Penguin.

Nove, Alec. 1986. *The Soviet Economic System.* 3rd ed. Boston: George Allen and Unwin.

Nove, Alec. 1987. "The Defense Burden: Some General Observations." In Jacobsen 1987, 175–86.

Nove, Alec. 1992. *An Economic History of the USSR: 1917–1991.* New York: Penguin.

Nove, Alec. 1994. "What Went Wrong with André Gunder Frank." *Review of International Political Economy* 1 (2): 345–50.

Nutter, G. Warren. 1962. *Growth of Industrial Production in the Soviet Union.* Princeton, NJ: Princeton University Press.

Odom, William E. 1998. *The Collapse of the Soviet Military.* New Haven, CT: Yale University Press.

OECD. 1993. *National Accounts for the Former Soviet Union: Sources, Methods and Estimates.* Paris: Centre for Co-Operation with European Economies in Transition.

Ofer, Gur. 1976. "Industrial Structure, Urbanization, and the Growth Strategy of Socialist Countries." *Quarterly Journal of Economics* 90 (2): 219–55.

Ofer, Gur. 1984. Review of *Industrial Innovation in the Soviet Union*, edited by Robert Amann and Julian Cooper. *Journal of Economic Literature* 22 (1): 138–40.

Ofer, Gur. 1987. "Soviet Economic Growth: 1928–1985." *Journal of Economic Literature* 25 (4): 1767–1833.

Ofer, Gur. 2003. "Communist Russia." In *The Oxford Encyclopedia of Economic History*, edited by Joel Mokyr. Vol. 4. Oxford: Oxford University Press.

Ofer, Gur. 2008. "Soviet Growth Record." In *The New Palgrave Dictionary of Economics*, edited by Steven N. Durlauf and Lawrence E. Blume. 2nd ed. Vol. 7. New York: Palgrave Macmillan.

Offer, Avner. 1987. "War Economy." In *The New Palgrave Dictionary of Economics*, edited by John Eatwell, Murray Milgate, and Peter Newman. Vol. 4. London: Palgrave Macmillan.

Okamura, Minoru. 1991. "Estimating the Impact of the Soviet Union's Threat on the United States-Japan Alliance: A Demand System Approach." *Review of Economics and Statistics* 73 (2): 200–207.

Okun, Arthur M. 1975. *Equality and Efficiency: The Big Tradeoff.* Washington, DC: Brookings Institution.

O.L.L. 1934. The International Aspects of German Economic Policy. *Bulletin of International News* 11 (3): 3–11.

Olsen, Arthur R., and Hailstones, Thomas, J. 1985. *Economics: Principles and Applications.* Cincinnati, OH: South-Western Publishers.

O'Neill, Mark. 2002. "The Soviet Airforce, 1917–1991." In *The Military History of the Soviet Union*, edited by Robin Higham and Frederick Kagan, 153–68. New York: Palgrave Macmillan.

Overy, Richard. 2010. *1939: Countdown to War*. New York: Viking.

Ozhegov, Aleksandr, Evgenii Rogovskii, and Iurii Iaremenko. 1991. "Konversiia oboronnoi promyshlennosti i preobrazovanie ekonomiki SSSR." *Kommunist* (1): 54–64.

Parrott, Bruce. 1983. Review of *Industrial Innovation in the Soviet Union*, by Ronald Amann and Julian Cooper. *Isis*, 74 (4): 600–601.

Parrott, Bruce, ed. 1985. *Trade, Technology, and Soviet-American Relations.* Bloomington: Indiana University Press.

Parshev, A. P. 2000. *Pochemu Rossiia ne Amerika.* Moscow: Forum.

Pavlova, I. V. 1993. *Stalinizm: stanovlenie mekhanizma vlasti.* Novosibirsk: Sibirskii khronograf.

Pavlova, I. V. 2001. *Mekhanizm vlasti i stroitel'stvo stalinskogo sotsializma.* Novosibirsk: SO RAN.

Pavlov, Valentin. 1993. *Avgust iznutri.* Moscow: Delovoi mir.

Pickersgill, Gary M. 1974. *Contemporary Economic Systems: A Comparative View.* Englewood Cliffs, NJ: Prentice Hall.

Pikhoia, R. G. 1998. *Sovetskii Soiuz: Istoriia vlasti, 1945–1991.* Moscow: RAGS.

Pipes, Richard. 1995. *Russia under the Bolshevik Regime.* New York: Vintage Books.

Pivovarov, Iu. L. 1997. "Szhatie intensivno ispol'zuemogo prostranstva: kontseptsiia makroregional'nogo razvitiia Rossii." *Vestnik Akademii nauk.* Seriia geograficheskaia 5, 63–74.

Polanyi, Michael. 1960. "Towards a Theory of Conspicuous Production." *Soviet Survey* 34, 90–100.

Polanyi, Michael. 1962. "The Republic of Science: Its Political and Economic Theory." *Minerva* 1 (1): 54–74.

Pollack, Jonathan D. 1996. "International Studies." In *Project Air Force 50th Anniversary (1946–1996)*, 39–42. Santa Monica, CA: RAND Corporation.

Pomer, Marshall. 2001. "Demise of the Command Economy." In *The New Russia: Transition Gone Awry*, edited by Lawrence Klein and Marshall Pomer, 139–70. Stanford, CA: Stanford University Press.

Pomfret, Richard. 2002. *Constructing a Market Economy: Diverse Paths from Central Planning in Asia and Europe*. Cheltenham, UK: Edward Elgar.

Posner, Richard. 1993. "What Do Judges Maximize?" *Supreme Court Economic Review* 3, 1–41.

Protasov, V. 1990. "Ne znaia brodu?" *Literaturnaia gazeta*, May 9.

Prybyla, J. S. 1965. Review of *Soviet Strategy for Economic Growth*, by Nicolas Spulber. *The Russian Review* 24 (1): 68–70.

Pryor, Frederic L. 1985. *A Guidebook to the Comparative Study of Economic Systems*. Englewood Cliffs, NJ: Prentice Hall.

Pugacheva, S. A., S. O. Botnera, B. S. Bukina, and A. B. Girshfel'da, eds. 1927. *Narodnoe khoziastvo i voina. Bibliograficheskii spravochnik*. Moscow: Tsentral'nyi sovet Osoaviakhima.

Putterman, Louis G. 1990. *Division of Labor and Welfare: An Introduction to Economic Systems*. Oxford, UK: Oxford University Press.

Rabkin, Yakov M. 1984. Review of *Industrial Innovation in the Soviet Union*, by Ronald Amann and Julian Cooper. *Slavic Review* 43 (1): 128–29.

Rassadin, V. 1999. "Sostoianie voenno-promyshlennogo kompleksa Rossii." *Voprosy ekonomiki* no. 7, 100–108.

"Rassekrechen 'rezerv MPS.'" 1992. *Gudok*, April 10.

Reddaway, Peter, and Dmitri Glinski. 2001. *The Tragedy of Russia's Reforms: Market Bolshevism against Democracy*. Washington, DC: United States Institute of Peace Press.

Rees, Edward Arfon. 2004. "Stalin as Leader 1924–1937: From Oligarch to Dictator." In *The Nature of Stalin's Dictatorship: The Politburo, 1924–1953*, edited by Edward Arfon Rees, 19–58. New York: Palgrave Macmillan.

Reynolds, Lloyd G. 1971. *The Three Worlds of Economics*. New Haven, CT: Yale University Press.

Reynolds, Lloyd G. 1988. *Economics: A General Introduction*. 5th ed. Homewood, IL: Irwin.

Richman, Barry M. 1967. *Management Development and Education in the Soviet Union*. East Lansing: Michigan State University.

Roberts, Paul Craig. 1971. *Alienation and the Soviet Economy*. Albuquerque: University of New Mexico Press.

Roberts, Paul Craig, and Karen LaFollette. 1990. *Meltdown: Inside the Soviet Economy.* Washington, DC: Cato Institute.

Robinson, Joan, and John Eatwell. 1973. *An Introduction to Modern Economics.* Maidenhead, UK: McGraw-Hill.

Robinson, Derek. 1986. *Introduction to Economics.* Cambridge, UK: ICSA.

Robinson, Derek. 1987. *Introduction to Economics (A Revision Aid).* Cambridge, UK: ICSA.

Rodionov, I. 1992. "Smelyi proekt." *Gudok*, November 4.

Rockoff, Hugh. 1998. "The United States: From Ploughshares to Swords." In Harrison 1998, 81–121.

Rohwer, Jurgen, and Mikhail Monakov. 2001. *Stalin's Ocean-Going Fleet: Soviet Naval Strategy and Shipbuilding Programmes, 1935–1953.* Portland, OR: Frank Cass.

Roland, Gerard. 2008. "A Review of János Kornai's *By Force of Thought: Irregular Memoirs of an Intellectual Journey." Journal of Economic Literature* 46 (1): 145–50.

Rosefielde, Steven, ed. 1981. *Economic Welfare and the Economics of Soviet Socialism.* Cambridge, UK: Cambridge University Press.

Rosefielde, Steven. 2002. "Back to the Future? Prospects for Russia's Military Industrial Revival." *Orbis* 46, (3): 505–6.

Rosefielde, Steven. 2005. *Russia in the 21st Century: The Prodigal Superpower.* Cambridge, UK: Cambridge University Press.

Rosovsky, Henry, ed. 1966. *Industrialization in Two Systems.* New York: Wiley.

Rostow, W. W. 1961. *The Stages of Economic Growth: A Non-Communist Manifesto.* Cambridge, UK: Cambridge University Press.

Rowland, Richard H. "Russia's Secret Cities." 1996. *Post-Soviet Geography and Economics* 37 (7): 426–62.

Ruffin, Roy J., and Paul P. Gregory. 1986. *Principles of Economics.* 2nd ed. Glenview, IL: Scott Foresman.

Ruffin, Roy J., and Paul R. Gregory. 1988. *Principles of Economics.* 3rd ed. Glenview, IL: Scott Foresman.

Rutland, Peter. 1985. *The Myth of the Plan: Lessons of Soviet Planning Experience.* La Salle, IL: Open Court.

Rutland, Peter. 1993. "Sovietology: Notes for a Post-Mortem." *The National Interest,* 31 (3): 109–23.

Ryzhkov, N. I. 1986. *O gosudarstvennom plane ekonomicheskogo i sotsial'nogo razvitiia SSSR na 1986–1990 gody.* Moscow: Politizdat.

Ryzhkov, N. I. 1992. *Perestroika: istoriia predatel'stv.* Moscow: Novosti.

Sah, Raaj Kumar, and Joseph E. Stiglitz. 1984. "The Economics of Price Scissors." *The American Economic Review* 74 (1): 125–38.

Sah, Raaj Kumar, and Joseph E. Stiglitz. 1987. "Price Scissors and the Structure of the Economy." *The Quarterly Journal of Economics* 102 (1): 109–34.

Samuelson, Lennart. 2000a. "The Red Army and Economic Planning, 1925–1940." In *The Soviet Defense-Industry Complex from Stalin to Khrushchev*, edited by John Barber and Mark Harrison, 47–69. New York: St. Martin's.

Samuelson, Lennart. 2000b. *Plans for Stalin's War Machine: Tukhachevskii and Military-Economic Planning, 1925–1941*. London: Palgrave Macmillan.

Samuelson, Paul A. 1976. *Economics*. 10th ed. New York: McGraw-Hill.

Samuelson, Paul A. 1980. *Economics*. 11th ed. New York: McGraw-Hill.

Samuelson, Paul A., and William D. Nordhaus. 1985. *Economics*. 12th ed. New York: McGraw-Hill.

Samuelson, Paul A., and William D. Nordhaus. 1989. *Economics*. 13th ed. New York: McGraw-Hill.

Sandler, Todd, and Keith Hartley. 1995. *The Economics of Defense*. Cambridge, UK: Cambridge University Press.

Scanlan, James P., ed. 1992. *Technology, Culture, and Development: The Experience of the Soviet Model*. Armonk, NY: M. E. Sharpe.

Schaffer, Mark E., ed. 1985. *Technology Transfer and East-West Relations*. London: Croom Helm.

Schama, Simon. 1989. *Citizens: A Chronicle of the French Revolution*. New York: Vintage Books.

Scherer, F. M. 2000. "The Emigration of German-Speaking Economists after 1933." *Journal of Economic Literature* 38 (3): 614–26.

Scherner, Jonas. 2013. "'Armament in Depth' or 'Armament in Breadth'? German Investment Pattern and Rearmament during the Nazi Period." *Economic History Review* 66 (2): 497–517.

Schnitzer, Martin C. 1991. *Comparative Economic Systems*. 5th ed. Cincinnati, OH: South-Western Publishing.

Schnitzer, Martin C., and James W. Nordyke. 1971. *Comparative Economic Systems*. Cincinnati, OH: South-Western Publishing.

Schnitzer, Martin C., and James W. Nordyke. 1977. *Comparative Economic Systems*. 2nd ed. Cincinnati, OH: South-Western Publishing.

Schnitzer, Martin C., and James W. Nordyke. 1983. *Comparative Economic Systems*. 3rd ed. Cincinnati, OH: South-Western Publishing.

Schnitzer, Martin C., and James W. Nordyke. 1987. *Comparative Economic Systems*. 4th ed. Cincinnati, OH: South-Western Publishing.

Schroeder, Gertrude E. 1972. "An Appraisal of Soviet Wage and Income Statistics." In Treml and Hardt, 1972, 287–314.

Schroeder, Gertrude E. 1983. Review of *Industrial Innovation in the Soviet Union*, by Ronald Amann and Julian Cooper. *Science*, n.s., 219 (4580): 46–47.

Schroeder, Gertrude E. 1995. "Reflections on Economic Sovietology." *Post-Soviet Affairs* 11 (3): 197–234.

Schultz, T. Paul. 1990. "Discussion." *American Economic Review: Papers and Proceedings* 80 (2): 445–50.

Schumpeter, Joseph A. (1942) 1976. *Capitalism, Socialism and Democracy*. Reprint, New York: Harper and Row. Citations refer to reprint.

Schwartz, Harry. 1949. *The Soviet Economy: A Selected Bibliography of Materials in English*. Syracuse, NY: Syracuse University Press.

Schwartz, Harry. 1950. *Russia's Soviet Economy*. New York: Prentice Hall.

Schwartz, Harry. 1954. *Russia's Soviet Economy*. 2nd ed. Englewood Cliffs, NJ: Prentice Hall.

Schwartz, Harry. 1965. *The Soviet Economy since Stalin*. Philadelphia: J. B. Lippincott.

Schwartz, Harry. 1968. *An Introduction to the Soviet Economy*. Columbus, OH: Charles Merrill Publishing Company.

Schweitzer, Arthur. 1943. "The Role of Foreign Trade in the Nazi War Economy." *Journal of Political Economy* 51 (4): 322–37.

Schranz, A. 1937. "Recent Tendencies in German Business Economics." *Accounting Review* 12 (3): 278–85.

Selke, Arthur C. 1936. "Geographic Aspects of the German Tourist Trade." *Economic Geography* 12 (2): 205–16.

Sen, Amartya. 1987. "Rational Behavior." In *The New Palgrave Dictionary of Economics*, edited by John Eatwell, Murray Milgate, and Peter Newman. Vol. 4. London: Palgrave Macmillan.

Sen, Gautam. 1984. *The Military Origins of Industrialization and International Trade Rivalry*. London: Pinter.

Shafiev, K., Lokshin, E., and Akopov, R., eds. 1960. *Politicheskaia ekonomiia sotsializma*. Moscow: Izdatel'stvo sotsial'no-ekonomicheskoi literatury.

Shakhnazarov, G. 1993. *Tsena svobody*. Moscow: Rossika-Zevs.

Shapiro, T. Rees. 2011. "Igor Birman, Economist Who Predicted Collapse of Soviet Economy, Dies at 82." *Washington Post*, April 20. https://www.washingtonpost.com/local/obituaries/igor-birman-economist-who-predicted-collapse-of-soviet-economy-dies-at-82/2011/04/19/AFh062EE_story.html?utm_term=.96f53b5ffcdd.

Sherman, Howard J. 1969. *The Soviet Economy*. Boston: Little, Brown and Company.

Sherman, Howard J. 1973. Review of *Western Technology and Soviet Economic Development, 1917 to 1930*, by Antony C. Sutton. *American Political Science Review* 67 (3): 1126–28.

Shulman, Marshall D. 1970. "The Future of Soviet Studies in the United States." *Slavic Review* 29 (3): 582–88.

Shlapentokh, Vladimir. 2001. *A Normal Totalitarian Society*. Armonk, NY: M. E. Sharpe.

Shlykov, V. 2001. "Chto pogubilo Sovetskii Soiuz? Amerikanskaia razvedka o sovetskikh voennykh raskhodakh." *Voennyi Vestnik*, no. 8.

Shlykov, V. 2002. "Chto pogubilo Sovetskii Soiuz? Genshtab i ekonomika." *Voennyi Vestnik*, no. 9, 5–63.

Shtromas, Alexander, and Morton A. Kaplan, eds. 1989. *The Soviet Union and the Challenge of the Future*. Vol. 2, *Economy and Society*. New York: Paragon House.

Siegelbaum, Lewis H. 1983. *The Politics of Industrial Mobilization in Russia, 1914–17: A Study of the War-Industries Committees.* New York: St. Martin's.

Siegfried, John J., and James T. Wilkinson. 1982. "The Economics Curriculum in the United States: 1980." *American Economic Review: Papers and Proceedings* 72 (2): 125–38.

Simakov, Dmitrii, and Zoia Kanka. 2002. "General Minekonomrazvitiia." *Vedomosti,* July 12.

Simonov, N. S. 1996. *Voenno-promyshlennyi kompleks SSSR v 1920–1950-e gody: tempy ekonomicheskogo rosta, struktura, organizatsiia proizvodstva i upravleniie.* Moscow: Rosspan.

Simonov, N. S. 2015. *VPK SSSR: tempy ekonomicheskogo rosta, struktura, organizatsiia proizvodstva i upravleniie.* 2nd ed, enlarged and corrected. Moscow: Universitet Dmitriia Pozharskogo.

Singer, H. W. 1940. "The German War Economy in the Light of Economic Periodicals." *Economic Journal,* 50 (200): 534–46.

Singer, H. W. 1941a. "The German War Economy in the Light of Economic Periodicals." *Economic Journal* 51 (202/203): 192–215.

Singer H. W. 1941b. "The German War Economy in the Light of Economic Periodicals." *Economic Journal* 51 (201): 19–35.

Singer H. W. 1941c. "The German War Economy in the Light of Economic Periodicals." *Economic Journal* 51 (204): 400–21.

Singer, H. W. 1942a. "The German War Economy, V." *Economic Journal* 52 (205): 18–36.

Singer, H. W. 1942b. "The German War Economy, VI." *The Economic Journal* 52 (206/207): 186–205.

Singer, H. W. 1942c. "The German War Economy, VII." *Economic Journal* 52 (208): 377–99.

Singer, H. W. 1943a. "The German War Economy, VIII." *Economic Journal* 53 (209): 121–39.

Singer, H. W. 1943b. "The Sources of War Finance in the German War Economy." *Review of Economic Studies* 10 (2): 106–14.

Singer, H. W. 1943c. "The German War Economy, IX." *Economic Journal* 53 (210/211): 243–59.

Singer, H. W. 1943d. "The German War Economy, X." *Economic Journal* 53 (212): 370–80.

Skidelsky, Robert. 1996. *The Road from Serfdom: The Economic and Political Consequences of the End of Communism.* New York: Viking Penguin.

Smith, Ronald P. 1980. "Military Expenditures and Investment in the OECD Countries, 1954–1973." *Journal of Comparative Economics* 4 (1): 19–32.

Solmssen, Georg. 1937. "A Plan for German Industrial Expansion." *International Affairs (Royal Institute of International Affairs 1931-1939)* 16 (2): 222–44.

Solo, Robert. 1978. Review of *The Technological Level of Soviet Industry*, edited by Robert Amann, Julian Cooper, and R. W. Davies. *Journal of Economic Literature* 16 (4): 1479–81.

Sorokin, G. 1946. *Sotsialisticheskoe planirovanie narodnogo khoziaistva SSSR*. Moscow: Gosudarstvennoe izdatel'stvo politicheskoi literatury.

Spiegel, Henry William. 1939. "German Tenancy Problems and Policies." *Journal of Land & Public Utility Economics* 15 (3): 333–42.

Spiegel, Henry William. 1940. "Wehrwirtschaft: Economics of the Military State." *American Economic Review* 30 (4): 713–23.

Spulber, Nicolas, ed. 1961. *Study of the Soviet Economy: Direction and Impact of Soviet Growth, Teaching and Research in Soviet Economics*. Bloomington: Indiana University Press.

Spulber, Nicolas. 1962. *The Soviet Economy. Structure, Principles, Problems*. New York: W. W. Norton.

Spulber, Nicolas. 1964. *Soviet Strategy for Economic Growth*. Bloomington: Indiana University Press.

Spulber, Nicolas. 1969. *The Soviet Economy: Structure, Principles, Problems*. Rev. ed. New York: W. W. Norton.

Spulber, Nicolas. 1991. *Restructuring the Soviet Economy: In Search of the Market*. Ann Arbor: The University of Michigan Press.

Spulber, Nicolas. 2003. Russia's Economic Transition: From Late Tsarism to the New Millennium. New York: Cambridge University Press.

Stalin, I. V. 1925a. "Politicheskii otchet tsentral'nogo komiteta XIV siezdu VKP (b)." In *Sochineniia*. Vol. 7. Moscow: Gosudarstvennoe izdatel'stvo politicheskoi literatury, 1947.

Stalin, I. V. 1925b. "Zakliuchitel'noe slovo po Politicheskomu otchetu tsentral'nogo komiteta." In *Sochineniia*. Vol. 7. Moscow: Gosudarstvennoe izdatel'stvo politicheskoi literatury, 1947.

Stalin, I. V. 1926. "O khoziaistvennom polozhenii Sovetskogo Soiuza i politike partii." In *Sochineniia*. Vol. 8. Moscow: Gosudarstvennoe izdatel'stvo politicheskoi literatury, 1948.

Stalin, I. V. 1928. "Ob industrializatsii strany i o pravom uklone v VKP (b)." In *Sochineniia*. Vol. 11. Moscow: Gosudarstvennoe izdatel'stvo politicheskoi literatury, 1949.

Stalin, I. V. 1931. "O zadachakh khoziaistvennikov." In *Sochineniia*. Vol. 13. Moscow: Gosudarstvennoe izdatel'stvo politicheskoi literatury, 1951.

Stalin, I. V. 1933. "Itogi pervoi piatiletki." In *Sochineniia*. Vol. 13. Moscow: Gosudarstvennoe izdatel'stvo politicheskoi literatury, 1951.

Stalin, I. V. 1946. "Rech' na predvybornom sobranii izbiratelei Stalinskogo izbiratel'nogo okruga goroda Moskvy." In *Sochineniia*. Vol. 3. Stanford, CA: Hoover Institution, 1967.

Starkov, Boris. 2000. "The security organs and the defense-industry complex." In *The Soviet Defense-Industry Complex from Stalin to Khrushchev*, edited by John Barber and Mark Harrison, 246–68. New York: St. Martin's.

Starr, Philip C. 1981. *Economics: Principles in Action*. 3rd ed. Belmont, CA: Wadsworth Publishing.

Starr, Philip C. 1984. *Economics: Principles in Action*. 4th ed. Belmont, CA: Wadsworth Publishing.

Steinberg, Dmitri. 1990. "Trends in Soviet Military Expenditure." *Soviet Studies* 42 (4): 675–99.

Steinberg, Dmitri. 1992. "The Soviet Defence Burden: Estimating Hidden Defence Costs." *Soviet Studies* 44 (2): 237–63.

Stephan, Paula E. 1996. "The Economics of Science." *Journal of Economic Literature* 34 (3): 1199–62.

Stigler, George J. 1978. "The Literature of Economics: The Case of the Kinked Oligopoly Demand Curve." *Economic Inquiry* 16 (2): 185–204.

Stigler, George. J. 1983. "Nobel Lecture: The Process and Progress of Economics." *Journal of Political Economy* 91 (4): 529–45.

Stigler, George J., Stephen M. Stigler, and Claire Friedland. 1995. "The Journals of Economics." *Journal of Political Economy* 103 (2): 331–59.

Stone, David R. 2000. *Hammer and Rifle: The Militarization of the Soviet Union, 1926–1933*. Lawrence: University Press of Kansas.

Stone, Norman. 1976. "Organizing an Economy for War: The Russian Shell Shortage, 1914–1917." In *War, Economy and the Military Mind*, edited by Geoffrey Best and Andrew Wheatcroft, 108–19. London: Croom Helm.

Strauss, Frederick. 1941. "The Food Problem in the German War Economy." *Quarterly Journal of Economics* 55 (3): 364–412.

Sutton, Antony C. 1968. *Western Technology and Soviet Economic Development 1917 to 1930*. Stanford, CA: Hoover Institution Press.

Sutton, Antony C. 1971. *Western Technology and Soviet Economic Development 1930 to 1945*. Stanford, CA: Hoover Institution Press.

Sutton, Antony C. 1973a. *Western Technology and Soviet Economic Development 1945 to 1965*. Stanford, CA: Hoover Institution Press.

Sutton, Antony C. 1973b. *National Suicide: Military Aid to the Soviet Union*, New Rochelle, NY: Arlington House.

Sutton, Antony C. 1995a. *Trilaterals over America*. New York: TAB Books.

Sutton, Antony C. 1995b. *The Federal Reserve Conspiracy*. New York: TAB Books.

Sutton, Antony C. 2003. *America's Secret Establishment: An Introduction to the Order of Skull & Bones*. Walterville, OR: Trine Day.

Sutton, John. 2008. "Market Structure." In *The New Palgrave Dictionary of Economics*, edited by Steven N. Durlauf and Lawrence E. Blume. 2nd ed. Vol. 5. New York: Palgrave Macmillan.

Sverdlik, Sh. B. 1990. "Vol'nyi ekonomist protiv vsei korolevskoi rati." *Ekonomika i organizatsiia promyshlennogo proizvodstva*, no. 12, 111–18.

Swain, D. Derk. 1990. "The Soviet Military Sector: How It Is Defined and Measured." In *The Impoverished Superpower: Perestroika and the Soviet Military Burden*, edited by Henry S. Rowen and Charles Wolf, Jr., 93–109. San Francisco: Institute for Contemporary Studies.

Sweezy, Maxine Yaple. 1939. "Distribution of Wealth and Income under the Nazis." *The Review of Economics and Statistics* 21 (4): 178–84.

Sweezy, Maxine Yaple. 1940. "German Corporate Profits: 1926–1938." *Quarterly Journal of Economics* 54 (3): 384–98.

Swianiewicz, Stanisław. 1965. *Forced Labor and Economic Development: An Enquiry into the Experience of Soviet Industrialization*. London: Oxford University Press.

Sykes, Charles J. 1990. *ProfScam: Professors and the Demise of Higher Education*. New York: St. Martin's.

Tatsioni, A., N. Bonitsis, and J. Ioannidis. 2007. "Persistence of Contradicted Claims in the Literature." *JAMA* 298 (21): 2517–26.

Taylor, Fred M. 1929. "The Guidance of Production in a Socialist State." *American Economic Review* 19, (1): 1–8.

Tedstrom, John E., ed. 1990. *Socialism, Perestroika, and the Dilemmas of Soviet Economic Reform*. Boulder, CO: Westview Press.

Temin, Peter. 1991. "Soviet and Nazi Economic Planning in the 1930s." *Economic History Review* 44 (4): 573–93.

"The Gap in Technology." 1978. *The Economist*, February 18.

"The Soviet Economy." 1979. *CHOICE: Current Reviews for Academic Libraries* (November): 1214.

Thomas, John R., and Ursula M. Kruse-Vaucienne, eds. 1977. *Soviet Science and Technology. Domestic and Foreign Perspectives*. Washington, DC: George Washington University.

Thomas, Robert P., and William V. Weber. 1990. *Economics: Principles & Applications*. Chicago: Dryden Press.

Thornton, Judith, ed. 1976. *Economic Analysis of the Soviet-Type System*. Cambridge, UK: Cambridge University Press.

Thornton, Judith. 1980. Review of *The Soviet Economy. How It Really Works*, by Constantine A. Krylov. *Russian Review* 39 (1): 103–4.

Tooze, Adam. 2006. *The Wages of Destruction: The Making and Breaking of the Nazi Economy*. New York: Viking.

Treml, Vladimir G., ed. 1968. *The Development of the Soviet Economy: Plan and Performance*. New York: Praeger.

Treml, Vladimir G. 1993. "Problems with Soviet Statistics: Past and Present." In *The Role of the Military Sector in the Economies of Russia and Ukraine: Proceedings of the Rand-Hoover Symposium, 1992*, edited by Charles Wolf, Jr., 3–19. Santa Monica, CA: RAND Corporation.

Treml, Vladimir G., and John P. Hardt, eds. 1972. *Soviet Economic Statistics*. Durham, NC: Duke University Press.

Treml, Vladimir G., Herbert S. Levine, and M. Marc Earle, Jr. 1977. "A Draft Proposal for the Creation of an Institute for the Study of the Soviet Union." Attached to National Intelligence Office/Europe memorandum. 12 January, 1977. CIA-RDP83M00171R000500230001-7. CREST System. National Archives at College Park.

Trotsky, Leon. (1937) 2004. *The Revolution Betrayed*. Translated by Max Eastman. NY: Dover.

Tsagolov, N., ed. 1970. *Kurs politicheskoi ekonomii*. Vol. 2. Moscow: Ekonomika.

Tsapkin, N. V., ed. 1972. *Planirovanie narodnogo khoziaistva SSSR*. Moscow: Mysl'.

Tsapkin, N. V., and V. I. Pereslegin, eds. 1967. *Planirovanie narodnogo khoziaistva SSSR*. Moscow: Mysl'.

TsSU SSSR. 1981. *Narodnoe khoziaistvo SSSR v 1980 g*. Moscow: Finansy i statistika.

Tukhachevskii, M. 1928. "Voina kak problema vooruzhennoi bor'by." *Bol'shaia Sovetskaia Entsyklopediia*. Vol. 12. At http://militera.lib.ru/science/tuhachevsky/index.html; accessed Feb. 7, 2016.

Tullock, Gordon. 1987. "Public Choice." In *The New Palgrave Dictionary of Economics*, edited by John Eatwell, Murray Milgate, and Peter Newman. Vol 3. New York: Palgrave Macmillian.

Ulam, Adam. 1974. *Expansion and Coexistence*. 2nd ed. New York: Praeger.

Unger, Aryeh L. 1998. "On the Meaning of 'Sovietology.'" *Communist and Post-Communist Studies* 31 (1): 17–27.

"Unreliable Research: Trouble at the Lab." 2013. *The Economist*, October 18. http://www.economist.com/news/briefing/21588057-scientists-think-science -self-correcting-alarming-degree-it-not-trouble.

Unsal, Erdal M. 1991. "The Heavy Industry Priority in Socialist Economic Planning." *Science and Society* 54 (1): 391–407.

U.S. Census Bureau. 1991. *Statistical Abstract of the United States*. Washington, DC: GPO.

U.S. Congress. 1976. Joint Economic Committee. *Soviet Economy in a New Perspective: A Compendium of Papers*. 94th Cong. 2nd sess. October 14.

U.S. Congress. 1977. Joint Economic Committee. *Allocation of Resources in the Soviet Union and China—1977: Hearings before the Subcommittee on Priorities in Economy and Government of the Joint Economic Committee*. 95th Cong. 1st sess. (Statement of John Hardt, Senior Specialist of Soviet Economics).

U.S. Congress. 1982. Joint Economic Committee. *USSR: Measures of Economic Growth and Development 1950–80*. 97th Cong. 2nd sess.

U.S. General Accounting Office. 1992. *Soviet Economy: Assessment of How Well the CIA Has Estimated the Size of the Economy: Report to the Honorable Daniel Patrick Moynihan*. Washington, DC: US General Accounting Office.

U.S. House. 1971. Committee of Education and Labor. *Higher Education Amendments of 1969: Hearings on H. R. 16098 and Related Bills before the Special Subcommittee on Education of the Committee on Education and Labor*. 91st Cong. 2nd sess.

U.S. Senate. 1982. Committee on Foreign Relations. *United States-Soviet Research Studies: Hearings before the Subcommittee on European Affairs of the Committee on Foreign Relations*. 97th Cong. 2nd sess. September 22.

U.S. Senate. 1991. Committee on Foreign Relations. *Estimating the Size and Growth of the Soviet Economy: Hearings before the Committee on Foreign Relations*. 101st Cong. 2nd sess. July 16.

Vayrynen, Raimo. 1992. *Military Industrialization and Economic Development: Theory and Historical Case Studies*. Aldershot, UK: Dartmouth.

Ventsov, S. 1928. *Narodnoe khoziaistvo i oborona SSSR*. Moscow: Moskovskii rabochii.

Ventsov, S. 1931. *Narodnoe khoziaistvo i oborona SSSR*. Moscow: Moskovskii rabochii.

Viljoen, S. 1974. *Economic Systems in World History*. London, UK: Longman.

Viotti, Staffan, and Rolf Eidem. 1978. *Economic Systems*. Oxford, UK: Martin Robertson.

Viscusi, Kip W., John M. Vernon, and Joseph E. Harrington, Jr. 1995. *Economics of Regulation and Antitrust*. 2nd ed. Cambridge, MA: MIT Press.

Vogel, Heinrich. 1968. "Satisfaction of Consumer Needs." In Treml 1968.

Vollweiler, Helmut. 1938. "Mobilisation of Labour Reserves in Germany: I." *International Labor Review* 38 (4): 447–613.

Von Hayek, F. A., ed. 1935. *Collectivist Economic Planning: Critical Studies on the Possibilities of Socialism*. London: Routledge.

Von Laue, Theodore H. 1964. *Why Lenin? Why Stalin? A Reappraisal of the Russian Revolution, 1900–1930*. Philadelphia: J. B. Lippincott, 1964.

Von Mises, Ludwig. (1922) 1981. *Socialism: An Economic and Sociological Analysis*. Jena, Germany: Gustav Fischer Verlag. Reprint, Indianapolis: Liberty Classics. Citations refer to Liberty Classics edition.

Voronetskaia, A. A., ed. 1969. *Industrializatsiia SSSR 1926–1928 gg. Dokumenty i materialy*. Moscow: Nauka.

Voroshilov, K. E. (1927a) 1936. "Oborona strany i sostoianie raboche-krest'ianskoi krasnoi armii." In *Stat'i i rechi*, 104–35. Moscow: Partizdat TsK VKP (b).

Voroshilov, K. E. (1927b) 1936. "Voprosy oborony i piatiletka." In *Stat'i i rechi*, 188–211. Moscow: Partizdat TsK VKP (b).

Vorotnikov, V. I. 1995. *A bylo eto tak . . . Iz dnevnika chlena Politbiuro TsK KPSS*. Moscow: Sovet veteranov knigoizdaniia.

Vucinich, Alexander. 1956. *The Soviet Academy of Sciences*. Stanford, CA: Stanford University Press.

Vucinich, Alexander. 1984. *Empire of Knowledge: The Academy of Sciences of the USSR (1917–1970)*. Berkeley: University of California Press.

Wade, Nicholas. 2009. "Researcher Condemns Conformity among His Peers." Tierney Lab, *New York Times*, July 23. https://tierneylab.blogs.nytimes.com/2009/07/23/researcher-condemns-conformity-among-his-peers/.

Waldron, Arthur. 2002. "A Chinese Famine Ignored." *The American Enterprise* 13 (6): 38–39.

Ward, Benjamin N. 1960. "The Planners' Choice Variables." In Grossman 1960, 131–64.

Ward, Benjamin N. 1967. *The Socialist Economy: A Study of Organizational Alternatives.* New York: Random House.

Ward, Benjamin N. 1979. *The Ideal Worlds of Economics: Liberal, Radical, and Conservative Economic World Views.* New York: Basic Books.

Wehner, Ing. Bruno. 1937. "German Regional Planning." *Journal of the American Institute of Planners* 3 (1): 9–12.

Whaley, Barton.1984. *Covert German Rearmament, 1919–1939: Deception and Misperception.* Frederick, MD: University Publications of America.

Whynes, David K. 1983. *Comparative Economic Development.* London: Butterworths.

Wilber, Charles K. 1969. *The Soviet Model and Underdeveloped Countries.* Chapel Hill: University of North Carolina Press.

Wilczynski, J. 1970. *The Economics of Socialism.* Studies in Economics. Chicago: Aldine.

Wilczynski, J. 1972. *The Economics of Socialism.* Studies in Economics. London: Allen and Unwin.

Wilczynski, J. 1977. *The Economics of Socialism.* Rev. ed. Studies in Economics. London: Allen and Unwin.

Wiczynski, J. 1982. *The Economics of Socialism.* London: Allen and Unwin.

Wiles, Peter. 1953. "The Soviet Economy Outpaces the West." Foreign Affairs 31 (4): 566–80.

Wiles, Peter. 1956a. "What Is to Be Done about the Success of Soviet Industry?" In Congress for Cultural Freedom 1956, 27–40.

Wiles, Peter. 1956b. "La Trahison du Clark." In Congress for Cultural Freedom 1956, 131–45.

Wiles, Peter. 1961. "Communist Economics and our Economics Textbooks." In Spulber 1961, 83–103.

Wiles, Peter. 1962. *The Political Economy of Communism.* Cambridge, MA: Harvard University Press.

Wiles, Peter. 1964. "Western Research into the Soviet Economy." *Survey* 50 (22): 69–81.

Wiles, Peter. 1967. "The Political and Social Prerequisites for a Soviet-Type Economy." *Economica* 34 (113): 1–19.

Wiles, Peter. 1976. *Economic Institutions Compared.* New York: Wiley.

Wiles, Peter, ed. 1988. *The Soviet Economy on the Brink of Reform: Essays in Honor of Alec Nove.* Boston: Unwin Hyman.

Wilhelm, John Howard. 2003. "The Failure of the American Sovietological Economics Profession." *Europe-Asia Studies* 55 (1): 59–74.

Williamson, Oliver E. 1985. *The Economic Institutions of Capitalism*. New York: Free Press.

Winiecki, Jan. 1988. *The Distorted World of Soviet-Type Economies*. Pittsburgh: University of Pittsburgh Press.

Wolf, Charles. 1996. "Defense Economics." In *Project Air Force 50th Anniversary (1946–1996)*, 57–59. Santa Monica, CA: RAND Corporation.

Wonnacott, Paul, and Ronald Wonnacott. 1982. *Economics*. 2nd ed. New York: McGraw-Hill.

Wonnacott, Paul, and Ronald Wonnacott. 1986. *Economics*. 3rd ed. New York: McGraw-Hill.

Wonnacott, Paul, and Ronald Wonnacott. 1990. *Economics*. 4th ed. New York: McGraw-Hill.

World Bank. 1991. *World Development Report 1991: The Challenge of Development*. Oxford: Oxford University Press.

World Bank. 2017. International Comparison Database. (2017) *GDP, PPP (current international $)* [Data file]. Washington, DC: The World Bank. Accessed at http://data.worldbank.org/indicator/NY.GDP.MKTP.PP.CD on 5/25/2017.

Wunderlich, Frieda. 1934. "New Aspects of Unemployment in Germany." *Social Research* 1 (1): 97–110.

Wunderlich, Frieda. 1938. "Germany's Defense Economy and the Decay of Capitalism." *Quarterly Journal of Economics* 52 (3): 401–30.

Zaleski, Eugène. 1967. *Planning Reforms in the Soviet Union, 1962–1966*. Chapel Hill: University of North Carolina Press.

Zaleski, Eugène. 1971. *Planning for Economic Growth in the Soviet Union, 1918–1932*. Chapel Hill: University of North Carolina Press.

Zaleski, Eugène. 1980. *Stalinist Planning for Economic Growth, 1933–1952*. Chapel Hill: University of North Carolina Press.

Zaleski, Eugène., J. P. Kozlowski, H. Wienert, R. W. Davies, M. J. Berry, and Ronald Amann. 1961. *Science Policy in the USSR*. Paris: OECD.

Zamagni, Vera. 1998. "Italy: How to Lose the War and Win the Peace." In Harrison 1998, 177–223.

Zauberman, Alfred. 1963. Review of *The Soviet Economy*, by Nicolas Spulber. *International Affairs* 39 (3): 446–54.

Zauberman, Alfred. 1967. *Aspects of Planometrics*. New Haven, CT: Yale University Press.

Zauberman, Alfred. 1976. *Mathematical Theory in Soviet Planning: Concepts, Methods, Techniques*. London: Oxford University Press.

Zausaev, V. 1998. Foreword to *Mezhregional'nye aspekty ekonomicheskoi reformy na Dal'nem Vostoke i Zabaikal'e*, by Ie. N. Galichanin. Khabarovsk.

Zhukov, G. K. 1969. *Vospominaniia i razmyshleniia*. Moscow: APH.

Zhuravlev, Sergei. 2009. "Rozhdenie krasnogo kolossa." *Ekspert*, December 28.

Zimbalist, Andrew, and Howard J. Sherman. 1984. *Comparing Economic Systems: A Political-Economic Approach*. New York: Academic Press.

Zoteev, Gennadii. 1998. "The View from Gosplan: Growth to the Year 2000." In Ellman and Kontorovich, 85–93.

# Index